WITHOUT RESTRAINT

How Skiing Saved My Son's Life

ROBERT C. DeLENA

AND

RYAN C. DeLENA

ESSEX, CONNECTICUT

An imprint of Globe Pequot, the trade division of
The Rowman & Littlefield Publishing Group, Inc.
4501 Forbes Blvd., Ste. 200
Lanham, MD 20706
www.rowman.com

Falcon and FalconGuides are registered trademarks of The Rowman & Littlefield Publishing Group, Inc.

Distributed by NATIONAL BOOK NETWORK

British Library Cataloguing in Publication Information available

Library of Congress Cataloging-in-Publication Data

Names: DeLena, Robert C., 1968– author. | DeLena, Ryan C., 2001– author.
Title: Without restraint : how skiing saved my son's life / Robert C. DeLena and Ryan C. DeLena.
Description: Essex, Connecticut : Falcon Guides, 2023.
Identifiers: LCCN 2022023460 (print) | LCCN 2022023461 (ebook) | ISBN 9781493066926 (cloth) | ISBN 9781493066933 (epub)
Subjects: LCSH: DeLena, Ryan C., 2001– | DeLena, Robert C., 1968– | Skiing—Psychological aspects. | Skiers—United States—Biography. | Children with mental disabilities—United States—Biography. | People with mental disabilities—United States—Biography. | Parents of children with mental disabilities—United States—Biography. | Fathers and sons—United States—Biography.
Classification: LCC GV854.2.D45 D45 2023 (print) | LCC GV854.2.D45 (ebook) | DDC 796.93092 [B]—dc23/eng/20220625
LC record available at https://lccn.loc.gov/2022023460
LC ebook record available at https://lccn.loc.gov/2022023461

♾️™ The paper used in this publication meets the minimum requirements of American National Standard for Information Sciences—Permanence of Paper for Printed Library Materials, ANSI/NISO Z39.48-1992.

The authors and The Rowman & Littlefield Publishing Group, Inc. assume no liability for accidents happening to, or injuries sustained by, readers who engage in the activities described in this book.

"It only looks like a mountain when you look at it from the bottom."

—RYAN C. DELENA, AGE 7

Contents

Preface

As a toddler, Ryan's emotional intensity, perseveration, and defiance caused my wife, Mary Beth, and I to seek professional help to nudge him onto the traditional pathway for success. Instead, expert assumptions about his intellectual limitations bound Ryan to a flawed system purportedly designed to aid him. If you are a parent, particularly a parent of a child with a disability, we hope you learn from our mistakes.

After writing separately, Ryan and I collaborated on a comprehensive examination of our journey. My recollections frame the entire story while Ryan's own words are revealed throughout the book in *italics*. All persons within the story are actual individuals; there are no composite characters. The names of some individuals and institutions were changed to respect their privacy and, whenever Ryan disputed my version, I deferred to him. His eidetic memory rendered extraordinary recall of life events, even those occurring when he was a toddler. Any editing of his work by me was purely grammatical or stylistic. By reliving our story concurrently, *Without Restraint* is part parenting memoir, part childhood memoir, but most importantly, it is a compelling story of struggle, enlightenment, and survival.

Through skiing and the adventures we experienced together, I learned everyone was wrong about Ryan, especially me.

—Robert C. DeLena

CHAPTER ONE

Never Complain and Never Give Up

"It is not the mountain we conquer, but ourselves."
—Sir Edmund Hillary

November 9, 2018. Unlike previous days searching for skiable terrain in Antarctica, our morning objective was easy to spot from the deck of the *Ocean Adventurer*. Not Your Matterhorn stood alone on a snowy peninsula requiring a long, steep skin to the summit. Clients onboard studied the peak excitedly and noted that our intense climbing efforts were certain to be rewarded with a 2,000-foot ski to the ocean on an untracked slope with forty degrees of pitch. The mountain itself was located atop a frozen plateau, approximately one mile from the rocky coastline, and climbers from Ice Axe Expeditions noted its similarity to the Matterhorn in Switzerland when they named it nine years prior. Personally, I thought it more resembled Mount Crumpit from *The Grinch Who Stole Christmas* because its sharply pointed peak twisted a quarter-turn, as if it was craning its neck toward the shore to spy on anyone bold enough to summit.

—◦—

The zodiac ride to shore was longer than usual. To locate a proper landing zone, we navigated around several large icebergs and through a field of smaller ice chunks, eventually settling on a ledge made of large boulders in the shadow of a steep, snowy slope. After a cautious climb over slippery rocks in our ski boots, it was time to gear up. Generally, after disembarking the zodiac, we clipped into our skis and began skinning up. Today, however, we first needed to climb straight up a snowy cliff face before we could start to skin. So, we kept our skis in hand and used them to stab the snow for support as we ascended. We then kicked steps up the cliff face, traveling for one hundred feet or so, and upon reaching the upper plateau, stopped to admire the peak in the distance before clicking into our skis.

After we negotiated the dicey cliff face, we assembled safely on the plateau and dropped our skis into position before securing the toepiece to our ski boots. We then clipped together in our usual order. Spaced by twenty feet of rope to prevent our team from falling into a crevasse, we climbed by employing a technique called "skinning," affixing a felt material made from mohair to the bottom of our skis and using special bindings that released at the heel. Our lead guide, Andrew, was positioned first. As always, I was right behind him, staring at his backside while he methodically ascended step by step, maintaining a pace I could withstand. We never conversed much during climbs, but every so often Andrew sensed that I was struggling and bellowed out, "Don't forget to look around!"

The anchor, or tail guide, to our climbing line, was Kurt, the director of operations for Ice Axe. Kurt was on a split-board, which meant he skinned up on a snowboard that divided into two halves before being reassembled for its intended purpose on the descent. Earlier in the week, I had the body-shaming misfortune of following this former college water polo player and his American flag Speedo during our ship's "polar plunge" into the frigid waters of the Southern Ocean.

Clipped just behind me as we ascended was my seventeen-year-old son, Ryan. He was already taller than me and, although he would never grow over six feet, he wasn't short. We shared some physical attributes like my broad shoulders and muscular frame, but unlike me, he had a six-pack of abdominal muscles and longer legs, which made him prettier and more athletic on skis. There is little question that he is my son because we greatly resemble each other facially with big brown eyes and long eye lashes, brown hair (before I went gray), a wide nose that originated generations ago in a small Italian village, and a cleft chin. However, his face is more angular, with a sharper jawline resulting in a more handsome appearance.

As we glided across the plateau toward Not Your Matterhorn, I wasn't able to see much of Ryan's face when I looked back over my shoulder. He had given up on sunblock after suffering a bad burn caused by the lack of ozone protection over Antarctica and was now covered by a ski mask, baseball hat, and sunglasses as if readied to rob a bank. Sunburn aside, Ryan had little trouble skinning up any mountain and was the strongest client-skier on the trip. He even skied as well as some of the guides, and Antarctica was unlike anything either of us had encountered in a ski resort. The runs were steep with variable snow conditions, but also presented life-threatening hazards such as hidden crevasses and the potential for avalanche. Yet, Ryan never appeared intimidated and skied every run aggressively, ripping through the glacial snow with beautiful S-shaped turns that left behind the evidentiary pattern of a highly skilled and technically proficient skier. I proudly wondered how many skiers in history had ever matched his progression from beginner to expert. He had moved from his first day of skiing on a beginner hill in Massachusetts to ski touring in Antarctica in under ten years.

As for me, skinning up mountains in Antarctica was brutal. We generally skinned over two thousand feet in morning ascents, and I spent most of the time begging for water breaks and asking Andrew, "How much farther?" Today, however, I vowed to be more positive, and with each sliding step, I quietly whispered my new mantra, which I had learned the previous evening during a presentation by a guide named Todd titled "Never Complain and Never Give Up." Todd's advice fueled me well into our second hour of skinning, just as we completed the approach to the base of the mountain. However, as the slope steepened, my incantation was soon replaced by the sound of my own labored breathing. We were just now beginning the ascent of Not Your Matterhorn, and as each sliding step began to increase in elevation, I found myself once again focused on the lengthy distance to the summit.

To occupy myself, I looked away from the peak and gazed to my left toward the icy waters below, relying on the icebergs floating in the bay for distraction. I spent the next hour studying each mass of ice, trying to pick a favorite, as we continued our ascent. While the top half of an iceberg is pure white, the part below the surface combines with the cobalt sea into a bright teal color like something from a child's paint set. Each has a unique design that is sometimes reshaped by the sun, and when melting on one side generates an imbalance, the iceberg topples, sending the previously submerged section out of the ocean and vice versa.

Although our ascents offered plenty of visual stimulation, Antarctica is remarkably silent—aside from the squawking penguins. As we neared the summit, we initiated a zigzag pattern to counter the slope, and rather than icebergs, I found myself marveling at Ryan. His movements were effortless and efficient. No matter the steepness or the snow conditions, climbing up was as much fun for him as skiing down. I could never relate to that aspect of his personality, and as I pondered how different we were, my thoughts shifted to the chaotic parenting journey that led to this adventure. Antarctica was, after all, just another attempt to make up for the terrible mistakes I made when Ryan was younger. Mistakes I worked tirelessly to correct but that gnawed at my consciousness with indelible feelings of regret, even when distracted by the most remarkable scenery on the planet.

〜〜

I am sure that everyone who travels to Antarctica has a moment or two when they consider what it took to get there, and as we slowly ascended Not Your Matterhorn, I contemplated my journey.

For me, when it came to the technical aspects of skiing, the nine-year career that led me to ski touring in Antarctica was without adversity, offering a direct line in pursuing my goals. However, it was never that simple. Like our morning zodiac ride across still water, I was forever mindful of the dangerous chunks of ice in my path. For my entire childhood, I was forced to navigate a field of doctors, teachers, and administrators who felt I was unable to walk the halls of any school without medication and constant supervision. Worse, many times I felt as though I was trapped by the ice floe as I was literally held in place until grown-ups deemed that I was ready to return to society.

Like most occasions when I reflected on my past, it was hard not to get angry, but by the time we neared the summit, I remembered that it no longer mattered where the experts thought I'd end up. What mattered was where I was now.

CHAPTER TWO

The Gift

"There must always be a struggle between a father and a son, while one aims at power and the other at independence."
—SAMUEL JOHNSON

October 13, 2000. Like all expectant parents preparing for their first child, Mary Beth and I were terrified. Friends who had completed the journey promised our initial appointment was nothing more than checking vitals and listening for the baby's heartbeat. Instead, after searching in vain for a minute or two, our nurse deadpanned, "Excuse me for one second while I grab your doctor." She was so matter of fact that I assumed she was simply misusing the Doppler machine, but, in an instant, our doctor appeared. He too attempted to locate a beating heart, and after failing, requested an immediate ultrasound to confirm everything was okay.

We left and nervously walked across the hall to the ultrasound facility. As Mary Beth checked in at the appointment desk, I studied the faces in the waiting area. Most would see images of healthy growing babies, with the anticipation of more significant moments to come. For the rest, hopes and dreams ended in the next hour. It was my first introduction to parenthood, lacking the slightest leverage to influence the result of the ultrasound, and I understood now why my grandmother sprinkled me with holy water as a child when I wasn't paying attention.

Mary Beth returned dejectedly. She shook her head slowly and exhaled with an exasperated sigh. "They're about to close for lunch and want us to come back in an hour."

We retreated outside and searched for a place to sit before settling on Au Bon Pain. Like most couples who start as friends, Mary Beth and I communicated easily, but as products of the television generation, particularly sitcoms, our conversations generally entailed outwitting the other to generate a laugh. This day, however, we stayed unusually quiet during lunch. Mary Beth ran her fingers through her short brown pixie cut while her dark eyes studied her day planner. She appeared to be counting days on her fingers to recalibrate her pregnancy calendar, which I referred to as the sex calendar, trying to discern the date of conception. Although she was a corporate attorney and not a prosecutor, she was interrogating her day planner, looking for evidence that our original conception math was off and making our baby too young for an audible heartbeat.

Occasionally, Mary Beth cross-examined me about my role in our baby's conception. "I feel like I am missing one time from late July."

"With me?"

"Thanks. That is super helpful." She wasn't amused and groaned slightly before diving back into the calendar.

With little else to do, my eyes wandered around the restaurant, eventually settling on a father-and-son pair a few tables away. The dad was busily cutting chicken fingers into tiny pieces as his son wiped grease onto his Red Sox shirt. The boy was wearing number 45 in honor of Pedro Martinez, but I doubted he was old enough to appreciate how the mood in the city was elevated every fifth day when Pedro was scheduled to pitch.

While I poked at my turkey sandwich, I prepared mentally for the outcome of the ultrasound. I knew miscarriages were common with first pregnancies and, after a few months of waiting, we could try again. Still, I wasn't ready to say goodbye to this baby. I had spent the last two weeks readying myself to be a dad and, certain we were having a boy, had already run through my list of firsts—first ball and glove, first Little League game, first high school game, and first game playing second base for Harvard University. I wasn't presumptuous enough to envision his first game in the majors, but the rest of the plan was etched in stone.

After lunch, we returned to the waiting room, and when Mary Beth's name was finally called, we traveled down a long hallway to the ultrasound room knowing life would be forever altered by the next few minutes. As images of our baby appeared on the monitor, the technician's tells showed: the unfurrowing of her brow with a slight exhale. She then offered play-by-play of the onscreen imagery, including our baby's large head, tiny body, and finally, a magnificent beating heart.

When the doctor walked in, he misread my pained expression and readied himself to deliver bad news. However, when the technician gave him the thumbs-up, he struggled to right himself. "Wait, so everything is good?" He then pointed at me before saying, "He looked so serious."

I faked a smiled back at him and let out a deep exhale. "That was pretty stressful."

The doctor smiled at me before fixing his eyes on Mary Beth. "The first of many stressful moments, my young friends." After he exited, while Mary Beth dressed, I took a deep breath and wondered how many excruciating near misses would be endured over this child's lifetime.

We departed with a black-and-white image of our baby on a thin piece of paper curled at the edges. It was too soon to determine the gender, but I remained convinced that we were having a boy because the profile in the image resembled me, so I assumed our baby would *be* like me in every possible way. He would study hard, get good grades, bat left, throw right, hate the Yankees, and beg to stay up past his bedtime to see the outcome of playoff games. I would soon learn, though, that there are no scripted plans when it comes to parenthood.

Even in the womb, our baby was beginning to show his stubbornness. He remained firmly in breech position, necessitating a Cesarean section. At Mary Beth's final appointment, our OB/GYN stated emphatically that most babies eventually spin around allowing for a vaginal birth, but this baby was different. Ryan Charles DeLena entered the world on May 7, 2001, on his terms. He was beautiful, loud, and strong-willed, and spent his first days screaming after several rounds of breastfeeding and even clumsier attempts at bottle feeding failed miserably. When Mary Beth finally surrendered, a lactation consultant settled on a special bottle called the Haberman Feeder used for babies with cleft lips.

The rest of Ryan's first year is a sleepless blur, but one thing I recall vividly was his love of pushing boundaries. From the moment he learned to crawl, our house morphed into a deathtrap, and soon every piece of furniture was tethered to a wall. He became obsessed with electrical outlets, stairs, fireplaces, and anything delicious discovered on the floor. If I averted my eyes for one second, he was inside the kitchen cabinets or behind the television ripping out the wires. So, when Mary Beth returned to work on a full-time basis, we hired a nanny to help care for Ryan while I continued to work from home. Fortunately, we found a sweet retiree named Fran who had raised children and grandchildren and lived close by.

Fran's job, aside from feeding and changing Ryan, was to keep him busy from 8 a.m. to 3 p.m. In the afternoon, I had primary responsibility until Mary Beth arrived home from work. However, since my workday didn't exactly end at three, my plan was to juggle business and fatherhood, occupying Ryan while I worked on the computer and made calls. That plan, however, lasted less than a week before I realized it was futile. No matter how many of Ryan's toys filled my office, he fixated on a button that opened the CD drive of my computer, wailing uncontrollably until he was allowed to push it. Luckily, he loved riding in my car and, if we drove long enough, he eventually passed out. The best part: he remained asleep as long the car traveled in excess of forty miles per hour, so I drove through neighboring towns like Keanu Reeves in the 1990s movie, *Speed*, cutting through parking lots to avoid red lights.

In September of 2002, when Ryan was sixteen months old, his sister, Abigail, was born. At the time, he seemed completely oblivious to Abigail's presence, preferring to explore every square inch of our home. Within a few months, every door, cabinet, and toilet incorporated childproof devices so complex that adult guests would exit bathrooms looking like they completed the SAT. We had tried numerous methods for containing Ryan, including swings and bouncy chairs, but he escaped the standard baby jail, made of interlocking plastic walls, by ramming his head into the joint sections until they snapped open.

Despite constant vigilance, parenting Ryan was a lot of fun. He spoke early on and developed an incredible vocabulary. With a few minutes of rehearsal, he memorized long strands of speech, reciting the

Pledge of Allegiance, or enumerating his Miranda rights during diaper changes. I also enjoyed teaching him lines from my favorite movies, so if you knew him back then you would witness Ryan launching into Hyman Roth's impassioned speech to Michael Corleone about the death of Moe Greene in *The Godfather II*. It led to some strange looks on the playground when Ryan honored Moe, lamenting to other toddlers that "there isn't even a plaque or a signpost or a statue of him in that town."

―❦―

My parents didn't believe in baby talk, and when I was still in diapers, they talked to me like I was an adult. Had things gone differently in preschool, Dad would have pushed me to read War and Peace *before my seventh birthday, and Mom would have asked me to intern for her company during middle school. I'm not saying they were particularly hard-driving or cruel. In fact, I only remember good times at home when I was really young.*

By the time I could walk, I wanted to discover the big world around me, which led to childproof locks on literally every door in our house. Whenever my parents told me I couldn't go into a specific room or closet, I assumed there must be something special about it, since I couldn't enter it until I was older. For example, when I was three years old, I became fascinated with a basket of grilling tools in our pantry. After several failed attempts to sneak in and climb the shelves, my mom finally let me hold some of them except for one particular tool she called the "Death Knife." This rather morbid name came from her desire to have me equate it with danger since it was sharper than the other tools, but her mistake was telling me only grown-ups were allowed to touch it. For the next week, I pleaded with her to let me hold it. She finally gave in and let me hold the long wooden handle with a sharp blade attached, taking it away after a few seconds. The problem was that I went into preschool the next day and bragged about holding the "Death Knife." A call was then immediately placed to Mom, forcing her to explain the nature of the knife, how it got that name, and why I even knew it existed.

―❦―

I was not surprised when Ryan's preschool director asked me to stay for a few minutes one afternoon to discuss his start to the school year. Ryan was attending the Sudbury Cooperative Preschool for a few hours on Tuesdays and Thursdays and was there less than a month when Mallorie, the owner, looked at me with concerned eyes and said, "There is something that I need to tell you after observing Ryan."

Mallorie had big blue puppy dog eyes to begin with, so she really looked unhappy about whatever she was about to disclose. I cut her off before she continued and without knowing anything, immediately came to Ryan's defense. "Isn't this . . . just . . . the terrible twos or something?"

She stopped me. "No, Rob, this isn't about misbehavior per se. This is much bigger." She then slumped her shoulders and softly exhaled, "Ryan is gifted."

As the word "gifted" struck my temporal lobe, I burst out laughing. "Jesus, I thought were going to say that something was wrong. Gifted sounds like a good problem to have."

"Well, it does come with some hurdles. My gifted son is a teenager now, and he was a very difficult child. He never listened to me or anyone. He still doesn't."

"I guess that does sound a lot like Ryan," I confessed. "So, what do we do?"

"Rob, this is going to change your lives forever. You and Mary Beth need to research everything about gifted children to prepare for the future."

I tried to appear dour but deep down I was thrilled about the prospect of raising a gifted child.

"I can promise you that we'll do all the necessary research. Especially Mary Beth. She loves research." By research, I really meant googling the differences between the starting salaries for graduates of Harvard versus Yale. "Mallorie, by the way, how did your son turn out?"

She forced a smile and sighed again. "He's doing well. He loves computer programming and this past summer he taught himself Hebrew."

Great, I thought to myself. *Ryan better not end up being a nerd like her kid.*

After racing home, I searched, "How do I know if my preschooler is gifted?" Even in the early days of the internet, dozens of websites with tests popped up. Most cited the following factors:

- a highly developed vocabulary
- a tendency to speak quickly
- the early use of longer, more complex sentences while using appropriate grammar
- early reading
- continually asking questions about what they see and hear, and wanting to receive thorough responses and explanations
- the ability to carry out multistep directions
- the ability to understand and participate in adult conversations
- the ability to change the language they use when speaking to different audiences

After digesting the checklist, Ryan certainly possessed the requisite criteria. Locally, I knew of several programs tailored to educating gifted children and looked forward to researching options while bragging to the world about my boy genius. However, there was one aspect to the articles on giftedness that I chose to ignore. Many of the articles included a caveat that characteristics of giftedness can be signs of an emotional problem or an early indication of autism.

———

Despite all I have been through, I am very close to my family. Dad and I have a unique relationship. When I was younger, he was often the only parent home, and he taught me about the history of everything, how to exercise, how to meet strangers, and just about every other lesson a boy learns growing up. He never hid the realities of the world from me and always gave me straight answers, even about things that would ordinarily scare a young child. With that kind of honesty, I never felt that I had to hide much from him. Plus, even if I did, he would see through it. I learned early on that he sees everyone for who they really are and isn't fooled by much.

Mom has always worked as a lawyer for biotech companies in Cambridge, Massachusetts, about an hour from our house during busy traffic hours. So, when I was young and went to bed early, I only saw her for a couple of hours in the early morning, a few minutes at night, and then on weekends. That didn't necessarily mean we had a distant relationship; it was just different from Dad. When I think back to Mom then, I picture her making breakfast in the morning and her attempts at making me and my sister laugh, which weren't always the funniest. Mom is your classic type-A, analytical parent, and no matter what problem or trouble I managed to get into as a toddler, she never believed in indulging emotional drama. Instead, her advice was usually "Suck it up and keep going."

If I fell climbing at the park, she would make sure I didn't break any bones, but she was not the type to douse me in Purell, smother me while I cried, and tell me to never try climbing that thing again. Instead, she dusted me off and told me to give it another try. I am sure psychiatrists pin it on her that I went on to become a ski mountaineer and a mountain climber—pursuits that require that decisions are made through an objective lens and where discomfort is simply accepted as a part of the process.

CHAPTER THREE

Not Otherwise Specified

*Throughout the evaluation, there were numerous instances of impul-
sivity, perseverative responding; difficulty shifting cognitive set to a
new set of tasks demand and reduced cognitive flexibility in generating
alternative solutions.*
—REPORT OF NEUROPSYCHOLOGICAL EVALUATION OF RYAN
DELENA BY DR. JANET SCHNEIDER, PHD, MS, PEDIATRIC
NEUROPSYCHOLOGIST (OCTOBER 1, 2004)

July 6, 2004. Prior to his birth, Mary Beth and I secured a coveted spot
for Ryan at the Treehouse School, a highly regarded preschool program
in the neighboring town of Concord, where we were impressed by the
energetic teachers and expansive facility. After enrolling him in summer
camp at Treehouse, which served as an introduction to preschool set to
begin in September, Ryan quickly ran into problems following directions
and melding with the other children.

At 2 p.m., I weaved my way through the elaborate system of traffic
cones and orange-vested teachers at pickup time, eagerly awaiting Ryan's
detailed description of every intriguing aspect to his new classroom.
Ryan's teacher smiled as she opened the car door, buckling him into his
seat for the ride home. I was in the process of turning my head to say
hello to him, when Kim, Treehouse's director, startled me by knocking on
the driver's-side window.

"Ryan had a great day," she said enthusiastically, before pausing. "Would you and Mary Beth be able meet with me tomorrow after drop-off?"

"Is there a class event?" I asked, fearing we missed something in the daily email update.

Her face grew more serious. "No, I just want to discuss a few things about Ryan's behavior today."

I quickly nodded and said, "Sure. I'll double-check Mary Beth's availability, but unless you hear otherwise, assume we're on." I then pulled out of the parking lot and engaged Ryan on his first day of camp, but as I drove, I replayed the short conversation with Kim in my head and felt uneasy. She never once said "gifted"; she said "behavior."

We met with Kim the following morning, and she relayed that, during Ryan's first day, he fixated on a giant farmhouse sink in the classroom. Rather than painting his assigned macaroni necklace, he insisted on repeatedly filling the sink, watching it drain over and over.

"Is that a problem?" I asked.

Mary Beth sensed that I was about to make a wiseass comment about Ryan failing to produce his quota of pasta necklaces and quickly interjected, "Kim, we know that he can be challenging, but he'll do better once he learns the class routine."

Kim smiled. "He absolutely will, and he's such a spirited and wonderful boy."

Spirited? She made him sound possessed, but I sensed that she was leaning on her years of experience and training. And now, having delivered the good news, she was readying the bad. She took a breath and asked, "Will you give us permission to have a pediatric neuropsychologist observe Ryan?"

I looked at Mary Beth blankly and prepared my response to Kim by first parsing the title silently in my head, arriving at a doctor who studies children with brain problems. It didn't sound like the title of someone called to determine where Ryan fell on Treehouse's scale of giftedness.

But, before I had the chance to respond, Mary Beth jumped in and said, "Sure. If you think it might be helpful."

Although we were alarmed by Kim's recommendation, when we left the meeting, I reflexively argued to Mary Beth that the administration at Treehouse was struggling to appreciate Ryan's intellect. "She doesn't get him because Ryan isn't scared to take a shit without permission." As proof, I cited articles that claimed educators often miss the brilliance of gifted children and instead focus on attention and authority problems.

Mary Beth clenched her teeth and narrowed her eyes. "You really think that is all that's going on with him?"

"Am I supposed to be worried because he doesn't aspire to middle management?"

Ryan typically viewed authority figures (including his parents) as speed bumps on the way to doing whatever he wanted. He had already suffered a *lifetime banishment* from a carousel in downtown Boston after insisting that he stand on the back of his assigned horse while riding, and then, after he was kicked off the ride, raced around for several minutes darting under and around horses, evading capture by the carousel staff.

"Banned for life!" screamed the sweaty, exasperated operator once he returned the escaped fugitive to parental custody.

"How are you gonna enforce that?" I countered. "Is there a 'Most Wanted' section in the back with pictures of naughty kids?"

"Easy," he claimed. "I'll never forget that fucking kid for as long as I live."

So, deep down, I was more concerned about Kim's reaction to Ryan's first day than I let on.

Ryan was observed later that week by Dr. Schneider, PhD, MS, who was recommended by Kim at Treehouse, and who appeared well-credentialed—having trained at Harvard Medical School and McLean Hospital. Mary Beth and I met with Dr. Schneider following her observation of Ryan that consisted of watching him interact with his classmates in the preschool room for two hours during camp. She was younger than I expected with an angular face, straight blonde hair, piercing blue eyes, and an aristocratic nose. Her firm handshake and rigid posture reminded me of a German dressage rider at the Olympics.

At our meeting, Dr. Schneider drew an oval on a yellow legal pad. She then bisected it from top to bottom, before explaining that Ryan was super bright in the left half of his brain and much weaker in the right half. She described Ryan's strengths as analytical thought, detail-oriented perception, ordered sequencing, rational thought, verbal-based skills, planning, math, science, and logic. She listed his weaknesses as intuitive thought, perception, random sequencing, emotional regulation, nonverbal based tasks, impulse control, and imaginative storytelling. I was baffled as to how she made that determination after watching him play, but it made sense. Mary Beth and I are both law school graduates and classic type-A people. Neither of us displayed the slightest hint of creativity, so it was reasonable that we had produced a toddler like Ryan.

Dr. Schneider quickly hatched a plan to formally test Ryan to determine his clinical issues. She recommended that he leave Treehouse after the summer, enrolling instead in a special preschool program in town, the Sudbury Integrated Preschool, which offered a highly structured program that combined neurotypical students and children with intellectual or emotional struggles. Naturally, we were skeptical, but Dr. Schneider seemed to know Treehouse and the Sudbury Integrated Preschool well, so if she felt strongly, one was better suited for Ryan than the other, we felt it wise to listen to her. Plus, we doubted Treehouse would allow Ryan to attend their program in the fall even if we chose to disregard her recommendation.

Dr. Schneider next conducted a series of tests on Ryan, including the Wechsler Preschool and Primary Scale of Intelligence test as part of a neuropsychological evaluation. The testing confirmed her yellow legal pad diagnosis, as Ryan scored highly on verbal tasks and well below average on some nonverbal problem sets. She concluded in her written report that the evaluation suggested developmental delay and reduced skills in the following areas:

1. pragmatic (social) language development and the ability to understand nonverbal social cues;

2. difficulty appreciating nonverbal information and discriminating and integrating visual information of increasing complexity;

3. difficulty with sensorimotor integration and aspects of motor planning control; and

4. difficulty with self-regulation of emotional, behavioral, and cognitive functions.

In a follow-up meeting, we heard for the first time, terms like "special needs," "autism spectrum," "Asperger's Syndrome," and "processing delay." She wasn't ready to label Ryan as autistic in the classic sense but revealed the "name of the game with a special needs child and a public-school program is to label his issues as *something* to access services from the town through an Individual Education Plan (IEP)."

Mary Beth and I nodded vigorously. She agreed from a legal perspective, and I agreed from a marketing perspective because the label was Ryan's ticket to services from our town.

"I want you to pay attention to this because it is important." Dr. Schneider fixed her blue eyes on me for some reason. "Ryan's label will fall under the umbrella of autism, but don't get too hung up on the official diagnosis."

I sat there, stunned. I flashed to something my grandfather used to say whenever I tried to wiggle out of a jam claiming a minor lapse in judgment. He was a former Marine and Boston cop and never indulged excuse making and would say, "Oh, it was a *little mistake*? Like being a *little pregnant*?" Dr. Schneider seemed to be leaning toward a diagnosis of *a little autistic.*

She then spent several minutes rifling through a large textbook on her desk called the Diagnostic and Statistical Manual of Mental Disorders ("DSM") before pausing on a particular section while she slowly nodded her head. She had discovered Ryan's ticket. Her formal diagnosis was Pervasive Developmental Disorder–Not Otherwise Specified ("PDD-NOS").[1] Her formal report stated, "Ryan will require intensive, therapeutic support to address these developmental concerns."

---

1. PDD-NOS is one of several subtypes of autism that were folded into the single diagnosis of autism spectrum disorder ("ASD") with the publication of the DSM-5 in 2013.

Dr. Schneider told us PDD-NOS occurred in conjunction with a wide range of intelligence in children, with most exhibiting significant challenges in social and language development. She conceded Ryan did not struggle with the language piece, but argued he was complex in terms of social pragmatics. PDD-NOS fit someone exhibiting some but not all the characteristics of autism or who presented with relatively mild symptoms.

In my mind, my gifted son had moved from early admission at Harvard to our town's preschool program for students with disabilities. Not surprisingly, processing terrible news about your child has stages of grief, and at this point, I was clearly in denial. I was sure he would outgrow whatever issues Dr. Schneider labeled, and I grew incredibly frustrated with my family and friends who asked dozens of times, "What's his diagnosis?" As if hearing the word "autism" provided questioners with comfort, revealing the socially appropriate emotional response while addressing Ryan's behavioral issues; issues that provoked side-eye glances between couples during playdates or whispers among relatives whenever Ryan melted down at a family function.

In the fall of 2004, following the advice of Dr. Schneider, Ryan attended the Sudbury Integrated Preschool. Ryan's teacher was an experienced and highly respected woman named Ellen who was clearly more comfortable around kids than adults. At our introductory meeting, she mumbled to Mary Beth and me that Ryan was "in the right place."

However, by the end of week one, Ellen admitted to me that she was "locked in a battle" with a boy she called "fascinating."

While Ryan played on the other side of the classroom, hoping to forestall heading home, she rolled her eyes and confessed, "Rob, in all my years of teaching, I've never seen a boy like Ryan. He studies every inch of the classroom. He peppers my teaching assistants with questions. He's fixated on blown light bulbs, leaky pipes, and is obsessed with the air-conditioning units behind the school."

"Doesn't that make him really smart and inquisitive?" I countered.

She squinted and tilted her round face from left to right and back again. "Sure, but he only participates when activities interest him and refuses when they don't. And he really struggles to transition from one activity to another, particularly when it is time to clean up." She sighed and her face grew more serious. "I think there might be underlying issues here."

"Like what?" I asked angrily.

She forced a smile. "I'm not sure, but hopefully Dr. Schneider can tell you more with additional testing."

My early childhood memories are mostly fragments of events, but the things I remember are such important pieces to the puzzle. The bottom line is that I was an interesting young kid, even if I was like other kids in a lot of ways. I didn't like to eat my vegetables. I explored my yard in search of anthills and spider-webs, but unlike other kids, I was fascinated by big machines, especially ones that sucked in air with giant fans. Whenever we went to a new house, I was less interested in playing with relatives or friends, and instead, wanted to see the basement because that's where I could find the furnaces and water heaters.

I suppose my interests made me unique, but what really made me so different from other kids was how hard it was to reason with me. Like any kid, my sense of right and wrong never went beyond typical parental reward and punishment. Unlike other children, however, I was far more willing to defy my parents because the benefit of getting what I wanted outweighed whatever my parents would do to punish me. At least, that is how the math added up before all the trouble started.

To survive the year, Ellen relied on every trick in her teaching handbook, even for her end-of-year theatrical production. In the play, Ryan received a small part with only one line, but Ellen worried he might disrupt it, entertaining the audience with improvisation. So, to keep him from commenting on stage during the performance, Ellen positioned an assistant teacher behind a cardboard tree from the elaborate set design, handing Ryan candy and gum to keep his mouth busy. By the second act, Ryan's mouth was so full, I worried he might choke to death.

Another aspect to my early childhood that stands out is that I hated to be inter-rupted when doing anything. If I was building with blocks, I wasn't finished until I did what I wanted with them, and good luck to anyone telling me oth-erwise. I also had an abundance of unfocused energy, which quickly translated into a hatred for sitting still, and made things difficult for me in preschool. I quickly got bored with my teacher, Ellen, and began wandering around the room to explore. Soon, a teacher's aide followed me everywhere. Had I known the implications of what I was doing, I never would have left that tiny chair and waist-high table, but at the time, my perception of consequence was only in the moment. If I was bad, I got a red card and had to give it to my parents when I got home from school. When my parents pulled the card from my back-pack, they were disappointed, but nothing really came of it. However, behind the scenes, the people around me were in the process of developing a plan that altered my life forever.

———

At the end of his first year at the Sudbury Integrated Preschool, we made a tactical blunder that would prove to be Mistake #1 in decisions about Ryan's care. As a four-year-old, Ryan was too young for kindergarten, and he required another year of preschool. Ellen suggested having him repeat the program, arguing it would help him better prepare for kindergarten. Dr. Schneider agreed, and Ryan restarted the program in September of 2005 but ran into problems almost immediately.

When Dr. Schneider observed him at school, she noted in her report that Ryan had a meltdown over the attendance board because "his picture was out of place." Her conclusion was he had regressed from her earlier observation conducted the previous spring, recounting that he transitioned easily that day from parent drop-off to the start of the school. Fifteen years later, rereading her report, it struck me as to why he was so upset. In the first half of the year, Ellen's students were required to Velcro a laminated checkmark next to their picture each morning as they walked in the door. However, during the second half of the year, the students were instead asked to place a checkmark next to the *written version* of their name. My belief is that Ryan was troubled by the pictures on the attendance sheet rather than written names, which ran counter to the attendance system of the previous spring. He had not "regressed" as Dr. Schneider's report suggested, he was simply frustrated by the unexplained regression in his classroom environment.

In addition to his irritation with the classroom reset, Ryan grew bored easily because the thrill of any "new" activity was lost on him, resulting in trouble. So much so, that by January of 2006, Ryan faced expulsion from preschool. Dr. Schneider quickly stepped in to negotiate a settlement with Sudbury's special education department, thereby allowing Ryan to finish the school year. In the compromise, the town agreed to pay for a teacher's aide dedicated to Ryan, and we agreed to try Ritalin, despite having refused medication in previous discussions. The teacher's aide helped Ryan finish the school year, but Ritalin acted like a double espresso and made his behavior a million times worse. After two days, we stopped it.

At the conclusion of the school year, we were advised by Dr. Schneider to consider private programs with a more therapeutic environment for his kindergarten placement. It was the first time that we heard the word *therapeutic* in conjunction with a school description. A word that sounded so beneficial, yet ultimately became a curse in Ryan's life.

CHAPTER FOUR

A Holding Environment

"What is not natural can be learned."

—Dr. Donald Winnicott

September 5, 2006. When Dr. Schneider proposed moving Ryan out of public school into a therapeutic environment, Mary Beth and I did not hear "therapeutic"; we heard "private." Like the classic study of wine drinkers rating various samples and told the price of each glass, we assumed the most expensive option for Ryan was best. After all, public school is free. The therapeutic programs we were exploring had tuitions nearing $75,000 and Sudbury was footing the bill—thank you very much.

After observing Ryan earlier in the spring, Dr. Schneider's *Report of Neuropsychological Re-Evaluation* recommended the following:

The nature and severity of Ryan's developmental difficulty indicates that he requires placement in a therapeutic school specifically able to address his needs. I have referred Ryan to the Spring Valley Therapeutic Academy, and program directors there have agreed he will enroll for September 2006. I strongly endorse this option for Ryan.

Based on the recommendation of Dr. Schneider, we enrolled Ryan in the Spring Valley Therapeutic Academy (SVTA). At the time, it seemed like the best option. It was close to home, drew from Sudbury and neighboring towns, ensuring potential friendships for Ryan, and even had "therapeutic" in the name. However, the school proved to be anything but therapeutic, resulting in big parenting Mistake #2.

SVTA was founded in the 1970s as an alternative to "reform school" for children who were intellectually or emotionally unable to attend public school with their peers. In its early years, SVTA managed emotionally troubled kids, allowing attendance at some version of school rather than banishing them to an institution. Most of the initial children at SVTA were developmentally delayed or behaviorally challenged, but at the turn of the twenty-first century, school systems (particularly in highly educated communities) experienced a dramatic rise in the diagnosis of autism spectrum disorder. As a result, local children with complex neurological profiles like Ryan's were increasingly extracted from public school, landing at SVTA.

The owners of SVTA were Harry and his wife Anne. Both had unkempt gray hair and resembled 1960s radicals who met in a commune, hatching an idea for an alternative educational experience for troubled youth. The third founder who ran the daily operations of the school was a man named Ira with a honed Brooklyn accent that reminded me of a Damon Runyon character. He was wiry and bald with sharp features and dark brown eyes that gave him a skeletal appearance, and he carried himself like hardscrabble kid who boxed his way out of the neighborhood. Ira spent his early career working in prisons and inner-city schools in Boston, further solidifying his persona.

SVTA utilized a "holding environment" in structuring an educational model for its student population. The school cited the work of Dr. Donald Winnicott (1896–1971), an English pediatrician and psychoanalyst who equated newborns held by their mothers to the "holding" environment of family, school, and society as children mature. It was easy to miss in the marketing materials that the holding environment referenced by SVTA signified that teachers and staff planned to *physically restrain* Ryan. In other words, teachers and staff were programmed to look for signs of emotional stress, offering students the chance to regain composure in a time-out or safe space, but should that fail, they were taught to pounce, grabbing students from behind and pinning them to the floor until they settled.

Similar to moving Ryan to the Sudbury Integrated Preschool and repeating preschool there, by allowing Dr. Schneider to steer Ryan to SVTA, we ignored our parental instincts and followed the recommendations of others. I appreciate why Mary Beth made these miscalculations because her successful professional career revolved around process and hierarchy, presuming those with more education and experience knew best. My parental approach leaned more heavily on instinct, but—in my desperation to cure Ryan—whenever a doctor or teacher held out the promise of a brighter day, I naively embraced it.

No matter our motivation, we made a terrible misjudgment assuming physical interventions performed at school when Ryan became upset helped him. Although we were motivated by all the right reasons in wanting to help Ryan, we were woefully uneducated on behavior control techniques, and it never occurred to us that there might be other options. To make matters worse, we acquiesced when SVTA insisted on training us in the proper technique for restraining Ryan at home. We even agreed to hire a full-time caregiver skilled in the fine art of restraint combat because that's what restraint is: two people having a physical confrontation where one side forces the other to submit. SVTA described it differently, calling it more of a "hug" for children unable to settle after becoming upset, but these hugs often resulted in elementary-school-aged children lying facedown on the ground with a grownup on top of them.

—◆—

Unlike my parents, I got a preview of life at SVTA when I was still at the Sudbury Integrated Preschool. A woman named Cara from SVTA came to observe me in class. She told me I was going to a new school in September with a big white barn, and I replied angrily, "I don't want to go to a new school! What about my friends? I like this school!" She then took me to the gym to watch me play alone with large foam dice on the basketball court and, after a few minutes, she told me it was time to put them away. When I resisted because recess wasn't over, she attempted to take them away from me, and when I pulled back, she grabbed my arm and reversed my body into a stress position.

I was terrified and tried to escape. Before I knew it, my feet were swept from underneath me and I was on the ground with Cara on top of me, pressing my body hard against the gym floor. I screamed loudly out of pain and fear, causing her to cover my mouth to muffle the disturbance. With her on top of me, I had trouble breathing and honestly thought I might suffocate. While all that was happening, she continued to ask me if I was "ready to be safe," but I didn't even know what she meant since she was the one who tackled me. Eventually, I submitted and after a while, she let go. I couldn't comprehend what had just happened, but something inside me knew things would never be the same again.

⸺

Ryan's first month at SVTA was relatively stable, and as Dr. Schneider correctly predicted, the heavily structured approach benefited him. School days were consistent, transitions previewed, and free play was highly supervised and scripted. In addition, we received daily reports documenting Ryan's day, including whether he was subjected to any "holds." When relevant, those reports described the circumstances surrounding the need to restrain him, but we followed up in the evening to glean his side of the story. In his version, Ryan generally accepted responsibility for whatever transgression led to his punishment, but his characterization of being held by a teacher sounded like the victim of near strangulation. Mary Beth and I attributed his passionate reenactments to child hyperbole because a five-year-old's description of a restraint that occurred hours before was prone to exaggeration.

From a purely educational standpoint, SVTA had success in motivating Ryan by leveraging his voracious appetite for information. Teachers and staff fostered the exploration of topics that interested him, and Ryan arrived home each day able to enthusiastically describe what he learned. That is why assessing SVTA in the beginning was so difficult. For every highlight, Ryan also chronicled the instances when he was restrained on the floor, and his face changed as he relived those incidents. He spoke in an angrier tone, which made sense, having made a mistake and been punished, but he never complained about his teachers or refused to get on the bus in the morning. Perhaps, he was just doing what the child of Robert and Mary Beth DeLena was supposed to do: toughing it out. Or, more likely, he was so desperate to make friends that he was willing to offset enjoyable moments at school with occasional physical pain.

———

At SVTA, holds happened every day, like training a dog. When I think about it now, giving the violent and demoralizing act of restraint a name like "hold" felt like naming a grizzly bear "Cuddles." It was an attempt to make it sound safe and, every time I did anything wrong, I was either put in timeout or a hold. Sometimes, if I so much as objected to what we were doing in class, I was put in a hold. If I stood up during a timeout, I was put in a hold.

One teacher, Sam, who assisted our class was always the most aggressive. He came off as having something to prove and was the most likely to cover my mouth, leave me with rug burns, and restrain me for prolonged periods of time. A female assistant teacher named Amy was more a fan of verbal abuse. She would often remind me during the holds that I was "just a little boy," so I felt small and insignificant.

The school director, Ira, was strange on every level. He was a sixty-year-old man with a bad case of toxic masculinity who clearly gained some twisted sense of pride from tackling little kids. He often bragged about the time he restrained five students at once, one under each limb and one pinned by his torso. At SVTA, students were forced to meet with Ira once a week in his upstairs office, and he also ate lunch with our class on Fridays. During my first lunch, he noticed my lack of height and came up with nicknames for me.

"Hey Ryan, how would you like it if I called you Pipsqueak?"

When I became embarrassed, he laughed at me in front of the whole table. I'm average height, but when I was little, Ira made me insecure about being short, and I started kneeling on chairs at the lunch table to feel taller. Soon, I kneeled everywhere I went. I never told my parents why, and they had me checked for hip problems because I never sat like a regular kid.

In my first year at SVTA, I was scared of Ira, but I refused to give in. I rebelled, pushing to do the things that I wanted to do, and I fought back whenever he put me in a hold. During one of our weekly meetings, I refused to play a board game with him, so he restrained me and rubbed it in my face that he could keep me still. In his best baseball announcer voice, he yelled, "And the sixty-year-old beats the five-year-old once again!"

Aside from the radical alteration to Ryan's school environment, other aspects of a structured behavioral model did initially improve life at home. At Dr. Schneider's suggestion, we searched for a new caregiver specializing in children with disabilities and, after interviewing several candidates, eventually hired a woman named Monica, a licensed ABA therapist. An ABA therapist is a person who uses Applied Behavior Analysis as a form of treatment. Applied Behavior Analysis is the process of studying behavior to put into place appropriate behavioral interventions. Consistent with SVTA, Monica implemented a behavioral model for Ryan predicated on reward and punishment including restraint.[1]

To her credit, Monica was incredibly consistent, managing to remain calm even in the most heated situations, and her systematic approach to parenting instituted predictability and routine in a house with neither. When our kids were young, Mary Beth and I employed a similar parenting strategy. We generally allowed Ryan and his younger sister, Abigail, free rein to do just about anything—only stepping in to put out fires. That parenting model may have benefited both kids later in life, but when they were young, Ryan ignited a lot of fires.

As a result, we saw improvement in Ryan's behavior during Monica's first few months. She was a master of laminated task schedules that included a reward at the end. Her use of positive reinforcement motivated Ryan to learn reading skills and to potty train—milestones that Mary Beth and I struggled to teach him. The problem, however, was that any time he failed on a task and hurt his chances of attaining the goal, he got emotional and Monica restrained him. In those instances, she followed the SVTA model precisely, asking Ryan if he "needed space" to calm down,

---

1. Restraint and seclusion have always been controversial aspects of ABA therapy. In 2010, the Association for Behavior Analysis International (ABAI) issued an official "Statement on Restraint and Seclusion" which stated, "Members strongly oppose the inappropriate and/or unnecessary use of seclusion, restraint, or other intrusive interventions. Although many persons with severe behavior problems can be effectively treated without the use of any restrictive interventions, restraint may be necessary on some rare occasions with meticulous clinical oversight and controls. In addition, a carefully planned and monitored use of timeout from reinforcement can be acceptable under restricted circumstances. Seclusion is sometimes necessary or needed, but behavior analysts would support only the most highly monitored and ethical practices associated with such use."

while warning him that his "body was getting fast." In other words, Monica was telling Ryan that he was becoming dysregulated, and if he failed to settle down, she was obligated to make him settle down.

Most of the time, despite Monica's admonition, the realization that it would now take him longer to attain whatever pot of gold was at the end of the chart was too much for Ryan to bear. He typically added something dramatic to demonstrate how angry he felt—knocking over a chair or throwing his juice box across the room. Once that happened, the next half hour was filled with yelling, screaming, and violence while she pinned Ryan on the ground until he submitted.

—⟡—

Abigail and I liked playing with Monica, but before she started working with us, she and my parents were trained by SVTA on how to properly execute restraints. Because I had already experienced a lot of holds at school, I begged and pleaded for them not to learn, but it was no use. Soon, I was getting violently restrained at school and at home every day. As a result, I was constantly terrified, never felt safe, and couldn't understand my world anymore. I began relying on my fight-or-flight instinct to survive day-to-day life, and anytime I sensed a threat, I either fought until I was too exhausted to defend myself or learned to run like hell until I was caught.

—⟡—

What bothers me most about the decision to restrain Ryan at home is that I was not raised in a house with any corporal punishment. My mother was home most days with me and my brother, Jon. Every so often, she snapped and fired a shoe across the room, but she never spanked us, and she bent over backward to ensure we were happy and healthy. My mother was also unable to rely on the "wait until your father gets home" threat because he was not a strict disciplinarian. His parenting model stemmed from abuse he suffered as a child and when called into a situation requiring a firmer hand, he used logic and reasoning to resolve it rather than physicality.

With the backdrop of my own childhood, why did I agree to a restraint-based punishment system for Ryan? If SVTA had suggested we restrain Abigail when she acted up, I never would have agreed in a million years. So, why was it different with Ryan? It flowed from the diagnosis. Once Dr. Schneider and SVTA established Ryan was a child with a disability, it opened the door to parent him differently. It shouldn't have, but it did.

— ❦ —

Abigail and I are very close today, but when she was younger, she had a talent for making trouble and still coming out on top. She could destroy whatever LEGO structure I was building or punch me in the stomach, and when I so much as pushed her back, she would scream at the top of her lungs and even cry on command—summoning my parents to her defense. Naturally, I was blamed, put in timeout, or restrained while she gave me a little smile.

— ❦ —

Undeniably, Ryan's behavior was different from Abigail's. He was out of control at times, never stopped moving, and was constantly in trouble for testing limits. Ryan was not the baseball player I expected. Instead, he used my power drill (without permission) to find out what the inside of a baseball looked like. When ideas materialized in his head, it was impossible to stop him, and he became defiant and irrational when he did not get his way. Abigail had her moments and certainly acted like a brat on occasion, but Ryan was relentless. Whenever parents recommended letting Ryan "cry it out," I laughed because Ryan could go for hours. In the interest of sanity, it was better to give in rather than fighting him for the rest of the day.

One piece of corroborating evidence SVTA used in justifying an ABA-based approach was a test performed on Ryan at Boston Children's Hospital called a "brain scan." This test was conducted in a small, secluded office by a neurologist named Dr. Doherty. Dr. Doherty revolutionized the use of electrodes strategically placed on a patient's head to register levels of brain stimulation. It was considered an innovative procedure by neurologists in the early 1990s that was seldom used by the time Ryan was tested, as most neurologists were now using MRIs. SVTA, however, swore by the genius of Dr. Doherty and, true to form, his testing identified "white matter" in one of the lobes of Ryan's brain.

At our post-testing meeting, Dr. Doherty concluded Ryan was bipolar like he was reading an x-ray of a cleanly fractured arm. He held up a spectrogram-looking chart with a pattern of shaded sections. "You see, this section indicates impaired processing. It fits a bipolar pattern and explains his issues relating to other children."

I wasn't convinced. "You can tell all that from flashing lights in his eyes?"

"Yes, of course. Your son's brain clearly misfires when processing stimuli and, since nothing can be done to correct it, you can only teach him to manage his abnormally slow or misfiring responses."

I looked at Mary Beth and hoped she would save me the trouble of telling Dr. Doherty that he was insane, but she sat quietly and began to tear up. Finally, I jumped in. "Are you saying it's hopeless?"

"Well, no, I am not saying that. I am saying that his inability to relate to others will help him when self-selecting a career. He might end up being highly successful at something like making furniture. Something that limits human interaction."

I looked and Mary Beth and whispered, "Furniture?" She turned her head and gave me a pleading expression that read, "Please don't say anything stupid." I nodded slowly and stood up, indicating that I was ending the appointment politely, but in my mind, I envisioned reaching across Dr. Doherty's desk to slap the electrodes on his bald head to determine *his* mental and emotional deficiencies.

Unsure of what to make of Dr. Doherty's conclusions, we asked Dr. Schneider to offer her opinion on the results of the brain scan. Fortunately, she was critical of the technology behind the test and cited the example of someone with trauma in a section of the brain that normally controls certain body functions and when damaged, other parts of the brain kick in to take its place.[2] She concluded any supposed analysis of

---

2. After researching Dr. Schneider's comment about damaged brains, I came upon the story of Phineas Gage on Wikipedia, a foreman on a railroad construction crew in Vermont in 1848. Gage was injured when an accident blew a thirteen-pound iron tamping rod through his skull. He survived, but much of his frontal cortex was destroyed. Initially, lacking a frontal cortex changed the

one lobe of Ryan's brain could never accurately forecast the rest of his life. That conversation left us feeling more upbeat about Ryan's future, but it was clear that SVTA accepted Dr. Doherty's report as gospel and planned to rely on it for justification in restraining him.

Every day, my parents received a written log of everything that happened during the school day. In those entries, I was painted as a troublemaker to justify the holds. No teacher was ever at fault in these writings.

After a restraint, I hardly remembered what I did to get into trouble in the first place and was never sure why some things got me restrained and not others. Sometimes restraint battles got really physical, and my teachers told me if I continued to act the way I was acting, I would end up in prison. I felt like a terrible person and often cried about my future, fearing I would hurt someone I cared about and would wind up spending my life in a cell. I thought everything was my fault.

Without question, we were wrong to assume SVTA knew more about Ryan than we did, even if parenting him the same way that we parented Abigail would have required endless hours monitoring his every move, anticipating trouble spots and, when he flared up emotionally, disarming him with an impassive demeanor. Clearly, it would have been really fucking exhausting, but I wish we had utilized that approach rather than pinning him to the floor until he lost the will to fight back. Instead, for the rest of 2007, and for all of 2008, Ryan's life was much the same. He was restrained hundreds of times at SVTA, dozens of other times by Monica, and Mary Beth and I also restrained him when we felt the SVTA protocol necessitated it. Those parenting scenes were particularly ugly because we were more emotional than Monica and only restrained

---

mild-mannered Gage into person lacking any impulse control with little deference for those around him. In time, however, Gage improved. He resumed working and was described as appropriately behaved. Psychiatrists believe his remaining frontal cortical tissue had taken on some of the functions lost in the injury.

him after something terrible transpired or when we just snapped like a guard in the Stanford Prison Experiment.[3]

To the outside world, we appeared normal. We traveled and saw friends and family, only accepting invitations to events and activities Ryan could handle. We kept Abigail on a traditional path—attending Treehouse, then public school, while playing sports and having playdates. I even coached her in softball, experiencing something that I always dreamed about with Ryan, except in baseball. Those moments on the field with Abigail were a distraction from the chaos occurring at home, but practices and games behind our middle school were constant reminders that my son was an outsider. He wasn't allowed in our town schools and was bused every day to a therapeutic school that manhandled him. So, despite my constant smile around parents of the girls that I coached, inside the walls of our house, the environment was tense and combustible. Ryan was kept happy with activities and places he enjoyed, but his behavior was modulated by the constant threat of restraint.

---

3. The Stanford Prison Experiment was a role-play simulation conducted by Stanford psychology professor Philip Zimbardo and held at Stanford University in 1971. It examined the reactions and behaviors of students in a two-week study of a simulated prison environment where some participants acted as prisoners and some as prison guards.

CHAPTER FIVE

The Magic Carpet

"Desperation is sometimes as powerful an inspirer as genius."
—BENJAMIN DISRAELI, BRITISH STATESMAN, 1804–1881

January 2, 2009. Parenting Ryan on weekends often resembled a hostage situation that necessitated ransom payments to prevent his constant movement and emotional intensity from inflicting discomfort. Ryan never targeted anyone intentionally but, when he was bored, there was no limit to the trouble he generated. Dr. Schneider characterized our seven-year-old's personality flaw as "lacking a contemplative pause" before acting, provoking every bystander in the vicinity.

To counter potential downtime, we relied on planning and improvisation. Planning meant trips to the Museum of Science, the Children's Museum, or the New England Aquarium—activities that killed time. However, the ride to and from a destination while he watched a DVD was often the most enjoyable aspect of the trip. Although witnessing Ryan soak in facts and new concepts was rewarding, his behavior in public places ranged from challenging to absolutely humiliating. He refused to share, take turns, or wait in line, and he pushed his way to the front of any public setting to better his vantage point. Particularly, when a destination contained an interactive area, Ryan's ability to foment discord was legendary, and we heard audible groans from other parents anytime he showed up for events at our town's community center.

On a weekend day without a planned activity or, worse, during school vacations, Ryan and Abigail played together in our house—well-stocked with toys—but that generally lasted a few minutes before Abigail was reduced to tears. Ryan was so amped during games or puzzles or building with LEGO bricks that whenever he perceived Abigail was performing better on a task, he would wreck whatever they were doing. As soon as the crying started, Mary Beth comforted Abigail while I removed Ryan from the situation, convincing him to go someplace he enjoyed like the playground or Home Depot to end the conflict.

Even on days when Ryan wasn't generating turmoil with his sister, we remained constantly vigilant to prevent him from climbing the walls of our house—and I mean that literally. Ryan loved to impress houseguests by spreading his legs, positioning his feet across our doorjambs, then shinnying up to touch the ceiling. Worse, he sometimes spread his entire body across a narrow hallway, parallel to the floor, using his hands and feet to ascend the walls, surveying the room below like a spider. Our house cleaner even suggested that we attend church services with her on Sundays after discovering handprints and footprints in unexplainable places.

I cannot recall exactly what precipitated tossing Ryan into my car on that cold January day, but it was just after lunch when I sped toward Nashoba Valley Ski Area, a tiny local hill with an active rental program for beginners. What fueled my brainstorm to take Ryan skiing remains a mystery, but we had attended several disastrous birthday parties over the years at a large indoor gymnastics studio near Nashoba and after another public humiliation, I must have driven by the ski area and filed it away as a possible activity one day to placate him.

⌒⌒

One day, during Christmas vacation, something happened that changed my world for the better on every level. Dad made a random decision to take me skiing at Nashoba Valley. It was located forty minutes from our house, and it stood just 240 feet high, but it was the tallest thing I'd ever seen. My guess is that Dad's expectations weren't very high in terms of my likely response to the sport because, over the years, attempts to find a hobby ended in failure, and sometimes tears. Our garage was a graveyard to every attempt, filled with baseball bats, footballs, basketballs, ice skates, and more.

After arriving at the ski area, we followed signs for ski rentals, and headed into a barn with corral-like dividers to funnel skiers and snowboarders through the rental process. We were then led like cattle through the rental procedure: standing next to a pole to measure height, stepping on a large scale for weight before placing our feet into a homemade measuring device. Ryan's zero-tolerance policy for anything tedious had me nervously awaiting the inevitable meltdown in front of other parents and their annoyingly well-behaved children.

By some act of mercy, we completed the rental process and stepped outside wearing the most uncomfortable ski boots in America. Then, after clicking into our skis and without really thinking about the next step, I pushed him toward the "magic carpet." If you haven't seen one, the magic carpet resembles an airport people mover, ascending to the top of the beginner hill. At Nashoba, the magic carpet is thirty-feet long with riders maintaining a standing position for one minute to reach the exit point. After reaching the loading area without either of us falling over, I nervously guided Ryan while he aligned his skis on the conveyor belt and, suddenly, we thrust forward, traveling uphill.

We remained upright for the ride up and disembarked without falling over. Then, as we stood in the middle of a slightly sloped hill, it dawned on me that I hadn't explained anything about skiing to Ryan because I never thought we would get this far. So, I grabbed him around his right shoulder and quickly twisted him to look at me.

"Ry, let me show you a couple of quick things." I often called him Ry, which was ironic because I intentionally selected a first name that people wouldn't shorten. I had gone through life as Robert, Robbie, Rob, and occasionally the dreaded Bobby or Bob, and wanted his name to hold true. "When you want to turn, lean your body slightly in the direction that you want to go, like riding a bike." My advice on turning was about as technically incorrect as it could be, but to be clear, I had skied very little in my own life. My godmother was a skier who enjoyed bringing kids from the city of Revere to the mountains of New Hampshire, and we traveled to her condo on two occasions during middle school. Also, during seventh grade, I took weekly YMCA bus trips with my brother to Bradford Hill in Massachusetts. However, by the start of high school, I stopped skiing entirely for fear of missing out on baseball season.

When I got off the magic carpet, I wasn't really sure what to expect. I'd never seen skiing in person, in fact, the closest thing to real skiing I'd ever seen was a winter-themed episode of Curious George *when I was a little kid. All I remembered from it was a scene when George goes straight down the hill, so I assumed that's what I was supposed to do. Dad tried to explain something to me, but between my hat and tight helmet over my ears, and the excitement about going down the hill, I didn't really catch anything he said.*

Ryan looked back at me blankly. The boy who usually spoke nonstop and who won arguments with pinpoint logic and staccato vehemence said nothing. Instead, his eyes wandered to the other skiers attempting to survive the short run to the bottom.

"Ry, pay attention for one second; I need to show you how to slow down and how to stop."

He turned his head to look at me. He looked silly standing there on skis, in an overstuffed winter jacket and wearing a bike helmet that I grabbed quickly from our garage lodged over a knit cap. "Listen. See how I point the tips of my skis inward to make a triangle? That will slow you down and help you stop."

"Yup."

His eyes once again moved down the hill. Like an alien from another planet who crash lands on earth, Ryan was scanning the landscape to assess every skier's strength and weakness.

"Ry, one last thing. If you fall . . . ." I dropped my body into the snow and began my explanation of how to line up my skis, relying on the slope of the hill for leverage to get back up. However, before I delved too deeply, Ryan looked at me, pointed his skis, and quickly pushed off with

37

one foot, rapidly descending in a straight line toward the bottom. He left me lying in the snow struggling to get up as he whizzed by dozens of beginner skiers who were falling around him like the opening scene of *Saving Private Ryan*. Then, rather than crashing into the orange snow fence at the bottom, he veered sharply toward the line of skiers waiting to load the magic carpet. I remember wondering if his sharp turn was purposeful or happenstance, but in either case, he finished by gliding to a stop near a cluster of skiers in the magic carpet line.

After breathlessly watching Ryan avoid slamming into the lift line, I shook off twenty-five years of rust and quickly raced to the bottom and derailed his plan to cut in front of other skiers waiting to load the magic carpet. He wasn't thrilled about heading to the back of the line, but rather than arguing, he peered up at me with a half-smile and shouted, "I want to do that again!"

We managed several more runs on the magic carpet without Ryan ever falling. I knew our day could end quickly with one crash, and most skiers fall constantly on day one, yet he seemed to ski faster with each run. He had little interest in learning how to stop and would ski as far as his momentum carried him, which resulted in dragging him back up the hill toward the magic carpet. Eventually, I grew weary and opted for a chairlift to take us to the very top of the hill, but on our first attempt, we suffered our first skiing mishap. After failing to realize he was too short for the approaching chair, I badly misjudged the loading process. When the chair hit us in the back of the legs, I fumbled Ryan and he fell off the lift, thankfully before it had ascended too high off the ground. He was unhurt but ordinarily the embarrassment of a falling in front of the entire lift line would have ended our day. Dr. Schneider and SVTA were always quick to point out Ryan's lack of awareness of other children's perspective, but he was always very cognizant of the judgment of other children whenever he failed at something. A public humiliation like falling off the chairlift should have ended our day. It didn't.

We lasted over three hours at Nashoba, and Mary Beth called several times, wondering if one or both of us was receiving treatment at a local emergency room. On the ride home, Ryan enthusiastically described how fast he skied. It was unfamiliar to have him conclude an activity with a smile on his face. As his father, it felt even more inexplicable. I know that sounds awful but, when he was seven years old, every single day involved emotional outbursts and conflict, often in public settings. For most of his early childhood, I possessed three emotional states: crisis, post-crisis, and waiting for the next crisis. In other words, anger, guilt, and anxiety. Yet, despite my nervousness heading into the experience, we enjoyed our time at Nashoba so much that we went back the next day. And, after we completed the rental procedure for a second time, we spent another hour on the magic carpet before arranging a private lesson to have one of Nashoba's professional instructors teach Ryan the proper technique for stopping. Although he was skiing well, he advanced as far as his momentum carried him or until he landed in the parking lot, and I wasn't having any luck teaching him to slow down, let alone snowplow into a stop.

Ryan was fine with a professional taking my place for an hour, but when a middle-aged woman with a British accent named Darcy introduced herself, sounding more like a nanny from a Disney movie, I was hardly optimistic. Ryan, however, didn't seem to mind and quickly headed off with his new friend, eager to show her what great a skier he was already, while I ducked inside for a much-needed bathroom break.

⸺ ❧ ⸺

My instructor watched me take one run on the magic carpet and I skied straight down as I did previously with Dad. She complimented my straight run but then explained to me that, if I wanted to be a good skier, I needed to make turns. Soon, I picked up a variation of a turn called a "pizza turn," and, after one more run on the magic carpet, we moved to the chairlift. My instructor then coached me through a handful of large "S-turns" as I descended an intermediate run.

⸺ ❧ ⸺

Upon returning outside, I scoured the beginner area unsuccessfully for any sign of Ryan, then skied several runs before heading back at the conclusion of his lesson. In a flash, Ryan and Darcy materialized, with Ryan finishing at my feet in a dramatic snowplow stop. Pleased with his progress, I asked Darcy how he did overall and waited for the usual code words to indicate how poorly he listened or followed the rules. However, instead of the typical, "Wow, he has lots of energy," or "Boy, he has his own ideas," Darcy said, as if she was describing afternoon tea, "Oh, we had such a time."

"Awesome!" I responded in the tone of an overindulgent but highly skeptical parent. "So, he did pretty well?"

"Oh, my goodness, yes!" she exclaimed. "He even made it down the expert slope."

I assumed Darcy was being sarcastic and let out a snort. I figured it was just a coaching ploy, one that I used when I coached softball, promising a girl with limited abilities that she would play at University of Florida one day. But, before I could match her comment with my usual snarkiness about Ryan skiing in the Olympics someday, Ryan interjected, "She isn't joking!"

⌁

The lesson went by so fast. On my last run, I asked if I could ski the trail with the large black diamond sign in front, knowing nothing about the symbol. She agreed, and we made our way over the blind roll of the hill to the really steep part. I didn't make it look pretty, losing a ski halfway down and struggling with my turns, but when I reached the bottom, another instructor had her eyes fixed on me. That instructor, whom I now know to be the ski school director, asked me if I really skied that run in my first lesson. I nodded, and when she gave me a high five, I looked at Dad, and asked, "Why is everyone looking at me?" Honestly, moving on skis felt so natural, I had no idea what a big deal it was to ski an expert slope on my second day of skiing.

⌁

Two weeks later, during the long weekend for Martin Luther King Jr., we headed west to Wachusett Mountain, a 2,000-foot ski area in Princeton, Massachusetts. Upon arrival, we encountered a packed parking lot and, as we headed toward the ski area, the lift lines were miles long. I thought, *okay, this is where it all falls apart.*

After I secured our rental gear, I ducked inside to ask an employee if there was a special pass or shorter line for kids with disabilities. That might sound ridiculous, but I was desperate. However, despite a few instances when Ryan dropped to the ground, surrendering all hope that the line would ever move, we managed to survive the long waits, skiing top to bottom several times without any meltdowns. As we concluded each run, he desperately hoped to get back up the lift as quickly as possible, but he was willing to trade something unpleasant to experience something he so badly wanted to do. It was the first time I had ever witnessed Ryan accept the concept of *waiting his turn* to do anything. That might not seem like a breakthrough for most children, but he was finally showing the maturity level of a seven-year-old, without meltdowns or unreasonable demands. Luckily, with each hour, the lines grew shorter, making the experience even more enjoyable. Ryan had improved immensely after his lesson at Nashoba, and I felt more comfortable with my turns as things were starting to come back to me.

In the aftermath of our day at Wachusett, I told Mary Beth that I was encouraged by Ryan's ability to self-regulate his patience level and persevere despite the long lines, and although it was more stressful than our time at Nashoba, it was still enjoyable. We laughed during the skiing portion and talked nonstop on the chairlifts up. Ryan remained as intense about skiing as he was about everything else and wanted to ski faster without falling. However, unlike other activities, his unrelenting drive for perfection wasn't causing him to unravel when things did not go as planned.

After conquering Wachusett, I was confident enough to purchase equipment for both of us and research ski resorts within driving distance of Sudbury. A few days later, we headed two hours north to Loon Mountain in New Hampshire and, as we pulled into the parking lot, I looked up at the ski area and took a deep breath. An afternoon of managing Ryan on a mountain was one thing, but the trails at Loon looked so steep and the two peaks comprising the resort were enormous compared to the ones we skied in Massachusetts. On the ride up, I had prepared myself by picturing each potential crisis with Ryan on the mountain. What if he is cold? What if he won't eat in the cafeteria? What if I lose track of him on the mountain? What if he gets hurt? As we headed into the lodge, I examined the cluster of trails funneling to the base and wondered about the trails near the top. This wasn't like Nashoba or Wachusett, where in both cases I was able to assess the hill/mountain from the parking lot. Loon was a step into the unknown, and as Ryan hurried toward the lodge, it dawned on me that I failed to account for one probable disaster scenario: What happens if *I* get hurt skiing at Loon and this experiment comes to an end?

—⌣—

Loon was so much bigger than Nashoba and even Wachusett. My desire to explore the vast terrain got us into trouble on numerous occasions. At Loon, I discovered "tree skiing" by taking Dad through an unmarked glade that ended at a closed trail, so we had to hike back up. Tree skiing got us into trouble again when Dad lost a ski on a trail called Undercut.

—⌣—

Fortunately, our day at Loon tested only one of my disaster protocols. On our way into the woods to try Undercut, I fell under the lift, losing a ski, and Ryan continued into the woods while I dug frantically to locate it. I screamed at him to wait for me, but Undercut was his only focus, and he never looked back.

—⌣—

He told me to go downhill while he looked for his ski. Little did he realize that the open section of the trail funneled into the most difficult woods on the entire mountain.

—⌣—

After finally collecting myself, I entered a steeper-pitched trail, but after several crashes resulted in a face full of branches and a bloody lip, I removed my skis and walked the rest of the way until I reached the groomed portion of the trail. I then raced to the bottom, but there was no sign of Ryan near the lift. My heart sank. He was gone, and I would never see him again. My mind flashed to the soon-to-be-held press conference where I would hold up his picture while explaining to the world why I allowed my troubled son to ski alone on a black diamond trail in the woods.

But before I reached the door of the lodge to call for help, I stumbled into Ryan. He was in the process of alerting a ski patroller that he had lost his dad. I wish I could take credit for teaching Ryan about the role of ski patrollers, if he got lost, but I never mentioned them. My protocol was less nuanced and was directed more at me than him. It had only one step: "Don't ever lose sight of Ryan."

On the ride home, I asked Ryan how he knew to seek out the patroller and inquired what he said to him.

"He had a red jacket that said Loon on the back, so he seemed like a good person to ask," he said clinically, logically, and without emotion. "I told him that I lost my dad in the trees."

"What did he say to that?"

"He laughed and told me not to worry."

——

After skiing at Loon, I was completely hooked. Nashoba and Wachusett were fun places, but Loon had trees to explore, and expert runs across two peaks with 2,000 feet of vertical drop. Loon even had a double black expert run that I wanted to try, but Dad said no.

As we drove home from New Hampshire, things outside my window looked different. I wasn't just seeing mountains and trees along the side of the highway; I saw places to ski and imagined myself slashing through the woods.

Dad laughed and agreed when I told him that mountains only looked like mountains when you looked at them from the bottom.

——

It might sound incredibly stressful, but that day at Loon was better than *anything* we had ever done together. After hundreds of hours wandering around Home Depot and attempting every activity under the sun to connect with him, only to have it fail tragically, I had just shared an activity with Ryan that he loved. Sure, dressing in the lodge, eating in the cafeteria, and waiting in lift lines reminded me how challenging he was, but once the skis were on his feet, he was no longer a boy with mental or emotional problems. He was happy.

CHAPTER SIX

Double Black Diamonds

"Never underestimate your own ignorance."
—ALBERT EINSTEIN

Over the next month, we skied every weekend at Loon. Each Friday, I laid out our equipment and consulted Mary Beth about coats, gloves, and face protection. On Saturday mornings, I tapped Ryan on the shoulder, and he quickly hopped out of bed. For years, Dr. Schneider and SVTA documented Ryan's struggles with transitions, warning change demanded "previewing" to allow him time to process any switch in "cognitive sets." To cement her point, Dr. Schneider used the analogy of an adult's commute home. Although traffic or crowded trains add stressors, the ride home allows sufficient time to shift from "work mode" to "parent mode." She advised us to warn Ryan well in advance whenever he was asked to move from one activity to another—an advanced warning so he was able to make a mental and emotional shift before having to make a physical one. Yet, each Saturday, he awoke, brushed his teeth, ate breakfast, and dressed before the car was even warmed up.

In short order, skiing became Ryan's favorite topic of conversation. At home, he drew pictures of mountains to demonstrate terrain at various resorts and began using strange words like "cornice" and "couloir" to describe impressive runs he planned to tackle. He found applications on his iPod Touch detailing trail maps for every ski resort in the country, and we spent long car rides to New Hampshire discussing challenging trails he wanted to ski. At this early stage of his skiing career, his primary goal was to ski a double black diamond trail, but I forbade him from attempting the only expert run at Loon because I was afraid to go anywhere near it.

For February school vacation, we traveled to Stowe, Vermont, and arranged for a week of beginner lessons for Mary Beth and Abigail, while Ryan and I planned to explore the vast terrain on Mt. Mansfield. Our hotel was located at the base of the mountain, which helped with ushering Ryan to and from the chairlifts with his equipment intact, but, from a skiing standpoint, Stowe proved more challenging than Loon. The resort has multiple double black trails and Ryan selected Hackett's Highway for his inaugural expert run, arguing it was shorter and less extreme than some of the others.

—◡—

After we arrived, we had dinner at the hotel, and I created a shortlist with a coloring pen, containing all the daunting runs I planned to tackle. Our server admired how I apparently selected the hardest trails on the mountain, but the next morning while riding the lift, Dad gave me the disappointing news that I was forbidden to ski any double black diamonds. He told me in five years, when I'd reached the age of twelve, I would be good enough to try them. In that moment, something changed inside me. I knew I had what it took to ski those runs, so this was no longer about following Dad's safety rules, it was about proving my skill. I was tired of people treating me like I couldn't do anything, so I decided to show everyone that I could accomplish whatever I put my mind to.

—◡—

Our first morning of skiing got off to a rough start. I was in the process of congratulating myself on getting Ryan out the door early, and we were waiting in a short line before our second run when a lift attendant pulled us out of line. Ryan had somehow managed to lose his lift ticket during our first run.

I looked at the lift attendant. "So, what should I do?"

The attendant pointed down a flight of metal stairs toward the lodge. "Just go in there and show them your receipt and get another one."

"What receipt?" I asked.

"The one they gave you when you paid, bro," he responded incredulously, as if I was the dumbest person on the planet.

Ryan sensed the conversation was headed toward a brick wall, and he fell to the ground and began to sob. I looked at the attendant and clasped my hands together indicating that I was now begging him to help me. "But we got the lift tickets when we checked into the hotel. There was no receipt. Can't we just do this run and ski to the lodge for a new ticket?"

"Look, dude. Just run down there. I can't hold up the line."

I bent down to console Ryan. Tears were now streaking down his cheeks and landing in the snow. "Listen, buddy, I have to run down there. Do you want to come with me?"

"No!" he yelled so everyone in the line knew the world had just wronged him. "I am not losing my place!"

I looked back at the attendant one last time and said "thanks" in such a way so he would realize he had just ruined my life. Then, I ran down the grated stairs in my boots and into the lodge. Whenever Ryan was upset or in pain, I morphed into an asshole, so I stormed to the front of the line and demanded another ticket, receipt or not, before hurrying back out to load onto the chairlift.

———

When we got off the lift, I made a sharp turn toward a trail called Hackett's Highway. It had a rectangular sign with a clearly printed "Experts Only" warning on it and, as I approached it, I heard Dad telling me to "Hold up!"

———

Still flustered and feeling guilty about my rude behavior during the lost ticket episode, I failed to realize he led us to the beginning of Hackett's Highway, and before I could talk him out of it, off he went.

———

I never stopped. Instead, I entered through the orange gate area. Soon, I meandered through rugged moguls, around rocks, and past a small waterfall cliff near the bottom.

⌒

At this stage, my image of double black trails included rocks, canyons, and possibly wolves, so I raced around on an intermediate blue run to try meeting him where he would likely emerge at the conclusion of Hackett's Highway.

⌒

Dad met me at the bottom, and I thought he would be mad, but he smiled and patted me on the helmet. From his reaction, I knew I had made my point. That night, I pulled out the same coloring pens, but, this time, I didn't make a list. I drew a picture of me skiing Hackett's. I then had Mom neatly write a few sentences describing the adventure. That picture and description are among the earliest entries to my series of detailed trip reports that I post on social media to this day.

⌒

After our week in Stowe, Ryan and I continued our Saturday adventures at Loon into the spring. With each week, I learned to minimize aspects of skiing that generated emotional flare-ups, allowing him to focus on the sport itself. He still grumbled through every second—from leaving the parking lot, to dressing in the lodge, to purchasing lift tickets, to lining up for the first chairlift of the day—but I found creative ways to limit the time that it took to get up the mountain and anything else that prevented him from ripping down the slope. I parked on South Peak, away from the main lodge, near a smaller lodge that was less crowded and with shorter lift-ticket lines. We avoided the bedlam of the main cafeteria, eating a quick lunch at a quiet restaurant located on the mountain, and I mastered the art of peeing while traveling on skis because Ryan absolutely hated losing precious minutes for bathroom breaks.

At the end of March, we decided to end our first ski season with a boys' trip to Sunday River in Maine. Sunday River is a massive resort by New England standards with eight skiable peaks and two hotels on site. We arrived Friday night and had an enjoyable ski day on Saturday. That night, Ryan was quiet during dinner, and I tried to cheer him up by talking about next season. In the morning, we quickly packed the car and checked out of the hotel before heading to the lifts. We then skied several of Sunday River's most challenging trails, displaying significant improvement since our first day at Nashoba.

After lunch, Ryan's mood soured, and during our first few runs, he more resembled the boy I parented away from the mountain than the boy I witnessed on ski days. He demanded to ski certain trails, got angry when I couldn't keep up, and even requested at one point to *"just ski alone."* Toward the end of the day, we argued after nearly colliding as we disembarked the chairlift. I lost patience and skied ahead, down a very steep run that was a mix of ice and slushy snow. Thankful that it was our final run of the season, my mind flashed to warmer weather, longer days, and coaching Abigail's softball team. In doing so, I failed to appreciate that Ryan was also processing the end of ski season. And when I looked back, he was crumpled in the snow, sobbing. Initially, I assumed it was a ploy to force one more ride up the chairlift. Side-stepping back up the hill to reach him, I curtly asked, "What's wrong now?"

In response, he looked up at me and screamed, "I don't want this to end! It is the only thing I have in my life that is any good!"

***

When I started skiing, I learned a lot about myself. I was a bit of an adrenaline junkie and liked to challenge myself and set goals. I also enjoyed being outside and seeing new places, and since skiing checked those boxes, it helped me realize what I was missing. Suddenly, there was more to life than the struggle of trying to conform at school and behave at home. I had skills to build on and never worried about being restrained or punished when I was skiing.

***

At that moment, when he finally verbalized his feelings, I was offered a glimpse into a child that I didn't understand. He had just disclosed that, for the first time in his entire life, he felt good about himself. Children are not tasked with weighing their internal happiness, so when Ryan articulated how he felt while skiing, it should have alerted me to how empty he felt *every* other day. He was savvy enough to understand, as a consequence of behaving differently, he was tackled several times per day until he surrendered. Instead, I chose to zero in on the aspects of his admission that I could use to my benefit. Ryan was happiest when he skied and was easier for me to parent on the slopes, while Mary Beth and Abigail were rewarded with a long break from his outbursts. But rather than analyzing the root causes of Ryan's unhappiness, on the long ride home from Sunday River, I selfishly concluded that we needed to find a warm-weather activity akin to skiing for similar results to naturally follow.

When the season ended, the time I spent away from skiing was often difficult. In the summer, I began doing gymnastics to pass the time. I learned different floor routines, flips, and other moves. Later that fall, a movie that featured a lot of parkour came out, and the sport became popular. Parkour involves turning your everyday environment into a jungle gym, using vaults, flips and jumps to travel from point A to point B. At SVTA, I used my gymnastics skills on the playground to do self-taught parkour at recess. However, even though I wasn't bothering anyone, my teachers weren't big fans of my antics, and my parkour career was limited to areas outside of school.

With snow a distant memory, we tried fishing, hiking, biking, golf, archery, and kayaking, but failed in unearthing an activity that effectively replaced skiing. Tensions rapidly mounted in our house, and our only reprieve was Ryan's attendance at the SVTA mandatory summer program, which ran for six weeks. Ryan felt ashamed that he was forced to endure "summer school" as part of his therapeutic placement and constantly reminded Abigail how easy her life was in "regular school." Although he never verbalized it, he must have also resented Abigail for never facing a program that physically restrained her. I failed to consider his perspective and focused instead on his absence Monday through Friday that allowed me to work in peace and afforded Abigail time to play with her friends without Ryan interrupting.

I was always incredibly jealous of my sister, who had summer vacations—something I didn't have the privilege of experiencing at SVTA. During recesses in the summer, my teacher Sam used a punishment he called "the scorcher." If you got a timeout during recess, you had to sit on a metal bench, exposed to the blazing sun and hot to the touch, for five minutes.

———

The summer of 2009 had one other twist. Monica was pregnant, and unable to restrain Ryan, so every physical intervention fell on me. It was such an odd dynamic to be working one minute, hear yelling, and in a flash find myself rolling around on the floor with Ryan. Often, I was amid restraining him without even knowing what caused Monica to summon me in the first place.

At some point in August, I began doubting the entire SVTA approach. When thrust into a situation that called for restraining Ryan, I felt myself becoming agitated because the fact that I was being asked to restrain him at all meant something negative had transpired. So, I raced downstairs as my heart rate surged and blood pressure elevated. At the crime scene, it was my job to put Ryan in timeout and, when he inevitably refused, arguing whatever had transpired was Abigail's fault, I was trained to jump on him from behind, holding him facedown while he fought for his life. The more he struggled, the angrier I became. The angrier I became, the more I utilized my physical dominance to constrict him, eventually forcing capitulation.

At the end of a restraint, I felt guilty and ashamed for inflicting pain over some stupid incident I hardly recalled. Ryan was usually covered in marks and rug burns, so I hugged him and told him how sorry I was for restraining him. Perhaps sensing my sadness, Ryan apologized, too. However, not for the incident in question—he apologized for being "such a bad kid."

CHAPTER SEVEN

Rolling a Stone Uphill

"Life starts all over again when it gets crisp in the fall."
—F. Scott Fitzgerald, *The Great Gatsby*

September 8, 2009. As Ryan began third grade at SVTA, we temporarily replaced Monica with a caregiver named Lauren. After graduating from Dartmouth College and a master's program at Bryn Mawr College, Lauren sought a yearlong nanny position while applying to medical school. Unlike Monica, Lauren lacked formal training under the ABA system and instead relied on her instincts to solve problems, generally avoiding the two-step punishment system of timeout followed by restraint.

At school, Ryan moved into a new classroom with students who were slightly older, falling between third and sixth grades. All were on IEPs, so much of the classroom work was student-specific, rendering grade level irrelevant. However, as the fall rolled on, Ryan's journal cataloging his day consistently described incidents of restraint. We attributed the increase to heightened expectations in his new classroom and changes at home with Monica on maternity leave.

As Thanksgiving neared, restraints during the school day escalated, which puzzled me since Lauren was surviving each afternoon without ever restraining him. Life at home wasn't perfect, but she kept Ryan busy playing Magic: The Gathering, solving advanced math equations, and discussing science and nature. Lauren found ways to incorporate Abigail into her "classroom," and afternoons remained relatively peaceful.

Although troubled by the rise in restraint incidents at SVTA, as temperatures dropped in December, I hoped the start of our second ski season would lead to more success at school. My misplaced logic assumed Ryan behaved differently at home, but rather, I should have appreciated that Lauren was disciplining him more successfully than teachers at SVTA. Yet, I focused instead on getting Ryan back on skis as soon as possible, and in early December we traveled to Sunday River to ski three trails of manmade mush.

By January, Loon was fully operational, and we took advantage of our season passes by skiing every Saturday. Ryan remained intense, and we bickered from time to time about when to break for lunch or when to head home, but I never faced a situation where he needed to be restrained. Mary Beth and I presumed skiing was simply the counterbalance to the trouble Ryan would always have in any school setting, so we skied as often as possible, including February school vacation in Vail, Colorado.

Lauren was also an experienced skier, and her brother Jay lived in Vail, so we invited her on the trip. On the flight to Denver, she confided that Jay moved to Vail several years prior for "one ski season" but decided to remain permanently. Although she never said it, I was sure her parents remained hopeful Jay would outgrow his ski bum phase, never bothering to consider whether he was *happy* in Vail.

⌐ ⌐

Lauren's brother lived in Vail, and she knew a lot about the mountain. Before we went, she made a trail map for me with arrows for runs she thought I would like. Then, on the plane ride to Denver, she gave me a crash course on skiing out west. She explained to me how cat tracks connected trails and different peaks, and where cliff bands were located and how to avoid them. Her last bit of advice was not-so-correct instruction on how to ski powder. "Just lean back super far," she told me.

⌐ ⌐

Given our limited skiing experience, Vail proved to be a little over our heads. While Mary Beth and Abigail took additional beginner lessons, Ryan led me into many precarious situations by dragging me down double black diamond runs including the back bowls. There, I was forced to choose between attempting a trail that appeared too difficult or refusing, stifling the development of the one activity that Ryan loved. In those situations, I explained to him that mastering the blue square runs would make him a better skier than simply surviving the extreme runs, but those conversations backfired.

As we stood over a double black run called Prima, I suggested an alternative. "Ryan, I am not sure about this one. It looks really steep, and the moguls are bigger than you are."

He bowed his head and his shoulders sagged. "So, you think I'm terrible?"

"Not at all, buddy. I'm just not sure you are ready for this one."

He looked up and readied his rebuttal. "Lauren thought Prima was doable for me. If you don't think so, you must think I stink at skiing!"

"No, I think you're a great skier for your age and you're getting better every day, but—"

"But you think I am terrible now?" He crumbled in the snow and began to cry.

"You know what? You're right. There is only one way to find out if you're ready. Let's do it."

—⁓—

At Vail, navigating the many lifts, bowls, and valleys was an immediate challenge for Dad, but I managed to find the first run on Lauren's map, a trail called Prima. She detailed it as a long mogul run with a difficulty level similar to that of the Stowe's double blacks. The part she left out was that Prima went on forever, and we skied for what felt like miles of leg-burning moguls before Dad got tired and made us stand in the middle of the trail for a ten-minute rest.

—⁓—

Although his experience level constituted *twenty* total skiing days, eight-year-old Ryan constantly sought expert runs even at Vail with 1,800 feet of vertical drop. I tried arguing that double black runs out west were more dangerous than New England, but he remained convinced that every open trail was doable, and his attitude went way beyond *wanting* to ski them. He *needed* to ski them.

That afternoon, we decided to meet Mom, Abigail, and Lauren for lunch at the top of the mountain in a lodge that overlooked an area called China Bowl. That bowl includes an "extreme terrain" run called Dragon's Teeth, named for its row of sharp cliffs that resemble teeth. I knew watching old ski movies that it was possible to drop a cliff on skis, though I had never tried it before.

From my seat at lunch, I had a perfect view of one of the smaller cliff sections shaped just like a diving board. I didn't tell Dad because he would have never agreed, but I planned to ski right off the end of it and land smoothly on my feet. So, after lunch, Dad and I descended into China Bowl, but when he saw the "extreme terrain" signs, he decided he was not skiing into that area and yelled at me not to go. I tried to explain that it was possible to go around the drop, but he was adamant about not going and told me that I shouldn't go either. I thought I had proved myself in Stowe, so I ignored him and dropped in and began working my way toward the line I wanted to take.

As Ryan headed toward a run called Dragon's Teeth, he warned me that it incorporated a giant cliff. Unable to stop him, I quickly searched for a way around while following his progress. When he reached a point where he was forced to jump from a small section of the cliff, about ten feet high, I stood motionless, unable to help him.

I located the rock feature to the left of me, which confirmed I was in the right place, but I knew so little about dropping cliffs that I didn't process the experience as dangerous or scary. I thought it would just be a small drop to a smooth landing, so I pointed my skis and slowly skied off the edge.

He hesitated for a second before launching, landing hard, and losing both skis.

The moment I hit the ground, both my skis ejected since I was using beginner equipment with low din settings that are meant to pop off easily to avoid injuries and not equipped to handle the forces associated with sticking drops. I began tumbling down the slope below with no equipment, but I didn't panic, even when I realized my equipment was scattered all over the place. I was just disappointed that I didn't stick the landing and wasn't looking forward to an "I told you so" from Dad.

On the climb to retrieve my equipment, a snowboarder noticed my predicament and asked, "Hey, little man, did you drop the cliff?"

I replied, "Yeah, but I lost my skis."

"No worries, it happens."

And, as I clicked back into my skis, it seemed strange that he still thought it was cool, even if I failed to land the jump.

My heart sank, watching him tumble down the hill, but he popped up, nonchalant. He didn't appear to be limping or crying. When he skied down to meet me, he scolded me for his "beginner equipment" and demanded "better skis for next season." I was happy to agree, and I marveled at his courage and toughness. I had spent four years listening to doctors and educators pontificate about his emotional fragility. I would have loved to see those learned professionals launch off a cliff, crash, get back up, and have their only complaint be about faulty equipment.

Even Dad congratulated me on my bravery for attempting Dragon's Teeth and told me that sometimes the courage to try is more important that the result itself. However, that was not the reaction at SVTA.

When I returned to school after our trip, I told my teachers about my failed attempt on Dragon's Teeth during our group therapy session, and the meeting quickly became a safety intervention. The teachers said I was a threat to myself and couldn't conceptualize danger just because I dropped a cliff. They even called for an emergency meeting with Ira, but he didn't know much about skiing either. I tried to tell him that those cliffs get dropped by skiers all the time and, unless every expert skier in the world is crazy, it wasn't fair to use this to measure my mental health.

On Ryan's first day of school following vacation, he was subjected to a "safety intervention." I learned about it when Mary Beth stormed into my office that evening, gripping his school journal. "Did you see this?" she asked.

"See what?" I responded cautiously, expecting the worst. "What did he do now?"

"They had an emergency meeting with Ira, Harry, and the teachers to discuss his inability to appreciate the risks of skiing."

I looked up at Mary Beth and shook my head. "What the fuck? Let me see it."

She handed me the dark blue marbled composition book, and I searched for an entry written by Ryan's teacher. At the emergency meeting, not only did Ira question Ryan's ability to properly assess the risks of his "aggressive" skiing, but he also questioned my ability to "properly supervise" Ryan on the slopes.

I slammed the book shut and looked up at Mary Beth. "Where the hell does he get off questioning me? He's taking the one positive aspect to this kid's life and making it negative by planting seeds of doubt about his own ability. Worse, he is making him doubt my judgment about taking risks!"

Mary Beth sighed and looked to counter my anger with something rational, but I cut her off before she uttered a word. "No. Don't try to defend it. I am seriously done with that fucking place."

Mary Beth gathered herself again and nodded. "I know, but we have to give it more time before you overreact. We need to first find another school before you do anything stupid. Okay?"

I agreed and refrained from confronting Ira or Harry about Ryan's skiing or my parenting. We continued our weekend adventures at Loon for the rest of March and, as our second season wrapped up just before April vacation, I fretted about another long stretch without an activity to placate him. As expected, there were difficult days at home, but nothing like his issues at SVTA. Multiple restraints were now part of his daily routine at school, and I was relieved when the SVTA summer program concluded, affording Ryan the month of August to decompress. Monica returned to work after Lauren departed for medical school, and we had our first discussions about eliminating the use of restraint at home.

CHAPTER EIGHT

The End of the Beginning

"Ryan has grand ideas of converting all those around him to think like he does, of capturing boa constrictors, of traveling to space, of saving lobsters and of taking over the world. Ryan requires structure and predictability to function at his best."
—MAJOR REVIEW FOR RYAN DELENA, 1ST GRADE, SVTA
(NOVEMBER 19, 2007)

September 7, 2010. At the start of fourth grade, I expressed further concern to Mary Beth that SVTA's restraint-based approach felt punitive and not therapeutic. Ryan was being physically assaulted long after whatever action led to restraining him in the first place, and he wasn't acknowledging his role in any misdeed before acquiescing to the proposed punishment. Instead, teachers forced him to pay for his sins by leveraging their size advantage, and all Ryan processed was the physical assault—not the events that led up to it. At SVTA, restraints came quickly and were used prophylactically while, at home, restraints were a last resort. But that depended on who was in charge and how bad a day the adult in question was having. Inconsistency in how and when punishment was meted out was confusing to Ryan and ran afoul of every parenting model ever tried.

Moreover, restraints were a constant source of stress among the adults in our house because situations ending in a restraint typically occurred when two adults were present. After school and through dinner, I was teamed with Monica, and nights and weekends, I was teamed with Mary Beth. When Ryan's defiance or misbehavior led to a restraint, one adult actively participated in a series of steps that led from verbal warning to failed timeout to wrestling on the floor. The second adult was a passive observer, lobbing advice to the other grown-up and simultaneously pleading with Ryan to submit. Occasionally, the passive adult provided physical assistance or traded places when the situation became too heated.

Interestingly, as an active participant, my conduct always seemed appropriate. It was only later when the adrenaline wore off that I found myself besieged by guilt, replaying the incident over and over, unable to justify it. However, when I witnessed Mary Beth or Monica execute a restraint, I immediately found myself questioning them afterward, arguing that the situation could have been avoided with a less violent approach. Mary Beth and Monica did the same when I was an active participant, particularly criticizing my level of anger and physicality. Therefore, the postmortem was a damaged child and one grown-up fighting with the other about how the incident was mishandled.

Initially, I raised doubts about SVTA's use of restraint during our weekly phone call with Ryan's teacher or assistant teacher. At the time, we enjoyed a productive working relationship with the school, so I felt comfortable probing for specific examples where a restraint had conditioned Ryan to follow the rules, avoid conflict, and act appropriately. His teachers provided a few examples where he bounced back after a restraint, but I argued that he was growing more physical during the altercations or fleeing entirely whenever he faced the prospect of grown-up intervention. Ryan's teachers passed along my concerns to the administration, which led to a series of meetings with Ira and Harry accompanied by Sudbury's special education coordinator.

Quite honestly, the turning point at SVTA materialized the instant I questioned their tactics with Ryan. Meetings previously filled with jokes and laughter became more businesslike and felt like depositions. Ira reminded us that we consented to SVTA's protocol, and under Massachusetts law, the school was permitted to restrain Ryan when he was in imminent danger or whenever he put staff in imminent danger. This led to further debate over the legal definition of "imminent," with Mary Beth arguing that a forty-seven-pound child was incapable of putting anyone in imminent danger and Ira rebutting that Ryan was a danger to himself whenever he became upset.

Mary Beth, once ambivalent about challenging SVTA, was surprised at how staunchly the administration dug in to defend their model. She argued to Ira that the reason Ryan was unglued in disciplinary situations was the threat of restraint itself—particularly the way SVTA used restraint immediately when a timeout failed. Suddenly, Mary Beth saw Ira and Harry in a different light, and for the first time, we aligned on challenging the school—citing numerous examples to Ira where Ryan was successfully deescalated using methods aside from restraint. These instances were not only occurring at home, but in summer camps and structured playgroups for children with disabilities, so we pleaded with Ira to try other methods like weighted blankets, sensory brushes, or deep tissue massage when Ryan became dysregulated.

Rather than relying on our input, SVTA fought back by challenging our parental approach. After dropping Ryan off one morning, Ira stepped outside to the line of cars and asked if I could stay for a few minutes. In his office, he skipped the usual small talk. "So, I understand from Ryan that you are trying not to restrain him at home anymore?"

"That's right. And, honestly, things are a lot better. No more hour-long battles on the kitchen floor."

Ira moved toward me. We were now separated by less than a foot. I am sure that was his method of intimidating children, but I held my ground and leaned in so that we were eyeball to eyeball. "You realize things are better in the short term because you are just letting Ryan have his way, right?"

My pulse quickened, and I could feel my face start to flush with agitation. "Maybe, but it still feels like a better result. We are negotiating solutions, and Ryan isn't spending his life pinned to the ground."

"Negotiating?" Ira's head snapped back, and he laughed. "You can't negotiate with terrorists! That kid will win every single argument, and eventually he'll be completely out of control and wind up dead or in jail for killing you!"

I turned and headed toward the door. As I grabbed the doorknob, I turned back to Ira. "I'll gladly die trying if it means proving you wrong about Ryan."

As I exited, I heard him mutter, "You just might."

The "dead or jail" threat from Ira was something that Ryan heard many times in his stint at SVTA. Although we never worried about Ryan intentionally harming someone, Mary Beth and I often warned Ryan that reacting physically sometimes produced unintended consequences, including accidental injury. Ironic, given that his teachers and caregivers were the ones using physicality to settle conflict, which caused him to react in kind. Truthfully, I worried more about Ryan committing suicide than harming someone else. His brain seemed to be in constant turmoil, and I wondered how anyone could live with that kind of pain, especially as he grew older and more isolated.

In a follow-up meeting later that month with me and Mary Beth, Harry (also an MD) contended Ryan was likely schizophrenic or psychotic, since he was unable to appreciate that restraints were meant to *help* rather than hurt him.

That statement caused Mary Beth to sit up straight and jump in before I had the chance to pounce. She was more measured than I would have been, but she did convey the lunacy of Harry's argument. "So, because he lives in constant fear of suffocation during a restraint, you think he is schizophrenic or psychotic for failing to appreciate the inherent value of restraints?"

"Precisely," Harry answered in a professorial tone. Like many academics I had met over the years, Harry acted as though he could answer a question about Ryan's mental health with certainty because of a study he read in 1979. "In fact, I think it would be valuable to have an independent psychiatrist observe Ryan at school and conduct some tests for schizophrenia and psychosis—like the Rorschach inkblot test."

"They still use the inkblot test?" I asked, stunned.

"Oh, sure. It is very insightful," Harry responded definitively.

I smirked at the thought of Ryan telling some shrink that he sees different ski trails at Loon and Vail for every image they showed him. Meanwhile, Mary Beth spoke up about wanting to check with Dr. Schneider first.

I interrupted her midsentence. "Harry, this will shock you, but I actually think that is a great idea. But what happens if your theory is proven wrong? Will you stop restraining him then?"

Harry looked off in the distance and rubbed his chin as though he was deep in thought about a prospect he had never considered. "Well, I guess we'll just have to see about that."

⁕

After I started skiing, my parents noticed I wasn't having as many behavioral issues outside of school, so they started restraining me less at home. Without the fear of being restrained every time I got in trouble or had an argument with Abigail, I had fewer physical issues at home. With the realization that restraining me less was making our house more peaceful, my parents began to doubt the methods of SVTA and, when they attended meetings with my teachers, began to pick apart the school's decisions. That made Ira mad, and he told me in one of my meetings that my parents were crazy if they thought I could exist without being restrained.

⁕

Fortunately, the independent psychiatrist found no evidence that supported a diagnosis of schizophrenia or psychosis but, hoping to lessen the frequency and intensity of restraints, we agreed to medicate Ryan. Harry initially recommended Risperdal, an antipsychotic used to treat schizophrenia, bipolar disorder, and irritability caused by autism, but we rejected it due to an awful side effect that caused some boys to develop breasts. He then suggested Abilify, an antipsychotic used to treat schizophrenia, bipolar disorder, depression, and Tourette syndrome. According to Harry, Abilify was used frequently to treat irritability associated with autism and presented a more palatable side-effect profile, so we reluctantly agreed to try it for a few weeks to determine its efficacy.

For the next few weeks, Ryan was more sedated; he sat in front of the television longer and played on his laptop for more hours of the day. As his body adjusted to the medication, however, he returned to his usual self and his general defiance or occasional conflicts with Abigail still led to the difficult parental decision of how to discipline or punish him. By this point, hardened by his time at SVTA, even on medication, Ryan reacted to piddling disagreements by running out of our house or raising his fists to signal he would not be restrained without a prolonged battle.

Eventually, Mary Beth and I stopped restraining Ryan entirely and asked Monica to do the same. Despite years of training with the ABA model, including a master's degree in special education, even Monica seemed open to trying another approach. She pressed for a plan for disciplining Ryan and forced me to admit there was none. So, instead, she adopted new methods for heading off issues with Ryan using discussion, reasoning, and even humor. Within a few weeks, the entire mood in our house felt more relaxed.

Even aware of the major changes at home, SVTA continued to restrain him. Ryan repeatedly arrived home from school scratched and bruised, and journal entries indicated he was out of class most of the day while long battles played out. From the start, SVTA had billed restraint as an effective method for *calming* emotionally unstable kids, but for Ryan the result was an incredibly warped fight-or-flight response. At the first sign of a mistake, he ran or prepared for a physical battle with an adult. How could SVTA argue it was helping him make better choices the next time? More importantly, what was it doing to his overall emotional well-being?

As we assessed changes to his behavior plan, Ryan began seeing a therapist named Dr. Norman on a weekly basis. Recommended to us by Dr. Schneider, Dr. Norman was new to the practice, with a gentle demeanor, soft voice, and a slight Southern accent. She was incredibly sweet, empathetic, and listened intently as Ryan described restraints as "threats on his life." He conveyed to Dr. Norman that he lived in constant fear of being suffocated, and she implored us to end the use of restraint by SVTA teachers and staff, arguing that Ryan was exhibiting classic signs of post-traumatic stress disorder.

When Dr. Norman's opinion was presented to SVTA, they pushed back even harder. In the school's eyes, we were not only questioning their approach with Ryan, but their entire school model. So, in response, Ira played his trump card. He prevented teachers and staff from restraining Ryan if we agreed to pick him up at school whenever he reached a point that ordinarily required it. Ira knew Mary Beth could not leave her job at a moment's notice and Monica lived forty-five minutes from the school, so anytime Ryan needed to be picked up, SVTA planned to call me.

⌐⟋⟍

The situation exploded during fourth grade. It was around mid-October, and my parents left a meeting with my teachers, looking furious. When I saw them, I was in the process of finishing a restraint, and my face was soaked in sweat and tears.

My parents even offered to pick me up at school every time there was a problem so they wouldn't have to restrain me. However, restraints were such a big part of their methodology that my teachers decided to make it impossible to attend school without them. If my parents wanted to play rough, so would they. Once the new system was implemented, they looked for any reason to send me home. One time that really stands out was after I tore a piece of paper in half, and they called it a "threat of violence." So, I was sent home during my first class; Dad hadn't even made the drive home yet.

⌐⟋⟍

On the Friday after we adopted the new system, Ira called me for the fifth day in a row to retrieve Ryan. Only this time, he called ten minutes after I had just dropped him off, and I drove back in a fury. Upon arrival, I grabbed Ryan's hand and stormed out of the administration building.

⌐⟋⟍

When he got to school that day, Dad grabbed my hand and we left without talking to Ira or my teachers. We didn't even stop at the front desk to sign out.

⌐⟋⟍

Just before we reached the front door, an assistant teacher raced after us because I forgot the journal used to document Ryan's behavior. When I looked back, she extended her arm to hand me the journal, but rather than accepting it, I told her to "save it for the litigation," and closed the door in her face.

⌐⟋⟍

We just left, and that was my last day ever at SVTA.

CHAPTER NINE

Paint Bucket

"I think it's a mistake to ever look for hope outside of one's self."
—ARTHUR MILLER

As I exited the SVTA parking lot, I called Mary Beth and, before she finished saying hello, I blurted, "He's never going back to that fucking school." Fortunately, Ryan was unwilling to ride in a car without a DVD playing and headphones, so he was unable to hear the heated conversation, particularly when Mary Beth accused me of overreacting before another school was lined up. We conferenced in Dr. Norman, and, while she agreed with the decision to leave SVTA, she warned us Ryan needed time to process leaving his friends and the routine of the school day.

After the call, I drove him to a park he loved, and then to lunch at an outdoor burger and ice cream place called Dairy Joy. As we stood in line, he requested his usual burger and fries, then smiled before adding "and the Paint Bucket Sundae." I chuckled and shook my head. Intended for eight or more people, I had refused the paint bucket request on dozens of occasions over the years but, on this day, I agreed to the sixteen-dollar ice cream.

As Ryan slowly consumed his mountain of soft serve, I informed him that we were removing him from SVTA. I confessed that we wrongly allowed his teachers to misuse restraints and concluded that it was "time to find a better approach."

He looked up, paused momentarily from shoveling ice cream into his mouth, and said, *"Finally."*

To have Ryan encapsulate his SVTA experience with a one-word reaction to exiting the program caused a surge of guilt to wash over me. I lowered my head and whispered, "Sometimes grown-ups make mistakes, too."

He nodded but seemed distracted. "Can we take home the paint bucket to show Mom?"

I smiled and countered, "Why, so you can get me into trouble?"

He laughed. "Yup."

Over the next few weeks, we hired a tutor for daily math and science lessons and asked Monica to incorporate more reading and writing exercises in the afternoons to ensure that Ryan didn't fall behind his fourth-grade classmates. In the interim, we searched for a new school and, after ruling out the places that utilized restraint, we were left with very few options.[1] Unfortunately, any school that deemphasized restraint refused to consider a student with Ryan's profile because his application had two strikes against it: (1) he attended SVTA, a therapeutic school with an ABA reward/punishment system utilizing restraint; and (2) he attended SVTA with a dedicated "one-to-one" teacher's aide.[2] In a sense, those strikes acted like a criminal record. Once less restrictive schools got wind of either element of Ryan's educational past, they assumed they could not handle him. That determination was made without ever vetting his case file.

Even on rare occasions when a school considered Ryan's application, his entire SVTA file was provided. That file was filled with incident reports documenting the hundreds of times Ryan was restrained and emphasized, in each instance, that he was out of control and restraint was necessary for safety's sake. So, after a month of researching and contacting possible schools, we lacked a logical next step.

---

1. Present day, Massachusetts limits the use of physical restraint and prohibits it to be used "as a means of discipline or punishment." But that does not mean it is banned entirely. It is "limited to the use of reasonable force as is necessary to protect a student or another member of the school community from assault or imminent, serious, physical harm." 603 CMR 46.03.

2. Ironically, we viewed the one-to-one teacher's aide as a bonus to living in a wealthy suburban town. Sudbury could afford to offer extra support for Ryan and the increased budget allowed SVTA to add an extra assistant teacher to his classroom.

Dr. Norman also used this downtime to tweak Ryan's medication. She felt Abilify was having little or no impact on his behavior and recommended instead that we try a low dose of a drug called Lamictal. Lamictal was the latest panacea in mental health medicine. It had been around since 1994 when it was approved as an anticonvulsant used in treating epilepsy. In 2003, it received FDA approval to be used on bipolar patients after medical professionals noted improvement in patients who did not respond to other mood-stabilizing drugs or antidepressants. Lamictal, however, came with serious potential side effects including Stevens-Johnson Syndrome, a rare, serious skin and membrane disorder causing skin to blister and peel—forming painful raw areas over the entire body including the eyes and mouth. The risk of death after contracting Steven-Johnson Syndrome is 5 to 10 percent, but Dr. Norman assured us that, by initiating at a lower dosage, she could quickly take him off the medication at the first sign of trouble. She claimed the positive results of Lamictal were startling and that it was worth trying.

Without school, Ryan spent most of the day by himself. Although I was able to monitor his activities until Monica arrived in the afternoon, my recruiting business was suffering the effects of the 2009-2010 economic meltdown, and I needed to react quickly to every client call and email. I tried to placate him with long movies, but eventually he got bored, and I would hear him in the kitchen filling bowls with water to freeze Abigail's toys in blocks of ice.

Since most children on our cul-de-sac attended public school, Ryan enjoyed Wednesdays because students were released at noon. One boy, named Mason, shared many of Ryan's interests, and the two boys spent significant time at our house and in our backyard.

⌒

After school and on weekends, I hung around with Mason. He lived down the street and he enjoyed science and nature like me. We soon became best friends, and he practically lived at our house for a while. We explored the woods of Sudbury, ate miserably hot peppers, jumped off things, and, like every kid born in the early 2000s, unearthed the world of social media.

Around the time I was nine, Dad started a YouTube channel for me under the handle "Extreme Ryan" so friends and family could see ski runs from my GoPro camera. Despite a few mean comments, the channel was well received and had a number of subscribers. Mason and I decided to film our exploits outside of skiing, uploading them to YouTube for additional content on my channel. Our first video showed us jumping off the decks behind our houses, but we ramped up to more challenging jumps like the one from Abigail's window. (Mason skipped that one.) Then, we filmed the hot pepper challenges, which were popular on YouTube.

―⸙―

One afternoon, while Ryan and Mason were playing with some of the other neighborhood kids, Ryan jumped off our deck into the lawn below. True to his analytical nature, he measured the height of the deck before he jumped and bragged to me afterward that it was twelve feet high. A few days later, he measured the distance from his sister's second-floor bedroom window to the ground. He theorized that the window jump was attemptable since the deck jump was completed so easily and noted for emphasis that the area below the bedroom window consisted of a deep layer of mulch, providing a much softer landing zone. I pleaded with him not to attempt it. Nevertheless, one afternoon when he was playing upstairs with Mason, he came bounding in the front door, and I reached the obvious conclusion about his grand entrance.

The leap from Abigail's window was Ryan's first stunt that frightened me. In my adolescence, thrill-seeking junkies usually died on motorcycles before they were old enough to vote, so I worried his next attempt would be off our roof. Yet, the window jump is a classic example of the complexity of Ryan's profile. It was a calculated gamble, completed successfully because he studied it prior to his attempt. There was a thoughtful, even logical approach to stunts like this one, yet, when other parents in the neighborhood, teachers, or Dr. Norman heard about Ryan jumping out of windows, their facial expressions read, "Someday soon, we'll attend your son's funeral."

―⸙―

Around the same time, we discovered video games, particularly Fruit Ninja, which involves swiping your finger across a phone screen to chop fruit in half. We came up with a brilliant idea to video Mason tossing apples and bananas at me while I diced them with a large knife. "Real-Life Fruit Ninja" was a big hit on our channel, but not in our neighborhood, and when neighbors saw the video, they stopped allowing their kids to hang out with me. Even Mason's mother said he needed a "break" from me.

—⁓—

Ryan's quest to become YouTube-famous complicated his status in our neighborhood. There was a big difference in having someone in the neighborhood tattle on Ryan for chopping fruit on our front lawn and having the same person report what they saw on the internet.

—⁓—

My parents were not upset about the video, aside from the wasted fruit, but did explain to me that not all parents have the same rules and that people get nervous about knives. When I explained that the knife was needed for the video, Dad replied, "You're not a famous internet star. Just stick to skiing."

—⁓—

Unfortunately, during Ryan's sabbatical, Abigail discovered that she received attention at school by discussing her brother's exploits. Now a fourth grader, Abigail was bright and pretty, but she wasn't one of the "cool" kids, and her hazel eyes were always serious. She struggled to fit in socially in the classroom and was a bit player in the drama playing out every day at home. So, tales about Ryan advanced her status with her classmates, fascinated her teachers, and in the process, reminded her parents of her existence. However, one afternoon, we were called into her principal's office to explain that the window jump, and amateur-sushi-chef-in-training video were neither dangerous nor the result of absentee parenting. Mary Beth and I assumed the meeting was conducted in confidence, but over the next week, we were instead introduced to the mandatory reporting requirements for educational providers under Massachusetts law. Abigail's principal reported Ryan's behavior to the Massachusetts Department of Children and Families (DCF) and we were forced to endure a three-hour home visit to determine if our house was a safe place for Ryan and Abigail.

Apparently Real-Life Fruit Ninja wasn't a big hit with state agencies in Massachusetts either. I came home from school one day to a serious lecture about my YouTube channel. Dad informed me that I needed to take down all the videos of parkour stunts and Fruit Ninja because I was going to "get in trouble with the state." He explained that the state was planning an investigation of our house and how I was parented. Mom told me a woman was coming to interview me because of my Fruit Ninja video and the jump from Abigail's window. She said if I didn't act safely when the woman was at our house, the state could put me in a foster home.

So, before the woman arrived, Dad put away all the power tools in the basement that I used to drill holes in things. He also put the axe away that I used to chop wood. I wanted to show the woman how safely I could use everything, but Dad said it was a really bad idea and told me it was okay to lie sometimes.

At our monthly parental meeting with Dr. Norman, we informed her of DCF's pending investigation. She was not surprised, and for the first time, asked us to consider a residential treatment facility to keep Ryan safe. When she asked how we felt about that possibility, Mary Beth leaned forward as if ready to ask a follow-up question, but I stopped her in her tracks and responded, "You can send Ryan to a group home after you pry him from my cold, dead hands."

Upon hearing that, Mary Beth sunk back into the couch, and gave Dr. Norman a look that said, "I wouldn't push this one."

When the woman finally showed up, she asked a million questions about things I did for fun and made me show her the stuff I played with inside the house. It took forever, but she seemed to like my description of the woods behind our house and my skiing stories. After she left, Mom and Dad were happy with how the meeting went. I was just glad it was over.

With the DCF investigation behind us, we agreed to have a state-approved school program conduct a forty-five-day evaluation to determine the next step in Ryan's education. He attended the Dearborn School in late October for purposes of this evaluation, and he lasted a day and a half. In the morning of his second day, Ryan had difficulty with a school assignment, tore his work into shreds, refused a timeout, and a staff member was called in to restrain him.

That evening, we received a call from the program director removing Ryan from the forty-five-day evaluation; we were stunned. Special education departments use forty-five-day evaluations as a *last resort*, and Ryan was unable to survive two days. On the call, I reminded the director that I grew up in a tougher town than Sudbury and how I attended elementary school in Revere with kids who went on to commit murder, so I could not understand how I produced a son that no school in Massachusetts would allow in the door unless it was run like a prison camp.

The problem with behavioral schools is that once you're in the system, you're stuck. If a school isn't working for you, the natural reaction of the special education system in any town is to move you to a more restrictive setting. The problem for me was a more restrictive setting meant more restraints, which would only trigger my fight-or-flight response even more; and once triggered, I was completely incapable of using logic to navigate my world. Not only that, but the only schools more restrictive than SVTA were residential programs, so I would lose my family forever.

At this point, running out of options and at our most vulnerable, we made major parenting Mistake #3, and this one was a fucking doozy. Once again, Dr. Norman strongly suggested we commit Ryan to a residential treatment facility, but this time, only for evaluation purposes.

She explained that Cambridge Hospital had a separate mental health facility for children and provided a safe environment for adjusting Ryan's medication while monitoring him twenty-four hours a day. Our understanding from Dr. Norman was Ryan would only need to spend a "short amount of time" at the hospital until the staff felt he was "more stable" and able to "try school again."

The bottom line is that we never should have hospitalized Ryan, but Dr. Norman played the one card she knew impacted our thinking. She led us to believe that without school, Ryan's behavior would decompensate, ultimately placing Abigail in danger. Although Ryan never intentionally targeted Abigail (aside from typical sibling conflict) and was rarely aggressive toward her, he was out of control at times. Most of Ryan's outbursts materialized when he faced a restraint and fought back or attempted to escape. In those instances, he reacted both physically and verbally, often threatening Abigail if she helped foster the conflict that led to the effort to restrain him.

Even during this period when we were no longer restraining him at home, Ryan was preconditioned to prepare for battle whenever he got in trouble. He defied all manner of discipline and tested to see how far he could push us before we broke down and restrained him again. When this occurred, the scene in our home was chaotic, and things in the house got broken. Clearly, Abigail was negatively impacted and exhibited signs of anxiety. She vocalized her fear that Ryan might harm her while he was "out of control," but she was not *afraid* of him. Yet, things needed to stabilize or there was a chance something bad could happen by accident.

As with SVTA and the decision to medicate Ryan, we hoped Cambridge Hospital would perform a miracle so Ryan could return to school, and everything would be "normal" again. Dr. Norman assured us Cambridge Hospital was nothing resembling an asylum from the 1950s, which provided some comfort, and I pictured an actual hospital with brightly colored group therapy rooms and loving staff. Instead, we willingly committed Ryan into the children's version of the state hospital depicted in *One Flew Over the Cuckoo's Nest*.

CHAPTER TEN

Randall Patrick McMurphy

"He who marches out of step, hears a different drum."
—KEN KESEY, *ONE FLEW OVER THE CUCKOO'S NEST*

November 8, 2010. The next day, prior to admitting Ryan, I first had to tell him. Over lunch at Friendly's, I tried explaining to my nine-year-old why this hospital stay would help him but couldn't manage a single sentence before my voice cracked and tears fell from my eyes. After regaining my composure, I assured him we picked a hospital that allowed us to stay with him at night, and I promised everything would be all right. He tensed up and cried a little but seemed to accept that it might help him. I even overheard him telling Abigail that he needed "to go away for a while," but "everything was going to be okay" and she "didn't need to cry" for him. At that moment, a boy deemed by learned professionals as lacking the ability to relate to other people seized the opportunity to comfort his younger sister and, after hearing that conversation, I retreated into the bathroom and vomited.

Dad took me to Friendly's and left Mom and Abigail home, which felt a little strange. As we sat in the booth, there was a general uneasiness about the situation. Then he hit me with it. He said Dr. Norman wanted me to go to Cambridge Hospital to try to get my medication right. I had heard about mental hospitals before, after my friend Joe at SVTA disappeared for a month and teachers explained where he was. Dad tried making me feel okay about it by saying he and Mom would be with me the entire time, but I got a bad feeling because it was the first time in my life that I saw Dad cry.

A few hours after informing Ryan of the decision to admit him to Cambridge Hospital, we arrived and began the admission process. We started in an emergency room of sorts with reinforced steel doors and grates on the windows, then moved from there to an individual office. It was empty except for a metal table with holes at the corners. It took me a minute to figure out that the holes provided staff with a place to handcuff patients when they were out of control.

The intake nurse walked in and, after introductions, checked Ryan's blood pressure and heart rate. She should have checked mine. She then turned her attention to Ryan. "Hi, Ryan. I know this is a really hard day, but I need to ask you a couple of questions. Is that okay?" Ryan fixed his attention on the nurse and muttered "fine" before looking away to examine the table he was sitting on.

The nurse continued, lowering her voice to a level somewhere between a whisper and a murmur. "Ryan, do you want to hurt yourself?"

"No!" Ryan's head snapped up, and he looked directly into the nurse's eyes.

"Do you want to hurt anyone else?"

"No!" he said emphatically before looking back at the table and tracing small circles on the metal surface. It seemed like he had more to say, but for the first time in his life, he looked defeated. He couldn't argue his way out of this one, and there was no use trying to run away since multiple reinforced steel doors blocked any possible escape.

The nurse then looked at Mary Beth and me, repeating the same questions about the likelihood of Ryan self-harming or whether we felt he was a threat to others. When we responded negatively to both, she looked puzzled as if to say, *Then, what the hell are you doing here?*

We walked into the hospital on the main floor and were directed into a small room that looked like a treatment room at a doctor's office, but this room had a feeling of hopelessness to it. I quickly noticed the big white button used to exit the room said, "For emergency use only." A nurse entered and talked to my parents for a little while and asked me a few questions, none of which I remember. Ordinarily, I can recall most anything from my life, but that day, my heart was beating so fast, and all of my focus was on the items in the room. Everything was made of metal and designed to withstand a hurricane. I remember wondering what kinds of things happened in this room to make the hospital reinforce every inch of it.

We were next led to a conference room to sign a series of documents. Mary Beth and I are both law school graduates and she is an excellent attorney, but things happened so fast and in such a surreal way that neither of us recognized the documents forfeited Ryan's freedom. By signing, we lost the right to discharge Ryan from the hospital without medical approval, handing his freedom and well-being to complete strangers. It is one of those moments in life that I constantly replay in my mind, replacing the outcome with a version that I wish had happened.

Upon completion of the paperwork, we were shown the facility, including Ryan's room. It looked more like a dorm room than a hospital room, with a narrow bed and open shelving for clothes. There was a desk bolted to the wall without a chair and a large window covered by a thick metal grate with a padlock. Outside of his room, the carpeted hallway led to a common area with a large TV playing children's movies. Some of the other patients were huddled there; very few seemed to have a parent present.

After a short waiting period, we were brought by elevator to the mental health ward. When the elevator doors opened, I was expecting something different. I pictured a room full of kids like me, maybe with toys or coloring books. Instead, we were funneled through a metal door, where my parents presented their IDs at the glass window. Then another metal door inside was remotely unlocked.

It opened to a long empty hallway with doors leading to bedrooms along each side. Most kids in the unit were older and looked like they could kill me with a single punch.

I was led to my assigned room. There was virtually no color in the room except for the gray walls, beige carpet, and brown desk bolted to the wall. The windows had thick metal screens and a big lock. I felt sick. This place looked like a prison, and I didn't understand why I needed to come to a place like this to change my medication.

That night, as the reality of my situation finally hit me, I burst into tears. I told Mom that I never thought things would get this bad. She gave me a hug, and I fell asleep.

———

Ryan's first full day in the hospital fell on a Saturday, and we were informed that his formal medical evaluation would begin on Monday. A man named Tony introduced himself and seemed to oversee the unit. He encouraged us to use the weekend to get situated and instructed Mary Beth and me on the process of entering and exiting the facility. Tony advised Ryan of the patient rules, provided information on the weekday schedule, and warned him to "be respectful of the staff." Ryan nodded in response and, after Tony walked away, we retreated to his room.

With nothing else on the schedule, we sat around and waited for someone to tell us what to do next. Nurses occasionally stopped in with medication (still on the low dose of Lamictal) and checked Ryan's vitals, but mostly we watched the clock. Since he was the newest kid on the unit, some of the other kids poked their heads into his room to meet him, providing a much-needed distraction. Most of the patients were Black or Latino boys between eight and fifteen years of age. I assumed they were diagnosed with some type of mental illness, but they readily described how they got in trouble at school for fighting and, rather than juvenile detention, were sent to Cambridge Hospital.

On Monday morning we finally met Dr. Jorgon, who oversaw Ryan's care. She was odd-looking, with a broad face and eyes that were far apart. As she introduced herself, her face grew even larger, yet somehow it remained in a constant state of furrow and frown. I tried to soften her all-business tone with my usual charm, but Dr. Jorgon never broke character. If anything, she seemed to like me less after meeting me and was bothered by the fact that Mary Beth and I were both lawyers, mentioning it several times.

Dr. Jorgon warned us, if we attempted to discharge Ryan without her approval, Massachusetts law allowed her to hold him for three business days and, during that period, afforded her the right to petition for an involuntary commitment. Before Mary Beth or I were able to clarify, Dr. Jorgon turned and hurried off without saying goodbye. I looked at Mary Beth and remarked sarcastically, "I don't think Ryan will be playing poker or watching the World Series." She stared back at me blankly, completely missing my Nurse Ratched reference from *One Flew Over the Cuckoo's Nest*, but based on the tears welling in her eyes, she seemed to grasp that Ryan wasn't leaving Cambridge Hospital until Dr. Jorgon said so.

Most days, Mary Beth and I alternated time at the hospital with Ryan, but there were instances when he was part of group therapy, and we used those opportunities to work or spend time with Abigail. At night, we took turns sharing a bed with Ryan, sleeping on a rubber-coated mattress, twenty-four inches wide with sheets that felt like sandpaper. On my nights with Ryan, I was often startled awake by the sound of patients screaming or sobbing. Occasionally, the yelling was followed by hospital orderlies rushing to a patient's room to extinguish the disturbance.

In Ryan's first few days under the care of Dr. Jorgon, not much happened. Aside from individual and group therapy sessions, most of the day was spent killing time in his room. We tried propping him up emotionally but that became increasingly difficult when we were unable to answer the most important question: when would he be released? Not knowing ourselves, we tried moving the target each day without upsetting him, making up reasons why he needed to remain for another day. We explained that his release hinged on Dr. Jorgon, but since she wasn't providing any information on the projected length of Ryan's stay, we injected false hope whenever possible to mollify him.

Toward the end of the week, Dr. Jorgon reported Ryan's refusal to participate in any of the group therapy sessions. To placate her, I theorized that Ryan was uncooperative because he was hoping that it might force her to release him sooner. Rather than empathizing with a confused and terrified child, Dr. Jorgon was angered and planned to increase his Lamictal to a much higher dose, claiming the medication would help Ryan "get with the program." When Mary Beth questioned whether it was a good idea to increase the dosage so rapidly, given the side-effect profile, Dr. Jorgon became incensed that someone without a medical background would dare challenge her authority over a medication decision. At one point, she snarled, "Are you a doctor in your spare time?"

At the start of the second week, Ryan began going stir-crazy. Every psychological profile conducted on him to this point recognized his need for black-and-white answers, so having a doctor refuse to provide any information as to his projected release date was mental and emotional torture. Quite honestly, it made little sense to me either. We had agreed to hospitalize him to stabilize his mental and emotional state, yet he was now the victim of a classic psychological conundrum. He was a hostage facing the psychological hurdle of uncertainty over when freedom might occur. Let's put in this way: a prisoner with a twenty-year jail sentence has hope of freedom one day, but a hostage without a fixed end date must search for a reason to have any hope at all. Ryan was no different, and he grew restless, and risked unraveling completely. He began to talk nonstop about potential ways to sneak him out of the hospital.

"Dad, can you bring the big suitcase tomorrow and pretend you brought me more clothes?"

Later in the week, when Monica and her husband came to visit, Ryan signaled that we should walk out together so he was hidden from the desk clerk when we exited. As he demonstrated his scheme by ducking between us, my heart sank. Ryan wasn't only expressing that it was possible to escape; he was relying on me to help him.

By the middle of the second week, we resorted to begging for his release. We offered to sign any waiver Dr. Jorgon could dream up, excusing her of any liability in the event Ryan harmed himself or anyone else. She wouldn't budge, wanting to first see Ryan exhibit perfect behavior at the group therapy sessions and monitored free-play time. So, after recognizing that she would never relent, I began to watch the night staff for opportunities to escape the facility with Ryan, noting in my phone when they took coffee breaks. I was certain we could escape the facility but then what? Mexico wasn't exactly an option, and any escape attempt might result in the state placing Ryan into foster care or in a more restrictive facility.

~

After a few days, I began to worry things weren't as they seemed. I was told by my parents that I would be at the hospital for one or two days, but there wasn't any talk about releasing me. They kept telling me that it wasn't up to them, but I wasn't sure if I believed them. Maybe they wanted me here? Without the ability to trust my parents, I was scared for my safety. I was trapped in a place with violent children and with adults who restrained me at the slightest sign of misbehavior. The prison-like environment drove me to my breaking point, so I stopped thinking logically and moved into survival mode.

On day eight, I gave up hoping for my release and tried to escape. After watching the office door all day, I noticed that when it opened, it connected to the room with the ID window. Perfect, I thought. When the door opened again, a woman walked out of the office, and I rushed in and pushed past her. In a single bound, I was on her desk. I then dove out the ID window and ran. I didn't care if I had to run through the city on my own with nowhere to go. I wanted out, and that's all that mattered.

However, I couldn't get past the second door and, while attempting to find another route, two guys burst in and yanked me off my feet. They dragged me back to the unit and shut the door. A few hours later, I tried escaping again, this time focusing my energy on getting around the second door, and as I raced away from the nurse, I checked different rooms to see if there was a shortcut I could use. Finally, I ran into an empty conference room and slammed the door shut. However, I was unable to lock the door, so I began piling chairs to form a barricade, but eventually the security guards pushed the door open and found me hiding under a table.

Frustrated by my second escape attempt, they dragged me to my room and locked it from the outside. After a few minutes, a nurse came in and gave me my medication, which happened whenever I acted up, but this time there were more pills than usual. She forced me to take them before leaving and locking the door again. I banged on the door, begging for them to let me out, but no one seemed to be listening to me. I kept kicking and punching it, but eventually I got really tired. I don't remember falling asleep, but when I woke up, Mom was there. She hugged me and made me promise not to try to escape anymore.

———

Toward the end of the second week, I entered Ryan's room and found him staring out the window while his tiny fingers grasped at the metal grate covering it.

"Do you think they would let me go outside for a few minutes and climb that big tree?" he asked.

Certain that he needed a glimmer of hope, I quickly changed the subject.

"Hey Ry, I'm thinking when you get out of here, we should take a trip out west. Maybe pick a place with the best early season snow?"

He immediately turned away from the window and looked at me with the hint of a smile. "Can we go anywhere?" he questioned.

I replied, "Sure, maybe not Alaska, but anywhere else in the country."

His eyes widened. "Alta and Snowbird?"

"Where are they again?"

"Utah."

I nodded in agreement and ensured him that we would pack for the slopes the minute we got home. He then sat down on the bed, grabbed his iPad, and loaded the trail maps for Alta and Snowbird to show me. We spent the rest of the day talking about every difficult trail he planned to ski. At one point, he leaned in as if to tell me an important secret and whispered, "Dad, have you ever heard of Devil's Castle?"

———

As the one-day hospital visit moved into its second week, Dad sensed the light at the end of the tunnel was fading, so he promised a ski trip to help cheer me up. He agreed to fly us to Utah as soon as I was released. I was happy to have something to look forward to, but Dad also used the ski trip to motivate me so I would follow hospital rules. "Try to be on your best behavior because you don't want to miss this trip," he kept telling me.

So, toward the end of the second week, I began to try—even doing good deeds around the hospital. I helped patients tie their laces when we had "roller skating day" in the hallways. I cleaned up the shreds of paper the nonverbal kid down the hall liked to tear. I participated in all the group therapy sessions, talking about my feelings, and doing the stupid role-playing exercises that Dr. Jorgon insisted we do. It must have helped, because later that week, my parents told me I was being discharged the next day. After taking a few minutes to be certain they were not lying to me, I literally rolled on the floor shouting "Yes!" at the top of my lungs. At least ten heads turned to the huge scene I was making. A staff member even smiled when he walked by and said, "I guess he heard the good news."

⌒⌒

At the end of the second week, Mary Beth and I met with Dr. Jorgon to discuss terms for Ryan's release. Dr. Jorgon wanted Ryan moved from the hospital to a Community-Based Acute Treatment (CBAT) facility.[1] CBATs operate much like mental hospitals except they are "unlocked," meaning families can remove patients anytime they want. Based on the criteria for CBAT placement, it is safe to assume Dr. Jorgon would not have agreed to a ski trip as the next step in Ryan's mental health journey, but I smiled and nodded while she discussed possible options for CBAT placement, knowing we never intended to set foot in any of the facilities she recommended.

Ryan's experience at Cambridge Hospital initiated a seismic shift in my parental mindset. For years, I had listened to the so-called experts, ignoring my instincts about a child I knew better than any professional paid to evaluate him. It had taken years, but finally, sitting alone in my basement on the night of Ryan's release, it struck me that doctors

---

1. Community-Based Acute Treatment (CBAT) is provided to children/adolescents who require a twenty-four-hour-a-day, seven-day-a-week, staff-secure (unlocked) group setting. For children and adolescents with serious behavioral health disorders, CBAT provides therapeutic intervention and specialized programming in a controlled environment with a high degree of supervision and structure. CBAT services are provided in the context of a comprehensive, multidisciplinary, and individualized treatment plan that is frequently reviewed and updated based on the member's clinical status and response to treatment.

and administrators at therapeutic schools were doing their best to help him but most had likely concluded he would wind up in a residential treatment facility. After all, life in a group home was the endgame for most of the kids in the "system." In the eyes of the experts, Ryan was a nine-year-old they had already written off, defining a pathway that was sure to include several different therapeutic schools, additional stints in mental hospitals, and ending as a permanent resident of a group home. It was a life Ryan would never willingly choose unless he was broken or medicated to a numbed threshold, involuntarily accepting a life of compliance.

On the contrary, watching him ski, I witnessed a version of Ryan others didn't know—thriving in an environment where risk and adventurousness were rewarded, not punished. *That* Ryan would be extinguished entirely by a residential treatment facility, so it was time to stop relying on others to fix him because the stakes were completely different for the experts. If a school or a medication failed to work and Ryan was permanently institutionalized, no one in the system would lose any sleep over it, and likely they had already anticipated it. No matter how intensely doctors or teachers wanted to help him, it was, after all, just a job for them; and given the litigious nature of American society, there was an undercurrent of liability avoidance in the system. As a result, doctors and school officials never took risks by altering treatment protocols based on Ryan's emotional needs. They stuck to the playbook and covered their asses by moving Ryan through previously defined treatment protocols and documented each step to prove they did everything possible to avoid a potential tragedy.

CHAPTER ELEVEN

Cliffed Out

"Rob and Ryan have a very playful relationship. They are often joking with each other, or Rob is praising Ryan for his successes of the day. Ryan loves spending time with Rob and often proudly speaks of Rob as being the 'strongest person alive.'"
—ORIGINAL PROFILE 1, SVTA (JUNE 11, 2007)

November 26, 2010. When my brother Jon was nine years old (the same age as Ryan during his stay at Cambridge Hospital), he spent two weeks at Massachusetts General Hospital after contracting a rare virus called Kawasaki Disease. He required antibiotics and cooling measures to bring down a high fever and eventually recovered. At the hospital, friends and neighbors brought him gifts, magazines, and candy. In contrast, when your child spends two weeks in a mental hospital, there are no visitors or presents. Neighbors have no idea what to say and avert their eyes, pretending not to see you.

As planned, Ryan and I ate a quick Thanksgiving brunch with Mary Beth, Abigail, and my mother before flying west to ski at Alta and Snowbird. Given the holiday week and last-minute nature of our trip, I worried about securing hotel accommodations, so when my brother mentioned a colleague, a DEA agent named Beau, with a condo near Alta and Snowbird, I happily accepted the offer of a free place to stay. Just before we departed for the airport, Beau called and provided directions to his place in Sandy, Utah, located "just down the road from the mountain." Beau's loosely described location, however, proved to be twenty-five minutes from both resorts. That might sound ungrateful because he was nice enough to offer it to us, but by the time we pulled into the parking lot having flown over five hours, I was spent. The act of managing Ryan—along with ski bags and luggage—was one thing, but he also added wrinkles to air travel such as his unwillingness to ingest any form of liquid that wasn't Juicy Juice (grape flavor).

We located Beau's unit; and after confirming the key was under the welcome mat, I opened the door to a giant bearded man in the kitchen, paint roller in hand, and someone who looked like his wife or girlfriend busily painting the other side of the room. After jumping backward and mumbling something about having the wrong unit, the man confirmed we were in the right place, explaining he lived upstairs and accidentally damaged the kitchen when a pipe burst several months ago. Beau surprised him with the news that we were using the unit over the holiday break, so he had sprung into action to repair the damage.

Ryan and I went to dinner to give our painting crew extra time and when we returned, I was happy to find the unit empty. With the two-hour time change, it was now hours past Ryan's bedtime, and after talking him into a quick bath, I filled the tub only to realize the water was ice cold. I turned the faucet in every direction, but there was no hot water; so, forgoing the bath, I crawled into bed with Ryan and forced myself to stay awake until he was out cold. I then phoned Beau, who contacted the property manager, and minutes later, another heavily bearded fellow arrived, demonstrating how to light the pilot on the water heater. Faced with the prospect of two massive Utah resorts that were sure to test our technical proficiency, this trip was risky enough from a skiing standpoint; but with Ryan only days removed from a mental hospital, I had little energy to oversee condo maintenance.

Ryan was so excited for his first ski day in Utah that he awoke at 6 a.m. We dressed quickly and arrived to find ourselves alone in the Alta parking lot. Much to our dismay, we discovered that, unlike back east, Alta did not open until nine a.m. Appreciating it was torture for Ryan to kill time waiting for anything, I allowed him to make his first Utah ski run between two parking lots after climbing up a small hill. Even in that parking lot run, Ryan was skiing in snow up to his knees. He was happy enough to climb up again for another run, but I felt butterflies in my stomach knowing skiing in Utah was a huge leap for both of us.

⌣

On my first run in Utah, I realized there was a whole level of skiing I hadn't reached yet. The year before, I conquered some of the hardest terrain at Vail, but we never got any big storms when we were there. Alta gave me the opportunity to test my skills on fantastic terrain such as Devil's Castle and Baldy Chutes, while skiing for the first time in fresh powder. However, my excitement was brought to a halt when Dad was in the process of buying the lift tickets. I looked up at the trail board near the lift; Devil's Castle, East Castle, Catherine's Area, and Baldy Chutes were all closed, meaning the entire upper mountain was out for this trip. Disappointed, I decided to head toward an area on the map with a dense collection of black diamond trails. While Vail was much bigger than anything I had ever skied, it had the layout of an East Coast mountain. In other words, trails were cut and included signs to indicate where to go, and everything on the trail map was true to scale. So, it was an easy adjustment. Alta, however, presented many firsts.

On our very first run, I searched for a trail that I remembered from the map in the "Blackjack Forest" area, but there were no trail signs indicating how to get there. I tried to lead us in the right direction, but as I ventured deeper into the trees with Dad, I realized there wasn't a defined trail, just a heavily wooded forest. To make matters worse, the snow was incredibly deep. Dad and I were still using basic beginner equipment, so our skinny skis included bindings that popped whenever they sensed a skier was in trouble. That setup was less than ideal in these conditions and Dad got frustrated when he fell twice before he decided to quit and told me that he was headed back toward the groomed runs. He'd done this before in the East and was comfortable allowing me to continue in the woods, so we planned to meet at the chairlift. However, skiing alone at Alta offered challenges Loon Mountain never did. As I skied down, I stumbled into a cliff area. In my research, I knew Alta had skiable cliffs, so I wasn't scared when I dropped over the edge of a big snow pile. However, there I realized that I wasn't in a cliff area at all—I was just skiing in steep snow. When I landed, my ski popped off while I rolled twenty feet. I wasn't hurt, but the powder was so deep that I couldn't hike back up to look for my ski without sinking. Each time I tried to climb back up the hill, I sunk to my thighs. Even when I tried to crawl, my knees sunk in deep, and I got scared. This was certainly a new experience, but that wasn't what troubled me the most. For the first time, I found myself in terrain that I wasn't sure I was good enough to ski. I called Dad in a panic. On the call, I cried and told him I was lost and couldn't get to my ski, and, worse, that I was terrible at skiing.

—⁓—

It wasn't usual to wait at the bottom of a run for a few minutes before Ryan showed up, but when my phone rang and I saw his name, I knew he was in trouble. I answered quickly but before I had the chance to ask if he was okay, he sobbed, "Dad, I fell and can't get to my ski. I thought I was good but I'm terrible!"

I tried to remain calm, focusing my questions on his physical status and location, but, unable to determine where he was stuck, I panicked and searched for help.

The lift attendant handed me a two-way radio, and I told the patroller that Ryan was a nine-year-old on the autism spectrum and roughly where we had separated. Although diagnosed with PDD-NOS, I played the autism card many times in his youth, usually to get him out of trouble with other parents at playgrounds, lifeguards at hotel pools, and once to secure a table at a packed Disney World restaurant when he was starving. That morning at Alta, I wasn't looking to extricate Ryan from an awkward social situation or attempting to stave off a meltdown to avoid public humiliation. He was trapped in the snow and already hysterical, so I needed to locate him as quickly as possible.

—⁓—

Dad tried to calm me down on the phone and attempted to determine my location so he could look for me. However, he was horrible at reading maps and never bothered to learn the names of any trails, so I wasn't surprised when he said he needed to get help from ski patrol. Luckily, in a few minutes, an upbeat ski patroller showed up to rescue me. She didn't seem gravely concerned and quickly retrieved my ski from its pinned position at the top of the steep slope. She helped me gear up, and we skied to the chairlift where Dad was waiting.

———

As I waited at the base of the mountain for ski patrol to rescue him, it registered that my brilliant solution to rehabilitate Ryan's spirit had lasted exactly one run. We had skied less than an hour and he was already upset and, worse, sounded ready to quit. Luckily, when he showed up with the patroller, he seemed to be in better spirits. I worried when Ryan overheard the patroller suggest that we stick to "blue squares" with names like Dipsey Doodle and Sugar Way and was pleased when he ignored her.

We headed back up the lift and neither of us mentioned our struggle in the trees. After that, we both skied better and managed to survive the rest of the morning without incident. That isn't to say I stayed on my feet the entire time, but with each fall, I quickly gathered myself without losing sight of Ryan. Over the course of the day, he grew more satisfied with his skiing in the deep snow, demonstrating a resiliency rarely evident in tasks at school. He was annoyed with the limited number of advanced trails and at one point attempted sidestepping to Baldy Chutes since no lift could take him there. He traveled halfway up before I yelled for him to come down. When he returned, he was still upset over the limited early-season terrain, so I deflected his angst by reminding him that a family we knew from home was skiing at Snowbird. I suggested crossing over to look for them, where we could also investigate whether Snowbird had more extreme runs.

Although Alta and Snowbird are separate resorts, there is a simple connection at the top of the mountain that allows skiers to cross over with a special lift ticket. Ryan and I, however, were skiing much lower near the Alta base, without crossover tickets, when he agreed to head to Snowbird. We assumed incorrectly that an easy lower trail connected the resorts, but after ten minutes of some very difficult tree skiing, we found ourselves on a paved road unsure of how to proceed. I wanted to abort and head back to Alta, but Ryan claimed by continuing along the road, we would eventually get to Snowbird.[1]

After another fifteen minutes of walking with our skis, we arrived at a series of condos. With the sun high in the sky and 8,000 feet of elevation, I was panting heavily. Eventually, we came upon an older gentleman who confirmed we were heading in the right direction. "The bad news is that you are still a half-mile from a place where you can ski onto Snowbird's property," he explained sadly. He also mentioned that he was a retired doctor and noted my labored breathing before asking, "Is there any history of heart problems in your family?"

When we finally reached a long, snowy hill leading to the base of Snowbird, the doctor was right: I was ready to collapse. We managed to ski to the bottom and, miraculously, we stumbled on our friends, Dylan and Melissa, just as they were headed to lunch. Their four kids were in ski school for the day, so I talked Ryan into eating with the adults before we went back to skiing. On the walk into the restaurant, Dylan recognized my strained pace and asked quietly, "Are you okay?" I gathered myself as we sat down and relayed the entire story. He looked shocked and repeated the same question a few times during lunch: "You *walked* here from Alta?"

We skied the rest of the afternoon at Snowbird, and I favored the layout over Alta. More terrain was open, including several double-black runs that Ryan loved and, more importantly, that I could avoid while keeping an eye on him. After our last run of the day, Dylan drove us to our rental car at Alta, and I was ready for an easier night but, once again, the water in the condo was ice cold. Reflexively, I reached for my phone to call the property manager, but with Ryan staring back at me in his underwear, I instead called Snowbird Village to see if there were any rooms available. The reservation specialist who answered snorted at me, "Um, yeah, the hotel is pretty empty at this time of year." So, I repacked the car, and we drove back to the resort to check in.

The next couple of days went well. Ryan was happier skiing with his friends from Sudbury, and it was reassuring to have Dylan and

---

1. Ryan's version of the story is that he wanted to turn back toward Alta, but I insisted that we keep following the road.

Melissa nearby. We ate meals together and adding a few drinks certainly helped me to decompress. I knew Melissa's brother suffered a psychotic breakdown years earlier during his freshman year at Boston College, so I was comfortable sharing aspects of Ryan's hospitalization with them. She emphasized that her brother was schizophrenic and nothing like Ryan, but I couldn't help wondering what it must have been like for her family. Although his emotional and mental issues eventually overwhelmed him, Melissa's brother made it to an elite college before he fell apart; so did that mean all the skiing in the world might not be enough to save Ryan?

Toward the end of our last ski day, Snowbird opened the backside of the mountain called Mineral Basin, a beautiful open bowl of trails that funneled to two lifts at the bottom. The trails are fairly difficult, but the resort groomed sections allowing more novice skiers to go back there. On this day, however, due to low visibility, it was impossible to discern the groomed runs, so Dylan, Melissa, Ryan, and I started out together but quickly lost sight of one another. In a matter of seconds, I found myself all alone. Although Mineral Basin is wide open, there were pockets of trees and some narrower trails, so I must have taken a trail that the others hadn't. *No big deal*, I reminded myself. Everything led to the same place at the bottom, and I would reconnect with Ryan there. However, after skiing back to the lift area, I didn't see anyone else, and after waiting for a few minutes, I started to worry. On my descent, I had fallen at one point, and it had taken me a while to dig out of the soft snow and get my skis back on. I even tried to call Dylan thinking I was stuck in the snow. When I finally reached the lifts, I figured the delay must have given the others enough time to reach the bottom and head back up, assuming I had already done the same.

Eventually, I gave up waiting and took the lift back up and skied down the front side of the resort to the village. It was a long ski down to the base and my mind raced. *I'm sure Ryan will be there. He is fine. Nothing to worry about. He knows the mountain better than I do. I'm sure he won't get lost in the middle of the Wasatch Valley as darkness creeps in.*

When I arrived, Dylan and Melissa were waiting for me, but there was no sign of Ryan. We chatted for a few minutes, and I tried to play it cool.

"What the hell happened to you?" Dylan wondered.

I told him about my fall. "I got tangled up and I was afraid if I took my skis off, I'd sink."

He laughed. "It isn't quicksand. Do you think they recover dozens of skiers' bodies every summer when the snow melts?"

I faked a smile. "How the hell should I know? I tried to call you. I even left you a voicemail to say goodbye and asked you to tell the world my story."[2]

He checked his phone, saw the missed call from me, smiled, and shook his head. "Hey, what do you think happened to Ryan?"

I told him that I was sure he would show up any second, but I was full of shit. Although Dylan and I had been friends for over twenty years, I was being "a guy" and didn't want him to see that I was scared. I love both him and Melissa, but they are maddeningly perfect. Dylan is six-foot-five, great looking, and good at everything because he never rests until he masters something. Melissa is as sweet as she is beautiful and, looking at them together in Snowbird, they could have modeled for the Gorsuch catalog. Worse, their four model children were off skiing with Lars the instructor, while I was standing at the base of a mountain wondering if my impaired child was lost in the Rockies because I fell and was afraid that my squat frame might sink in the snow.

When another twenty minutes went by without him, I told Dylan and Melissa that I was running to the bathroom, but instead I ducked inside the ski patrol office. As I approached the desk, an older, weathered patroller with blond hair and blue eyes glanced up from his paperwork.

"Can I help you?" he asked casually.

I tried to match his vibe. "Hey, yeah, not an emergency or anything, but I'm having trouble locating my son. We got separated in Mineral Basin."

"How old?" he asked as if running through a drill he had conducted a million times before.

---

2. Dylan kept that voicemail for years and would play it occasionally to mock me. I was very happy when he finally converted from a Blackberry to an iPhone and my panicked message was lost to history.

"Nine," I replied ever-so-nonchalantly while hiding the thoughts exploding in my mind. *Just your regular nine-year-old. Nothing to see here. Autism? Mental hospital? I'm sorry, what?*

"Name?"

"Ryan." *Just regular old Ryan.*

He stopped taking notes. "Wait, I think we have a Ryan in the shack at the top of Mineral. Let me give them a call."

———

On our last afternoon at Snowbird, we took the lift to the Mineral Basin tunnel and descended blindly over the backside. I say blindly because, while we were on the lift, clouds and haze rolled in, with lighting so flat that it was difficult to tell where to go. We skied one run to the bottom but, on the way down, got separated. At the bottom, I didn't see Dad, Melissa, or Dylan, so I stood and waited. After a while, I assumed they must have ridden up one of the two lifts before I got there and were waiting at the top. So, I hopped on the main lift to the top of Mineral Basin.

When I got to the top, no one was there waiting for me, so I skied down into Mineral one more time to look for them. On the way down, I ended up in one of Mineral's many cliff areas. I remembered seeing High Stakes Cliffs on the trail map and decided to check it out. I tried to weave my way through, but eventually found myself above a significant drop. After recognizing that hiking out wasn't an option, I pointed my skis downhill and dropped. What I didn't realize was how shallow the snowpack was so early in the season and when I hit the snow, I instantly double ejected out of my skis, tumbling swiftly down the apron below. When I got up, I wasn't hurt but there was a huge hole in my jacket from the jagged cliff. I climbed back to my skis, but one of my poles was stranded on a big rock above me.

———

I waited while the ski patroller called the office at the top of the mountain. When they answered, he asked if they still had Ryan in the shack and as he nodded, he handed me the phone.

"Hi, this is Ryan's dad." I paused and waited for him to say, "Oh, so you're the idiot that lost his kid." Instead, he introduced himself and told me Ryan was fine.

"He got a little turned around and then got cliffed-out." He responded as if he was telling a funny story, not a dire one, and I felt the muscles in my face release. He reassured me that Ryan was unhurt, but since it was so late in the day, the patroller asked for permission to ski Ryan back down to the village.

I stumbled outside to curious looks from Dylan and Melissa. I told them that I found Ryan and that he was heading down. Then, I exhaled like I had just been dug out after an avalanche, looked at Dylan, and asked, "What the fuck does cliffed-out mean?"

———

Two ski patrollers arrived, helped me get my gear together, and said they would help me find my dad. Apparently, he had gone to the tram side to look for me, and when I wasn't there, he called ski patrol. By that time, they already had me in their hut. They told him I got "cliffed-out" in Mineral when I reached a point on the cliff where I had no possible options to ski down, so I was forced to jump. Luckily, I was uninjured thanks to the extra padding in my puffy coat, but if I wanted to be a big mountain skier, I had more to learn. Not just about skiing but about navigating mountains and planning routes from below.

———

Despite the High Stakes Cliffs debacle, the trip served its intended purpose, and Ryan's lifeless hospital room with grates on the windows was a distant memory. He did well on and off the mountain, even managing the comedy surrounding the condo experience. He handled the challenging aspects of the trip that Dr. Schneider predicted he would always struggle with, and that SVTA, Monica, and his parents witnessed him wrestle with every day. Airport lines, a long flight, a spontaneous switch to a hotel, failing to ski well initially at Alta before being forced to walk to Snowbird, and running into trouble in Mineral Basin were all potential triggers that he had dealt with successfully. I never once threatened him with restraint and, although he was certainly more stubborn and emotional than other kids at the resort, including Dylan and Melissa's children, he never stood out on the mountain or in the hotel as a child with a disability. To prove it, I could have asked every skier at Snowbird to guess where Ryan spent the previous week and there wasn't the slightest chance that anyone would have landed on "a mental hospital."

His dad, on the other hand, was mentally and physically exhausted, and very much looked forward to the long flight home. Not that flying with Ryan was easy, but at least it buckled him in place for a few hours.

Right as our plane began to taxi, Ryan looked at me and said, "Dad, my legs are really itchy." I responded nonchalantly that Utah is very dry and leaned forward to grab some moisturizer out of my bag. But just as I started to unzip my carry-on, I thought better of it and quickly sat up. "Let me see your legs."

Ryan reached down and pulled up both of his pant legs. From my vantage point, I was only able to see a few inches of skin from the hem of his pants to the top of his socks, but what I was able to see was covered in a terrible rash. I loosened my seatbelt and quickly stretched across my seat to lower his right sock. His skin was bright red with raised bumps, and the rash traveled to the point where his sneakers covered the rest of his feet. I lifted his pants and was slightly relieved when the rash stopped halfway up his calf. I then executed the same drill on his left leg and found his skin less inflamed but still irritated.

"What is it, Dad?" He asked with a tinge of fear in his voice.

"I'm not sure, buddy. I think it might be . . ." My voice trailed off. I stopped to look again.

I immediately went into denial. I examined the bumps more closely this time and began thinking of possible explanations out loud to Ryan, before refuting them to myself.

"Dry skin?" *But why there?*

"Maybe your ski boots were too tight?" *No, there is no way that could happen on both legs.*

"Maybe you were allergic to the detergent in the hotel sheets?" *No, how could it only affect his lower legs?*

It was time to face reality. The only plausible explanation for Ryan's rash was Lamictal. He was not yet blistering like the kids who died from

Stevens-Johnson syndrome, but it was clearly an allergic reaction to the increased dosage that Dr. Jorgon insisted on. Frantically, I sent a text to Dr. Norman on my Blackberry and sat, silently unsure of what to do next. I focused my energy on the top left-hand corner of my Blackberry, demanding that it blink its red flashing light to indicate a response, just as pilot came over the speaker to announce that we were next in line for takeoff.

Should I alert the flight attendant?

Maybe they could turn the plane around on the runway?

But, then what? Do we call an ambulance and head to a Salt Lake City hospital?

My Blackberry vibrated and began blinking, thankfully. Dr. Norman replied, "Stop taking [the Lamictal] immediately."

Just then, the flight attendant wandered by. "Sir, you need to put that away."

Shit, now what? In 2010, planes lacked Wi-Fi, so once our plane took off, my only recourse would be alerting the pilot to make an emergency landing. *Fuck, should we just get it over with and ask to get off now? But, if this was a life-or-death situation, wouldn't Dr. Norman have texted that or tried to call? Focus, Rob. She only said to stop taking the Lamictal. She didn't say anything about a hospital. Okay, fine, no more Lamictal. Now, get that panicked look off your face before Ryan senses that something is wrong.*

I spent the next five hours nervously studying Ryan, praying his eyes didn't begin to blister.

When we landed, Dr. Norman confirmed that I should head home and not to the emergency room. That was a good sign, at least. However, it spelled the end of Lamictal. All the misery endured at Cambridge Hospital had officially accomplished *nothing*. Ryan was put through two weeks of hell only to aggressively increase the dosage of a medicine and trigger a side effect that could have killed him.

As we drove home from the airport, I was emotionally exhausted but drew on my reserves to be furious. For the entire forty-minute ride, I gripped the steering wheel so tightly that it left indents in the leather covering. Ryan drifted in and out of sleep, while my jaw muscles flexed, and I re-litigated the decision to hospitalize him.

When Dr. Norman pushed for a hospital stay for purposes of evaluation, I assumed she knew better. When Dr. Jorgon insisted on the higher dosage of Lamictal, I acquiesced, and if not for an itchy leg, Ryan might have succumbed to a side effect that I knew was a possibility. Even if the likelihood of dying from Stevens-Johnson syndrome was remote, it ignited the same set of emotions I experienced leaving the hospital. Only, this was an even louder wakeup call. Expert input was one thing, but it was time to stop searching for miracle cures to Ryan's behavioral challenges. He was never going to be the child that I expected. No special school program or medicine was going to make him captain of the baseball team or an investment banker. Ryan was the boy that I got, and he was suffering. It was up to me to help him and watching him on skis gave me reason to believe that I could help him. It was time to take charge of the medical and educational decisions surrounding his care, even if assuming that level of responsibility raised the stakes to the highest possible threshold.

What if ignoring a doctor's advice led to Ryan's suicide?

Or, what if his actions harmed someone else?

CHAPTER TWELVE

The Extreme Club

"Every person has the right to live, work, and learn in an emotionally and physically safe environment."

—BRIDGER SCHOOL

December 1, 2010. We returned from Utah to the news that several therapeutic schools were interested in meeting Ryan. Unfortunately, those institutions not only utilized restraint, but relished it as a behavioral deterrent, so we begged the special education department to find *one* restraint-free therapeutic school willing to interview him. We argued to the coordinator that Ryan presented better in person and hoped a successful interview might convince a less restrictive program to give him a second chance.

After a slew of rejections from restraint-free programs, the town eventually convinced one school called Milestones to meet Ryan. However, when he climbed to the top of a play structure on his tour and refused to get down, the meeting ended in a quick rejection. Despite promising to act appropriately at the interview, Ryan sabotaged his chances by pushing the limits of Milestone's disciplinary policy to test the staff's reaction. Burned by previous assurances from every adult in his life, Ryan wanted proof that the program would not restrain him.

Although he made his point on the tour, without another restraint-free program to assess, we were dispatched on several horrifying campus tours of schools willing to consider him. There, we witnessed isolation rooms and behavior modification systems based on tokens earned and spent like inmates at prison commissaries. One particularly awful school utilized an assembly line of staff to restrain students in a large "discipline room" resembling a steel cage match at a WrestleMania event.[1]

In our search for an appropriate school program, we also faced a major decision with respect to Ryan's medication. After his allergic reaction to Lamictal, Dr. Norman recommended transitioning him to lithium, a widely accepted option in treating bipolar disorder that lacked the terrible potential side effects of Lamictal. The primary side effect was dry mouth, but the reason we resisted initially was the frequent blood draws required to monitor the lithium level in Ryan's system. Although he was more tolerant of needles than most nine-year-olds, it was a big ask to have daily, weekly, and later monthly blood tests. Dr. Norman also recommended a second medication called Seroquel used to treat certain mental/mood conditions such as schizophrenia and bipolar disorder. Seroquel had a ten-year history of pediatric use, and its main side effect was weight gain, so it appeared safer than other options.

As evidenced by his behavior at the Milestones interview, Ryan still feared restraint during episodic conflict and, when he got upset, his emotional state was so dysregulated that Dr. Norman argued medication remained the most prudent course of action. I wasn't happy with medicating him after the Lamictal allergic reaction, but Mary Beth felt strongly that lithium and Seroquel were safer, so I was willing to try them. With the combination of medicines, Ryan became extremely sedate. He pleaded to ski on weekends but, during the week, was content playing Minecraft, staring blankly at his computer screen for hours. Within a few weeks, we noticed bloating in his face and around his midsection. Soon, he was carrying an extra twenty pounds and, while that is hard on any person, it was particularly difficult for a boy who prided himself on athleticism.

---

1. Rooms like this still exist in Massachusetts. Although schools cannot use restraint as a means of punishment or discipline per se, restraint and/or isolation is allowed when a student is a threat to themselves or others. Prone restraints (facedown on the ground) are further limited by statute but are used when certain conditions are met.

Several nasty commenters on his YouTube channel referenced his weight. I quickly deleted the comments before Ryan read them, but I worried about future posts on other social media platforms that I was unable to monitor.

In January of 2011, Sudbury's special education coordinator convinced us to tour the Bridger School. Bridger's use of restraints was a dealbreaker when we investigated it originally, but we agreed to a visit, and the school presented better than we expected. The campus was more expansive than SVTA and resembled a suburban private school with multiple buildings and facilities. Classrooms on the tour were more traditional than other therapeutic schools we visited, with rows of desks and teachers lecturing in front of whiteboards.

Monica previously worked in the residential section at Bridger and worried us with her description of the student population as tough city kids kicked out of Boston public schools. On the tour, however, the other students turned and smiled at Ryan and seemed excited by the prospect of someone new joining the class. Unlike SVTA, it did not appear many of the students were on the autism spectrum, and I questioned Mary Beth as to why Sudbury recommended a school for students defined by behavioral challenges that largely resulted from socioeconomic circumstances, but we both agreed Bridger was Ryan's only option.

Prior to enrolling at Bridger, Mary Beth and I attended a long meeting with the administration to discuss strategies for dealing with Ryan when he became upset. The meeting took place in a small conference room with a dozen people densely seated around a long mahogany table, and while I was in the process of assuring the administration that Ryan was not the least bit dangerous, my phone vibrated. I ignored it, but it vibrated again. Monica was calling, knowing we were in an important meeting at Bridger, so something was clearly wrong. I politely excused myself, mumbling something about extinguishing "a quick work fire."

As I made my way outside, Monica frantically explained that she and Abigail were locked in a bathroom because Ryan was trying to break down the door to confront them. Monica, who rarely overreacted, sounded scared, so I offered to call the police. Despite threatening Ryan with law enforcement involvement a few times over the years, I never seriously considered calling 911 to quell a meltdown.

Abigail decided it would be funny to lock me out of the house. When I couldn't get in the front door or the basement slider, I went around to the garage to see if that door was open. It was locked as well, so I went back to the front door and started banging on it. When it was clear that Monica wasn't coming to rescue me, I picked up a rock and tried breaking one of the glass panels next to the door. I hoped that I could reach through the broken panel to unlock the door, but when I banged the rock against the glass, it didn't break. I was about to try again when Monica came to the door and promised if I put the rock down, she would open it. I agreed, but when she let me in, I charged back into the house to locate Abigail.

Monica then chased after me, grabbed Abigail, dragged her into the bathroom, and locked the door. I started kicking the bathroom door, and Monica told me she was calling Dad. I knew my parents were in an important meeting and if they found out there was a fight at home, especially while Monica was pregnant, the punishment would be a nightmare. So, I decided that I needed to stop her from calling and body-slammed the door with my hip as hard as I could. Abigail started screaming, and Monica yelled something about calling the police.

Just then, I snapped back into reality and thought, "Holy crap, they called the cops on me!" So, I dipped out the back door and grabbed my scooter to escape down the street. When I reached the end of the cul-de-sac, I ditched the scooter in some bushes and ran for the woods. In a few minutes, I saw a police car make a slow circle and stop. The officer stepped out of his car. I knew that he would never find me in the woods because I had mapped every inch of it and knew of endless thickets and swamps where I could hide. But running away to the woods also meant that I couldn't go home, which was how this whole thing started in the first place.

Finally, I darted out of the woods onto a neighbor's porch to feel safer. Surprisingly, when the officer approached, he didn't tackle me as I expected. Instead, he sat down on the steps and talked to me in a quiet demeanor. He was really nice about the situation and told me that he had a sister that drove him crazy, too. So, I surrendered and headed home.

To an outsider, an emotionally troubled child attempting to attack a sibling likely meant another trip to Cambridge Hospital. However, I remained convinced Ryan was damaged by SVTA and his irrational responses to conflict were a by-product of fearing for his own safety. Perhaps I was being naïve, but I felt hopeful that Bridger would better condition Ryan to regulate his emotional swings during periods of escalation. Ryan, on the other hand, was very skeptical of Bridger because we were honest with him about the school's use of restraints. He was willing to give it a try, but whenever we discussed the school, his body language was rigid with a healthy dose of PTSD paranoia. Who could blame him? His parents and doctors had already failed to deliver on promises with respect to the Sudbury Integrated Preschool and SVTA, so he had every reason to suspect that this was another trap.

When he finally hopped into the gray van for his first day at Bridger, I was relieved to have him back in school and out of the house for a few hours during my workday. I remained optimistic that Bridger offered Ryan a fresh start and hoped new classmates and the desire to fit in might pressure him to modulate his behavior. Not surprisingly, he got off to a shaky start and was restrained several times in the first couple of weeks. By this point, we were so sensitive to even hearing the word "restraint" that we demanded a meeting with Ryan's teachers, but the administration at Bridger was able to justify the circumstances around each episode.

While the school agreed Ryan was deeply impacted by restraints at SVTA, the administration argued that his normal fight-or-flight response was so out of whack that the school *needed* to restrain him to help normalize his reactions. Bridger's justification sounded catch-22ish to me, but as we assessed each situation, there was a point during the buildup of the conflict where Ryan should have backed down and deescalated long before he was restrained. Bridger's protocol altered the methodology employed by SVTA, who would have restrained him long before he had an opportunity to calm down. The problem was that Ryan was so fearful of being restrained that, the minute he got into trouble for something small, he lashed out or ran.

Out of all my options for potential schools, I liked Bridger the best, and so did my parents. Unlike SVTA, Bridger used restraints as a last resort rather than a method of control. So, I was actually looking forward to going back to school.

I'll never forget my first day at Bridger. Earlier that week, we had the biggest snowstorm of my life, and the snow was up to my chest as I walked around at recess. In my first week, I was given a math assessment test. I quickly realized how easy it was, so I asked for a sheet of scrap paper. I took the scrap paper and wrote out algebraic equations, and then solved all of them. For a year after Monica had her baby, I had a babysitter named Lauren. While Monica taught me to read, Lauren helped my math skills progress. Maybe a bit farther than they needed to, considering I was so young. The teacher monitoring the assessment noticed I was spending more time on the scrap paper than the actual test, so she sent a teacher's aide to check on me. He took the paper and called the head teacher. He told her I was making up my own math, and he didn't know if any of it was right. She checked it and, one by one, approved each answer. She said in a very surprised voice, "This is all correct!" I apologized and offered to finish the assessment. She replied, "You can put that down now." After that, I was given my own private math class, where I learned algebra and geometry instead of addition and subtraction.

Aside from academics, I soon realized that my struggles were far from over. When I came to Bridger following the hospital and years at SVTA, I was broken. I ran or fought at the first sign of trouble and could barely trust my parents, let alone new people. At Bridger, the first time I got in trouble, they called in two guys named Greg and Dave. They provided school security and only appeared when there was trouble. I tried to run away from them and then fought back when Greg grabbed me before I reached the door. Believe it or not, after that first encounter with Greg and Dave, I wanted to return to SVTA. Although I was restrained hundreds of times at SVTA, it was usually by my teachers. At Bridger, Greg and Dave's only job was to restrain kids. They were both really big and never cracked a smile.

Teachers at Bridger worked diligently to earn Ryan's trust, talking through problems before they escalated. It took months and, ironically, what helped him adopt better strategies for conflict resolution was the influence of other students. Most led difficult lives, residing with foster families or in state-run facilities, and many were abused or neglected. With every reason to resent Ryan for having socioeconomic advantages, his fellow students protected him by teaching him to "go along to get along." They implored him to relent on small issues with teachers and demonstrated the benefit of backing down during periods of conflict, rather than magnifying punishment by fighting back or fleeing.

In his own way, Ryan was a big influence on other students at Bridger. Foster care, group homes, and schools with residential facilities were hardly bastions of free expression. These kids were conditioned to choose compliance over retribution, so Ryan reciprocated by teaching them to advocate, question, and buck the system at every turn. He had the courage to speak up, not only when he believed he was treated unfairly, but anytime he thought his classmates were treated unjustly.

Outside of the classroom, Ryan backflipped while disembarking swings, walked across the top pole of the swing set like a balance beam, and climbed to the top of the massive tree in the middle of the Bridger campus. Originally, he did this to get noticed by his peers, and the administration referred to his physical prowess as his "social currency." What Bridger's administration did not foresee, however, was once Ryan had the other students' attention, he cashed in chips by teaching his class-mates to *fly*. He formed an "Extreme Club" and soon, dozens of students were using recess to test their boundaries and conquer challenges instead of mindlessly sitting on a swing and waiting for someone (who was never coming) to push them.

Aside from worrying about restraints again, my biggest issue at Bridger was deciding who I could trust. Every new person, even the other kids, seemed like a threat. At first, I had trouble relating to the other kids because many of them were going through struggles I couldn't begin to comprehend. While most people at SVTA struggled with mental health, many of Bridger students suffered from parental abuse or neglect. Some of the kids were taken from their homes and lived at school full-time. In the first few weeks, a few of the kids resented me for having a home, let alone both parents.

Over time, my peers became more accepting and didn't see me as an object of jealousy. My self-taught parkour came in handy when I naturally displayed it on the playground. The teachers at Bridger always thought I was showing off, but I was just having fun the only way I knew how. Suddenly, everyone wanted to learn, so I decided to teach them by inventing a progression system, starting small and finishing big. I called it the "Extreme Club," and there were twenty levels. One through five were basic jumps and vaults; six through ten involved balancing, climbing, high jumps, and landing in parkour rolls; eleven to fifteen were demonstrating proficiency in beginner flips; and sixteen to twenty were various completed flips and advanced moves. In retrospect, I was not qualified to teach any of this, and I'm lucky no one got hurt, but I must have done something right because, by my second year, I had twenty people in the club. Many were pretty good, but only a couple managed backflips and side flips off the picnic tables on campus like me.

Although people didn't know what to make of me in the beginning, I quickly gained popularity within the school and finally felt connected. In return, I taught my friends to believe in themselves, to be more confident, and how to discover their true capabilities. I appreciated how difficult things were for them, so I hoped these lessons gave them a chance at a decent life.

⌒⌒

Outside of Bridger, Ryan's life was steady. He still saw Dr. Norman weekly and remained highly medicated on lithium and Seroquel, but without the chaotic use of restraint at home, afternoons and evenings were more sanguine. Non-skiing weekends still presented challenges, but Ryan was able to fill warm-weather days in the woods and wetlands behind our house. His quest to explore, document, and map the entire area included Mason, his friend from the neighborhood, and Max, a boy from Bridger. Although friendships were few and far between at Bridger due to restrictions surrounding contact between students outside of school, the administration allowed students to see each other away from school with parental permission. This was often difficult to obtain since many of the students moved frequently between different foster homes, so Ryan was fortunate that Max's adopted mother allowed him to visit on weekends.

While things were certainly better than they were at SVTA, life was far from perfect for Ryan. He gained significant weight because of the medication, which was poorly timed because Bridger was his first introduction to crushes and even actual dating. He seemed forever caught in a cycle of liking girls who liked someone else, and since Max was particularly handsome, any girl Ryan liked always seemed more interested in Max. Initially, Ryan viewed Max as his "sworn enemy," but over time they became close friends. We were quick to praise him for putting aside his jealousy and accepting Max as a friend.

Later that summer, one of my best friends, Max, began going through troubles as well. Max was in the same year as me at Bridger. We began our friendship after we realized a girl we were fighting over wasn't worth the trouble. We decided we were better off friends, and he spent most weekends at our house. Max was two years older, and he started seeing a girl that his mother didn't know about. For most of that summer, he snuck out to see her, but when his mother found out, a fight broke out and Max was sent to a residential program.

The hardest part of attending school with people who have issues is watching them suffer. Therapeutic schools market themselves to parents as being a safe haven for kids who are different. However, being constantly surrounded by kids who were abused at home, suicidal, or intellectually disabled made it hard for me to make lasting friendships. I got used to watching people I cared for disappear from my life at a young age, but this was different. Max was adopted by someone who appeared to love him very much. Then they had one fight and she stuck him in a group home. I have to admit that part of me worried it might happen to me. I was doing better at home since my parents stopped restraining me, but we still argued about things, and I still fought with Abigail. What if one bad argument pushed them over the edge and I wound up in a group home? Dad always promised that would never happen, but he also told me that SVTA and Cambridge Hospital would help me. Could I really trust him?

Although it had been over two years since Ryan was restrained at home, he struggled to accept that we would never use it again as a deterrent. He also remained on high alert about any decisions regarding his care, fearing that he might be dragged back to the hospital. He constantly spied on us and acted increasingly paranoid whenever conversations between Mary Beth and me were conducted in hushed tones. Often, those conversations were about topics that he wasn't yet ready to hear but had little to do with his actual treatment. For example, during Ryan's time at Bridger, Monica informed us that she was relocating to California. Mary Beth and I hoped to conduct the initial candidate screening before informing Ryan and Abigail that Monica was leaving us. Eventually, we settled on a twenty-four-year-old woman named Chloe. Like Monica, Chloe was ABA trained. She worked in a special education classroom as a paraprofessional and, during her final interview where we allowed Ryan and Abigail to participate, Ryan asked her if she restrained kids at her school. When Chloe answered that sometimes she restrained them to keep them safe, Ryan looked at her and pointed toward the door and yelled, *"Get out!"*

Chapter Thirteen

Hang Me, Oh Hang Me

"Ryan is beginning to identify what his body needs but requires much adult supervision in the moment."
—IEP Progress Report for Ryan DeLena, Bridger School (June 2011)

December 30, 2012. *When I was eleven years old, Dad and I really got into skiing, and we researched different places to go. I looked for mountains with cool expert runs and Dad looked for resorts with hotels near the lifts. We went to some interesting places including Mammoth, Jackson Hole, and Whistler. At Mammoth, I got Dad in a bit over his head because I wanted to ski a well-known expert run called Hangman's Hollow.*

Hangman's is always difficult, but when we arrived in Mammoth, the early season snow coverage was thin, so it was really challenging. The run started with big cornice drop that formed a wall of snow at the top before narrowing to a tight couloir (a steep, narrow gully on a mountainside) lined by a rock ledge. The overall snowpack was firm, but a soft layer of windblown snow filled the chute.

I took one quick look at Hangman's Hollow and refused to go. We then skied down a different trail, and Ryan spent the entire gondola ride up for our second run seething. Randomly, we met Stacy Cook (a three-time

Olympian ski racer) on the gondola ride up, and she asked if Ryan missed breakfast because he seemed "hangry."

As soon as the gondola doors opened, Ryan headed back to Hangman's Hollow. I knew eventually he would force me to ski it, so I leaned over the cornice wall and examined the rest of the run, which narrowed between two rock bands at its steepest point and resembled an elevator shaft.

"What if I ski around and meet you at the bottom?" I asked with twinge of guilt.

"Dad, I shouldn't do it alone. What if I fall in the couloir and need help?"

This wasn't a typical debate won by an eleven-year-old with emotion. Ryan had logic on his side, and he knew it. As his father, I couldn't let him try this one solo. "All right, just give me a few seconds to look at this friggin' thing."

I stared down the couloir again. Every fiber of my being wanted to turn away, but I stood there motionless. I couldn't disappoint Ryan.

Coined in the Alps, the term *couloir* translates in French to "passage" or "corridor," but luckily for me, early-season conditions had yet to build a massive cornice wall at the entrance, so it didn't look impossible. It required that I remain upright for an initial twenty-foot drop down the side of a wall that was over fifty degrees steep. And, even if I managed to successfully negotiate that obstacle, I would then land in the actual couloir, *mellowing* to a slope nearing forty degrees. A forty-degree slope might not sound so bad to a sophomore in geometry class but summoning the testicular fortitude to angle my body down the mountainside standing on two planks of wood, I froze up. This was steeper than anything we had skied to this point, and I felt like an elephant refusing to climb up a hill, only my mind was objecting to the physics of skiing *down* anything greater than forty degrees.[1]

---

1. When I was a kid, my dad worked nights in a parking lot behind the old Boston Garden. The lot sat in the shadow of a long wooden ramp that delivery trucks used to enter the arena. When plans were drawn up for the new Boston Garden, a similar ramp was constructed out of cement with the same slope to walk elephants into the building whenever the circus came to Boston. Elephants have an internal fear of slopes over thirty-six degrees because anything greater requires too much energy to move their enormous bodies uphill. Apparently, Hannibal experienced this firsthand in 218 BC when he attempted to cross the Alps to invade Rome.

To this day, Ryan's GoPro video titled "Extreme Ryan (11 Years Old) Saves Dad on Hangman's Hollow" most accurately encapsulates our early skiing relationship.

When he finally started his GoPro, he announced to his followers, "Hangman's Hollow. Arguably the hardest trail on the map!" He then paused, which indicated to me that he was still unsure about this one. That indecision was hinted at in his next question. "Okay, now who is dropping in first?"

"Me, I guess?" As if I had any choice.

"Only if you want!" he replied happily, knowing he received the answer he was seeking.

We then spent a few seconds searching for the best way to start the run. We debated various ways to launch off the top of the cornice wall into the couloir, but I wasn't attempting anything that required airtime.

"Hey, Dad, I found a real nice spot to drop in."

Although he encouraged me to jump, I eyeballed a side-cutting sneak attack rather than a frontal assault and carefully slid down the cornice wall into the couloir. I survived, but when I made my first turn, I slipped for an instant before catching myself. That near-fall rattled me, and for a second, I forgot about my son, who was preparing to drop in.

Ryan then announced to his followers that he was ready to launch from the top of the cornice wall. "Okay, here we are." He then yelled to me standing in the middle of the couloir about twenty yards below him. "Are you going to watch? I found the perfect spot!"

I wanted to reply, "No, I am busy trying not to die," but I turned and watched him jump into the couloir. When he landed, he let out a couple of whoops, but after pausing to examine the rest of the run, he appeared to quickly sense how narrow it was, particularly as it approached the rocks.

With the rest of the couloir left to ski, we stood next to one another and debated how to best proceed. After a few seconds, I skied first and dived into the teeth of the run with one aggressive turn in the soft snow. However, as I shifted my weight into my second turn, my skis caught on the hard-packed Sierra Cement beneath the soft layer and I spun into a violent crash, plummeting down the elevator shaft.

"Careful!" screamed Ryan, fearing I was headed straight for the volcanic rock lining the couloir. His breathing then moved into a full pant, and he raced down the couloir to help me. He paused about fifty feet above me and yelled, "You all right?"

——❦——

Unfortunately, Dad's hard charging on Hangman's Hollow lasted two turns before he fell and lost a ski. He spun around on his back with his head pointed down the slope. Then he just kept on sliding. He traveled a hundred yards straight down with his gear in a "yard sale" all over the slope. Luckily, he slid straight down and never crashed into the rocks.

——❦——

"Yeah, buddy, I'm great." *I just need to find the rest of my body.*

With Ryan paused in the middle of the couloir to assess how best to gather my skis and poles, he ran into a snowboarder who was gracious enough to stop in the run to help gather my equipment. Ryan got right to the point. "Can you give me some help up here?"

The snowboarder, who was fifteen feet below my skis, recommended the obvious and suggested that Ryan grab them on the way down.

Ryan then paused to assess the location of the skis. Although they were twenty feet apart horizontally, they were at same vertical location on the hill. Ever the scientist, Ryan informed the snowboarder, "It's going to be kinda' hard. They're both at the same angle." In other words, *This run will be much less interesting for my viewers if I have to grab a ski, then sidestep across the slope to Dad's other ski.*

The snowboarder bowed his head as if to say, *Why the fuck did I stop to help this guy?* But he relented and began to climb back up the hill on his hands and knees toward my skis. Ryan watched him struggle for a bit before appreciating that he had to at least get one of the skis. He then proceeded down, and upon reaching the first ski, pushed it to the snowboarder. The snowboarder pointed at the second ski, but seeing where the snowboarder was positioned, Ryan said, "I don't know if I can do that. You're kinda' in my way."

The snowboarder's shoulders slumped once again. He then climbed across the hill toward my second ski. He struggled to grab it but when he was finally in possession of both, he asked Ryan to bring them to me.

"No, I'm on video. I don't want to stay here too long."

Not the answer the snowboarder was anticipating.

Ryan continued down to me. The poor snowboarder was left negotiating the most difficult run on the mountain while carrying two giant powder skis to me.

When Ryan and I reunited, after a short debate about a missing pole, he checked to see if I was okay, but then quickly zeroed in on his second most pressing concern. "We're still gonna' post this on YouTube, right?"

Completely defeated, I wiped away the snow and sweat from my face. "Seriously? I looked like an idiot."

In response, Ryan raised his voice. "You didn't look like an idiot, Dad! This is the hardest run on the entire map! There's no shame!" So, I gathered my possessions and my pride and agreed to let him post the video.

Ryan then happily turned his attention back to his viewership. "Well, I got some nice turns in there. Sorry if the video was a little slow to all my viewers; I had to get Dad's skis. So, I am going to turn off the camera now, and until next time, this is Extreme Ryan."

To most, Ryan's reaction might seem out of place because he shifted his focus so quickly from my health back to his goal of becoming YouTube famous. Children with his supposed profile can lack empathy for the misfortune of others. Yet, Ryan's immediate reaction to my fall stood in stark contrast. When he yelled "Careful!" he was obviously scared for me. Then, later, when I was feeling sorry for myself and asked him not to post my fall on video for the world to laugh at, he stopped to console me. He wanted so badly to post the video but first addressed how I might feel about it.

He was clearly aware that my body and my ego were battered by Hangman's Hollow.

━ ⌣ ━

Next run, I decided to tackle Hangman's Hollow alone. Dad seemed a little shaken up after he fell, so there was no need to put him through it again. Plus, his fall ruined my GoPro video of the run, and I really wanted to make a good one for my channel.

Once I knew I could ski it, I really attacked it on my next run.

On the Mammoth trip, I realized that I was a much better skier than Dad. Several commenters on YouTube pointed it out after watching videos of us skiing together at different places, but I never really thought about it until Mammoth. He wasn't able to ski really steep runs like Hangman's Hollow, and he struggled a lot in the trees. The problem was that mountains out west were so big with so many great runs that Dad and I had a lot of arguments about when to stay together and when to separate. I knew he wanted to stay with me, and I didn't want to hurt his feelings, but I remember thinking that maybe it was time to speak up and tell him that it was okay to let me do these runs alone.

I survived Mammoth and logged plenty of skiing with Ryan back east in late 2012 and early 2013. For February break, our entire family traveled to Wyoming and, after my near-death experience at Mammoth, I sought help. I hired a guide in Jackson Hole to take Ryan to all the runs he wanted to do, and when a burly thirty-something dude with longish hair named Jake met us at the ski school, I was optimistic. However, from the start, Jake seemed reluctant to commit to any sort of plan.

"So, Jake, Ryan is hoping to ski Corbett's Couloir and some of the harder double blacks off the tram."

Jake looked at Ryan and then back at me. "Yeah, we'll probably play it by ear and see what's open today. A lot of those runs are condition dependent."

I wanted to tell Jake not to bullshit a bullshitter but bit my tongue and hoped the half-day of guiding would go better than I expected.

When our entire family flew to Jackson Hole in Wyoming, there was one famous run called Corbett's Couloir that I was dying to attempt. Dad wasn't sure I could do it, so he hired a guide to take me down the run, but no matter how many times I asked the guide, he made excuses for why I couldn't do it.

At first, he said it was closed. Then, when I pointed out to him that there were people skiing it, we skied over to Corbett's and he said, "The line is too long. Let's do something else and come back." But every time I asked when we were going back to it, he found something else to ski instead.

At the end of the lesson, he acted like he was disappointed that we ran out of time before we could attempt Corbett's. But I knew he never intended on allowing me to try it. He never even gave me a chance to prove myself—he just decided from the outset that I was too young or too small. Afterward, when I was skiing with Dad in the afternoon, I felt bad about myself. I wondered if I would ever have the trust of grown-ups, including my own parents, to do anything. Dad gave me more freedom on ski trips, but even he said no when he thought something was over my head. How would I accomplish anything in skiing if I couldn't attempt the hardest runs?

Unlike Ryan, my progress as a skier in the 2012 and 2013 seasons was incremental. Constantly forced into situations above my ability level, I cautiously slid my way down the difficult slopes with poor technique and created bad habits. I spent our trips avoiding steep runs or runs with hazards like trees or rocks, but there were times when I felt obliged to stay with Ryan. First descents at new destinations or runs late in the day when the light was fading compelled my presence. But even when Ryan was not responsible for forcing me onto expert slopes, I still managed to put myself in precarious situations through inexperience (i.e., stupidity).

On the Jackson Hole trip, we accidentally separated, and I wound up on a very steep pitch dotted with trees and exposed rock. The snow cover was very thin, resembling a series of plateaus that necessitated jumping and landing, one by one. Each plateau jump was about ten feet, connected by narrow channels of snow and ice about two feet across, which flowed from one to another like snow slides. I managed to ski down the first couple successfully, but after reaching a point that involved too narrow of a slide and too big of a jump, I made the rookie mistake of taking off my skis and wrapping them in my arms to slide down to the next plateau on my ass. I assumed that I could slide then stop to reassess how to tackle the next one. However, sliding on my ass worked a little too well and as

I slid down to the next plateau, I shot across a patch of ice, launching down to the next plateau, and the next, and the next. Certain I would end up dead or paralyzed, when I finally came to a stop and was surprisingly unhurt, I stood up and screamed, "I can't be killed!"

Unfortunately, the glow of survival lasted a few seconds before realizing one of my skis was three plateaus above me. Since there was no way for me to climb up to retrieve it, I called Ryan and then ski patrol for assistance. The problem on both calls, however, was that I couldn't remember the name of any nearby trails, so I advised the patroller to search an area "with lots of trees and rocks," which led to a predictable retort: "Sir, Jackson Hole has a lot of trees and rocks."

—◆—

I never understood why Dad refused to learn the trail map for any resort that we traveled to. Whenever we got separated and tried to reconnect on the phone, I would get frustrated and tell him to just meet me at the base. He was like a guy that wouldn't use the GPS in his car. It wasn't a big deal in the East because mountains usually led to roads if he really got lost. But out west, he could be lost for days.

—◆—

Although I was incredibly proud of Ryan's development as a skier, it was humbling. He was so much better than me. Especially on our trips out west, I wanted to stay with him and ensure his safety on extreme runs, but in doing so I was putting myself in danger. The logical move was to separate and trust that he would be okay. He exhibited freakish balance on skis and never panicked or cried out for help when something was steep. Shit, I panicked and cried out all the time. So, why was it so difficult to let him go alone? Was it because of his diagnosis? If he was a "normal" kid, would I have granted him more freedom? Certainly, that was a factor. I was aware of how the experts in Ryan's life looked at me. They believed that I was in denial about his issues and was too permissive, and they would be lined up to point fingers at me should Ryan get hurt on the slopes. Maybe by staying with him I hoped it would be me that got hurt and not him.

On the flight back from Jackson Hole, I thought about my debacle, getting lost and plummeting down the rocky slope. I could have easily been killed because I did something stupid. Ryan would have never made the same mistake on skis. He studied every resort before we traveled. He memorized the trail map. He skied aggressively but was never out of control. He never tried to show off to look cool in front of other skiers. Hell, my main concern was looking cool in front of other skiers. (Well, maybe not *cool*, but I never wanted to look bad.) Ryan didn't care. His goals were internal. As a result, he skied better than me or almost anyone else on the mountain. Maybe it was time to accept that he had earned something on skis that he was never allowed to experience in school or at home: the freedom to take risks and make mistakes.

CHAPTER FOURTEEN

I Have Just the Guy

"I never teach my pupils; I only attempt to provide the conditions in which they can learn."

—ALBERT EINSTEIN

March 15, 2014. I am not much of a planner. For me, there is something thrilling about improvising when encountering the unexpected. That said, Ryan's lousy experience with a hired ski guide in Jackson Hole pushed me to be more proactive in organizing our trip to Big Sky, Montana. The reason skiing in Big Sky necessitated hiring a guide was an insane run called Big Couloir. With a fifty-degree pitch and 1,500-foot vertical drop, Big Couloir not only *required* a skiing partner, but also avalanche gear, including a beacon. And anything that mandated equipment to assist rescuers in locating your buried body was not for me. I'm sure it seems crazy, then, that I would allow my twelve-year-old to attempt Big Couloir, but in the five years I had spent watching him ski, he had yet to encounter any ski run that was too difficult. Quite honestly, I was more nervous about traveling to a new destination, which always tested my desire to have things run smoothly. Since this was our first time traveling to Montana, I fretted more about missing our connecting flight than I did about Ryan surviving Big Couloir.

However, since Big Couloir greatly exceeded my ability level, I knew that Ryan's only chance to attempt it was to find a guide willing to partner with him. So, the day before we were set to travel, I called the ski school at Big Sky, pleading for the right guide for a private-lesson day. Without delving into detail about Ryan for fear of limiting the experience, I requested someone to guide my "complicated son." The director assured me that he had "just the guy," strongly recommending that we hire Ben Brosseau for the entire day.

<hr>

In the spring of 2014, Dad and I took our first trip to Big Sky. The 11,000-foot summit of Lone Peak in Big Sky boasts some of the most technical inbound terrain outside of Europe, but there was only one line that I had my eyes on: Big Couloir. The 1,500-foot rock-lined couloir was unlike anything I had seen before, especially growing up in the East. Sure, we have couloirs in New England—places where a glacier or a rockslide has left behind a seam or vertical crevasse—but few couloirs in the world were like this one because it was meant to be skied. It was the perfect pitch and positioned precisely on the mountain to avoid sunlight while allowing strong winds to funnel in hundreds of inches of snow. You even had to sign out with the ski patrol to let them know you were attempting it before you could drop in. Since Dad was pretty clear that he wasn't joining me, we agreed on hiring a guide.

<hr>

We arrived in Big Sky just after midnight. With the time difference, it felt much later, and Ryan fell asleep as I unpacked. The next morning, we awoke just as the sun was beginning to light the summit of Lone Peak, far and away the most prominent mountain comprising Big Sky resort. After a quick breakfast, we headed outside to the ski school meeting place, and remained there for a few minutes watching other skiers match up with their instructors or guides. While I nervously studied the tall, pointed, craggy mountaintop where Big Couloir originated, Ryan rocked back and forth in his skis. Clearly, he was apprehensive that this Ben guy would emerge, take one look at him, and find an excuse to deny his conquest.

To be honest, I feared the same result. I had already practiced a speech in my head, pleading with Ben to allow Ryan to ski the ridiculous run, no matter how risky. Although, I had moved beyond thinking Ryan needed to be cured by some special school or doctor, there was still a part of me who believed that he *needed* these victories. Hackett's Highway became Dragon's Teeth and Dragon's Teeth became Hangman's Hollow and Hangman's became Big Couloir. With each mountain conquered, he progressed as a person with glimmers of independence and emotional resilience. I knew how badly Ryan wanted this one, and as we waited for Ben to emerge, I knew how badly I wanted it for Ryan.

Suddenly, a guide walked out of the ski school and headed in our direction before pausing to ask, "Are you Rob?" He introduced himself as Ben. He was boyish looking with a deliberate and unworried manner. Everything about him seemed to move fluidly, gliding in the snow when he walked like he was raised in ski boots. He had strawberry-blond hair that peeked out from under his bandana, blue eyes, and a fair, almost pinkish complexion. His throaty voice reminded me of John Lackey, who was pitching those days for the Red Sox, and I imagined the conversation that was about to happen. I pictured Ben saying something Midwestern like "aw, shucks" when he found a way to shatter Ryan's dream of skiing Big Couloir.

After introductions, I quickly summoned enough courage to inform Ben that we traveled a long way so Ryan could ski Big Couloir. For some reason, I incorporated a French accent when I said "couloir," but as soon as it passed from my lips, I waited for Ben to laugh or shake his head emphatically. Instead, he quickly scanned Ryan from head to toe, and as I prepared my pleading rebuttal, he casually remarked, "Okay, let me just run inside and get him an avalanche beacon." And off he went, effortlessly gliding back into the building.

Ben returned and secured a backpack onto Ryan with all of the necessary equipment, and before I knew it, the three of us loaded the lift and headed up the mountain to ski a few practice runs. On those initial runs, Ben assessed Ryan to make sure he could handle a run like Big Couloir, but he never said it. He actually didn't say much of anything. His quiet demeanor reminded me of a cowboy, doing his job without a whole lot of unnecessary chatter. When I asked him questions, he provided polite and thoughtful answers in a succinct manner, but Ben was not a guy who sits next to you on a plane and spills his life story. To get that, I spent the day peppering him with questions like a witness on cross-examination.

I didn't have much luck with the last guide in Jackson Hole because he never looked at my ability; instead, he doubted me based on my age and height. Ben was different. He never questioned my talent and immediately grabbed an avalanche beacon before we headed for the tram. After we got to the top, we began with a test run down "The Bowl" to assess my readiness for the couloir, so I skied hard and fast, trying to ride the fall line as much as possible. Ben must have liked how I skied because, after we rode back up the tram, we proceeded to the patrol shack to sign out for Big Couloir.

Ryan remained quiet during the practice runs, but I could tell he liked Ben. Unlike his guide in Jackson Hole and most grown-ups Ryan had encountered, Ben wasn't lecturing him on why he wasn't old enough or experienced enough to tackle expert runs. When he provided advice, it was couched around Ryan's goal, saying things like, "When you ski Big Couloir, you'll need to be a bit more cautious as you enter the run because the top section can be firm and icy." Ryan melded so easily with Ben that I was comfortable when they left me at their assigned time. Though, as they skied away toward the entrance of the famed run, I whispered to the ski gods, "Please let this go well." Rather than concern for his safety, my nervousness centered on Ryan skiing to his incredibly high standards. Since skiers were allotted a defined time slot to ski Big Couloir, Ryan had only one chance at success because we couldn't just jump back on the chairlift for a second attempt. Should he tumble or ski it timidly, he would never get over it.

I quickly skied down the other side of Lone Peak before working my way toward the bottom of Big Couloir, where I would wait and watch. Several skiers managed to complete the run without incident before one skier fell just as he neared the halfway point. He spent several torturous minutes climbing back up to retrieve a lost ski. That delay provided me with just enough time to consider what the rest of the trip would be like if Ryan suffered a similar fate.

After a half hour, we got our time slot. Patrol gave us the go-ahead and we traversed to the entrance. Ben took the first drop as a gusty wind blew across the rocky ridge, then he stopped at the bend and waved me on. He warned me that the top section was sketchy, so I slowly crept in and made my first turn. The snow was windswept and firm, so I focused on keeping my edges as I descended. After we paused at the midsection, Ben said the rest of the run had much better snow, and on the lower half I made better turns.

When I caught a glimpse of a tiny dot that looked like Ryan, I snapped picture after picture, as he made defined and purposeful turns down the extremely steep upper section. At the halfway point, he paused to reconnect with Ben and the two tapped poles in a "skier's high five." Ben next instructed Ryan on the intricacies of the second half of the run, and Ryan charged down, making sweeping turns toward the finish. With each turn, I felt a sense of relief, knowing he would be pleased with his aggressiveness and technique. At that moment, Ryan might have been the best twelve-year-old skier on the mountain, but that meant far less than being the happiest twelve-year-old skier on the mountain. For the first time, he had set a goal for himself, pursued, and accomplished it without any adults questioning his skill or sanity.

As Ryan reached the bottom, he smiled and let out an "Oh, yeah!" I tapped his ski pole with mine and told him how proud I was, and he smiled back and said, "That was amazing!" Ben arrived soon after and congratulated him. While the two of them exchanged a fist pump, I studied Ryan's face, and something was different. I couldn't quite put my finger on it, but he seemed comfortable in his own skin for the first time since he was a toddler. As other skiers funneled past and nodded in approval, recognizing Ryan's accomplishment, I thought, *No one here has any fucking idea what this kid has been through to get to this day.*

Over 150,000 viewers on YouTube have watched "Extreme Ryan Skiing Big Couloir in March of 2014." It bothers Ryan that so many people have viewed it because, as he matured, his later videos contain more dynamic skiing. Yet for me, the most significant seconds of the video take place before any skiing starts. As they are standing on top of Big Couloir, Ben directs Ryan to recognize the snow conditions and urges him not to "ski it fast, but ski it well." He reminds Ryan that being safe is the most important part of the run, and instructs Ryan to give him a twenty-five-second head start and wait for him to signal. Ben then skis down the top section and sets up halfway down while Ryan counts aloud. When he eventually receives the thumbs-up from Ben to start skiing, Ryan whispers to himself before he drops in, "I've wanted to do this for so long."

We ate a celebratory lunch, and I quietly shook my head at one point when Ryan asked Ben a question.

"Do you think I am ready for Little Couloir?"

Given that Little Couloir is one of the most intimidating ski runs on the planet, and much steeper and dangerous than Big Couloir, I feared that Ben might laugh or dismiss Ryan out of hand so I interjected. "Can't we enjoy the moment? You just skied Big Couloir as a friggin' twelve-year-old!"

Ben jumped in before I could continue backpedaling. He spoke slowly and softly with his deep croak. "Ryan, based on what I saw today, you will definitely ski Little Couloir soon. I just need to see you ski more advanced terrain, so maybe we can make it a goal that we work on together?"

I poked at my fries and thought to myself, Ben had just delivered the *perfect* answer to Ryan. He said no to Little Couloir while saying yes, and he also ensured that we would be coming back to Big Sky to ski with him again.

After lunch, Ben led Ryan on a hike across the top traverse of Lone Peak so they could ski runs only accessible from the ridgeline. They were gone over two hours; when they materialized, both were all smiles. Ben took great pictures of Ryan hiking on the ridge and, although he looked young and out of place, he was not. He was exactly where he needed to be and despite only knowing Ryan for a few hours, Ben understood.

─ ⌣ ─

It was an amazing day. I set out to do Big Couloir and did it. For once, no adult tried to talk me out of it or stop me, and something I'd only seen in pictures became a reality for me. From that point, we were in love with Big Sky, and it marked the beginning of many future adventures. More importantly, Ben became a reliable partner and role model. When I look back on it, he was the first adult who believed in me.

───⌣───

It had taken Ryan five years to move from the magic carpet to Big Couloir, years that included two therapeutic schools, medication, and stint at a mental hospital. From my vantage point, his life was traveling on parallel tracks, non-skiing, and skiing. In school, Ryan was a student with a disability who most adults assumed required constant supervision and a future that surely included some form of adult intervention. He was restrained less and less but still seemed unsettled at Bridger. The kids at Bridger were good-hearted, but many were raised in traumatic circumstances, and the vibe always felt combative. Mary Beth and I attended meetings and science fairs at the school, constantly watching giant men with radios racing around from crisis to crisis and could not imagine Ryan learning much in such a tense environment. Fortunately, he was a curious and highly motivated learner. Outside of Bridger, he independently studied rocks, minerals, nature, geography, and anything related to skiing. As parents, we took note of it and built on his passions whenever possible. With his formal schooling in such chaotic environments, in many ways, Ryan was teaching himself. He learned from his parents and caregivers, but mostly he acquired facts by researching people, places, and things that interested him. Quite honestly, we were tempted to homeschool him, but homeschooling Ryan would have denied him the socialization he truly craved.

On the contrary, the skiing version of Ryan was not only free of the disability label, he was Extreme Ryan.[1] He could ski any run no matter the difficulty and could do it alone. He was, frankly, a much better skier

---

1. Ryan's nickname was hatched in Vail. Skiing out west for the first time in 2010, he continuously pushed me to ski double black diamond runs. Those runs were always marked by a sign with EXTREME in bright red letters. At some point, I started calling him Extreme Ryan on the trip and the name stuck. Today, Ryan's social media profiles encompass the name, although he seems embarrassed by it now that he is a young man.

than his dad and, often, this twelve-year-old kid was supervising *me*. More importantly, when we were on ski trips, I witnessed a more manageable and independent Ryan. I could take credit, but the reality is travel and the nature of skiing forced me to be more hands-off. As a result, he wasn't just happier on the mountain, but during every aspect of his time away from home and school, signaling that he desperately craved a less restrictive parenting and educational approach outside of skiing.

In seventh grade, I asked my parents about school options aside from Bridger. I wanted to find a school where they didn't restrain students at all, where I wasn't forced to walk in single file lines to class and could use the bathroom without supervision. I especially wanted a place where I could see a friend outside of school without getting permission from parents, school administrators, and the government. My mom told me any school that we found would likely be as restrictive as Bridger and SVTA. I spun on that sentence for weeks, as my hope of a normal life away from skiing quickly faded.

Chapter Fifteen

Redefining Collaborative

"Our mission is to provide our students with an enriched learning experience that is student-centered, collaborative, and academically challenging. Our belief in fostering a treatment environment based on the principles of trauma-informed care, as well as our strong organizational efforts to eliminate restraint and seclusion, reinforce a treatment culture sensitive to the needs of our students."

—Parsons School

September 3, 2014. As Ryan approached the end of seventh grade, we again pressed Sudbury for a restraint-free program, and the Parsons School—a school that previously rejected him when he left SVTA—agreed to an interview. Located approximately one hour west of Sudbury, Parsons had a large campus with a student population of local day students from suburban towns west of Boston and a small percentage of residential students from all over Massachusetts. On our tour, students presented with a variety of social and emotional issues. Some were on the autism spectrum, while others appeared more behavioral. I suspected the rest of the student body attended Parsons (especially as residents) due to challenging family situations.

After his time at Bridger and with a more presentable case file, Ryan was accepted and began eighth grade in their middle school. Parsons employed restraint "only when necessary" and, in its marketing materials, touted the use of Collaborative Problem Solving ("CPS") in navigating student-to-student relations and student-to-faculty interactions. CPS is an often-cited method for dealing with difficult children, particularly those on the spectrum, and it was recommended to us originally by Dr. Schneider when she first began treating Ryan, suggesting we read a book titled *The Explosive Child* by Dr. Ross Greene.

The CPS model is based on conflict resolution through mutually agreed-upon rules of engagement for disagreements arising between adults and children. In the model, issues are labeled A, B, or C. Issues falling in the A category concern safety and security with the adult having the final say. Issues falling in the C category allow the child a clean victory without any debate. Issues in the B category are more complex, forcing the child and adult to compromise. Personally, I thought the entire premise was overly simplistic because parents make this calculation every day without ruminating over it. If your child wants to play in traffic, you say no. If your child wants to play in a puddle, you say yes. If your child wants to jump in a puddle near some traffic, you make a judgment call. Not exactly earth-shattering, but the fact that Parsons relied on CPS instead of more draconian behavioral deterrents sounded encouraging.

The problem was, prior to Ryan's enrollment, a staff member was charged with sexually assaulting students, and the program was revamped in response. But the administration at Parsons never bothered to let anyone know that school's methodology and behavior model had been completely altered. CPS was replaced with a reactive staffing model predicated on constant adult supervision, relying on traditional ABA methods including restraint and isolation. At the eighth-grade level, seats were assigned for classes and lunch, and Ryan was not allowed to leave class for a drink of water without a chaperone. Even when we pointed out to the administration that lithium made him constantly thirsty, the school wouldn't give in, and when Ryan was thirsty, he would get irritable. When he was irritable, he would get into trouble.

———————

I began eighth grade at the Parsons School. The reason we settled on Parsons as my next school was the school's use of Collaborative Problem Solving. However, there was nothing collaborative about it. The school is a dictatorship, and most days, it felt like a prison. At Parsons, you walked everywhere in single file, and you couldn't go to the bathroom without someone standing by the door. In my first week there, I went to the bathroom without asking and they nearly kicked the door in. I heard a teacher outside telling another, "Wait, I hear him peeing. I think he really had to go."

Parsons was a terrible experience from the start, but during my first few weeks, one aspect of my daily life that kept me sane was a girl named Miranda. She was my first "girlfriend," and I use the term loosely because we never actually went on any dates. We just acknowledged our interest in each other and talked on the phone sometimes. Her foster parents always came up with excuses to prevent us from ever meeting on weekends, so school was the only time I saw her, but just knowing she was there made the hour-long ride to hell doable.

However, once teachers figured out that I liked Miranda, they used it to get me to stop disobeying the rules. They told Miranda that she wasn't allowed to talk to me until I got my act together, and if she talked to me, she'd be in trouble, too. For an entire week, I couldn't figure out what I did to make her ignore me. Luckily, when I called her over the weekend, she confessed that she wasn't giving me the silent treatment but was forbidden to talk to me until I behaved better in class. After hearing that, my initial relief turned to rage: these jerks were willing to manipulate Miranda to make me comply with their rules.

＊＊＊

Just after Ryan's enrollment at Parsons, Dr. Norman moved to Chicago and recommended a new psychiatrist for Ryan named Dr. Marcus Delgado. From our initial consultation, it was clear that Dr. Delgado practiced very differently from Dr. Norman. Dr. Norman wasn't a bad psychiatrist, but she was inexperienced and extremely cautious in her approach. She struck me as never wanting to be wrong about Ryan yet lacked the confidence to be right about him. On the other hand, Dr. Delgado's iconoclastic nature caused him to question everything to do with Ryan's care. Although he appeared young, with his jet-black hair and dark eyes, he had practiced for over fifteen years, earning a reputation for challenging authority figures in schools. He even questioned the prior recommendations of Dr. Schneider and Dr. Norman—recommendations followed blindly by Mary Beth and me. Although it was uncomfortable explaining our parenting choices, the fact that Dr. Delgado confronted them along with the decisions of doctors and educators was a refreshing change.

A few weeks into treating Ryan, we met Dr. Delgado for a parental consultation. At the meeting, he asked us to identify the demonstrated benefit of each medication Ryan was taking, probing whether it was eclipsed by potential damage to Ryan's physical well-being. By this point, Ryan was taking lithium and Seroquel and, before she moved, Dr. Norman added Prozac to counter some of the sadness he was experiencing. I went along due to Prozac's benign safety profile, but Dr. Delgado was deeply concerned that Ryan's cholesterol was off the charts. He scrutinized Ryan's diet, illustrating the importance of proper nutrition, and spoke very bluntly about Ryan's overall health. He predicted that the side effects of lithium, Seroquel, and Prozac would eventually prove fatal, since each caused weight gain and led to elevated cholesterol levels and blood pressure.[1] He then inquired about Ryan's formal diagnosis.

"Is Ryan bipolar?" Dr. Delgado's tone shifted. His thick Colombian accent was replaced by a flatter, sharper inflexion that punched each syllable like lawyer on cross-examination, asking a question he already knew the answer to.

Mary Beth and I answered at the same time. She seemed relieved that I was the one fumbling, and her voice trailed off as I continued. "I don't think so. I mean, we always saw plenty of highs, but he never suffers bouts of depression. Don't you need both to be bipolar?"

"Typically, yes. You would see mood swings in a patient that is bipolar." Dr. Delgado was now leading both witnesses. "So, you aren't seeing that rollercoaster with Ryan?"

Mary Beth and I again spoke up in concert, but she hesitated long enough for us to answer sequentially. I was more direct and simply said, "No."

She interjected, "Not really. Ryan can get sad occasionally, but it is usually the result of an event. He is generally pretty happy and energetic."

---

1. People who use antidepressants have a 14 percent higher risk of heart attacks and strokes and a 33 percent greater risk of death, according to findings in a meta-analysis of seventeen studies that was published in 2017 in the journal *Psychotherapy and Psychosomatics.*

In classic Mary Beth fashion, she agreed with me but left herself some legalistic wiggle room.

Dr. Delgado sat up in his leather desk chair, pitched forward, and readied for the kill. "So, why is he being medicated like a child who *is* bipolar?"

Mary Beth and I looked at each other, hoping to be the one who got to dodge the question. She piped up, thankfully. "Well, I suppose originally we medicated him because he was so out of control, and we had issues with an allergic reaction to Lamictal, and this current combination of medicines seems to be helping him attend school without many complaints from his teachers."

Upon hearing that, Dr. Delgado paused to remove his glasses. He wiped his eyes, and I wasn't sure if he was disgusted with our parenting or if he was expressing empathy. Finally, after several torturous seconds, he spoke. "So, the decision to medicate him with two antipsychotics and an antidepressant was made so he could attend a flawed school program without causing disruption?"

I nodded and spoke up before Mary Beth had a chance to counter. "Basically, yeah." What I really wanted to say was "Guilty as charged, your honor."

As we exited the office following the appointment, I stopped Mary Beth in the parking lot. "I think he is onto something with Ryan's medication. I know skiing is different, but the kid that I see on the mountain and away from school does not need to be medicated."

She stiffened and countered, "Look, if he wants to dial back some of the medication, I have no issue, but removing all of the meds at once seems a little aggressive."

I wasn't surprised by her cautious reaction. Mary Beth always viewed Ryan's issues clinically and logically and generally avoided risk. She wasn't swayed by emotional arguments, so I countered in measured terms. "Aside from the cholesterol and the other health concerns, once he reaches adulthood, you know Ryan won't take any meds, so whatever benefits you think we see now only masks challenges he'll face as an adult when it is removed from the equation."

Mary Beth nodded begrudgingly and climbed in her car. It felt like one of those "agree to disagree" moments in any marriage, but in the coming weeks, she granted Dr. Delgado permission to begin eliminating Prozac.

※ ※

Medication for mood disorders isn't selective. It doesn't just limit sadness and anger; it dulls happiness as well. As Dr. Delgado decreased the medications, I felt like I was recovering from an awful illness. Before, I had spent a lot of time on the couch feeling out of shape. I didn't have the energy to work out. The real measure of how much the meds were limiting me was when I didn't even feel happy while skiing. Now, I was finally experiencing the world in its true colors again, and once my energy returned, I put it to positive use: I began a rigorous training program to become a badass ski mountaineer.

※ ※

Ryan began exercising regularly and completely altered his diet by eliminating takeout, fried foods, and beef jerky. In response, his LDL cholesterol lowered significantly. More importantly, without Prozac, his mood never soured, so Mary Beth agreed when Dr. Delgado next suggested tapering Ryan's dosage of Seroquel.

Dr. Delgado's involvement in Ryan's mental and physical well-being materialized at a critical juncture as he was approaching puberty. Clearly, the three medicines Ryan took daily were exhibiting negative side effects evident in his cholesterol, weight, and body fat. Moreover, these medicines were muting his emotional response to stimuli during a growth period that would impact the way he viewed relationships for the rest of his life. Ryan was a thirteen-year-old boy like any other. He wanted his friends to like him and was navigating his romantic aspirations. Initially, I believed medication helped him by dampening the volatility in his emotional profile. Yet, Dr. Delgado pushed me to reassess my thinking. What good is medication if it limits your ability to feel? How could Ryan learn to process and successfully manage disappointment, even heartache, if he was never allowed to experience emotional pain?

Dr. Delgado's involvement shook me from indifference about Ryan's treatment by the staff at Parsons. Maybe "indifference" is the wrong word, but I had gotten lazy about the issues Ryan was facing at school because his attendance at Parsons felt routine and allowed me to focus on other aspects of my life—including Abigail's struggles with anxiety as well as my small business. Most likely, however, the heavy doses of antipsychotics were muting Ryan's reactions, so despite the flaws in Parsons' approach, he wasn't complaining much about school. He got in the van every morning without any hesitation, and when he came in the door at 3 p.m., he never said much about his day. Unlike the administration at SVTA, who provided daily written communication, and Bridger, who provided weekly updates by phone, Parsons only contacted us in the event of a problem. Certainly, there were plenty of moments like that, but overall, our communication was limited to quarterly IEP meetings.

At one of Ryan's weekly meetings with Dr. Delgado, he came out of the session where I was waiting in the lobby. Dr. Delgado asked Ryan, "Is it okay for me to speak to your dad for a minute before you go home?" Ryan agreed, and I ducked into Dr. Delgado's office.

"How do you think school is going?" he asked innocently, but I could tell it was one of his loaded questions—and not loaded like a pistol, loaded like a cannon.

I took the bait. "Okay, I guess. Ryan doesn't say much, and the school only calls when there's a problem."

"A problem for who? Ryan or the school?"

"The school, I guess. Whenever he does something bad, the principal calls."

Ready . . . Aim . . .

"What about problems for Ryan? Are you asking him about his day? Is he talking to you about how his day is structured and how the staff reacts when he fails to comply?"

I felt compelled to defend myself. "I always ask him about his day when he gets home, but he usually just shrugs and says 'fine.'"

Dr. Delgado smiled and patted me on the back while he guided me toward the office door. As I exited, he said, "You might want to ask him more questions."

Fire.

Chapter Sixteen

Follow the Leader

"Tell me and I forget. Teach me and I may remember. Involve me and I learn."

—Benjamin Franklin

January 1, 2015. When Ryan was in the second grade, he was asked in a school project to name his hero. Most of the students at SVTA listed David Ortiz or Tom Brady. The rest honored mom or dad. Ryan's project stated, "No one. Why would I waste my time looking up to someone else?"

Despite a natural inclination to forge his own path, the mentor-mentee relationship between Ryan and Ben continued to blossom. Whenever we traveled to Big Sky, Ben greatly enhanced Ryan's technique with small tweaks in his balance and body mechanics while also addressing the preparation and tactical decisions necessary for making safe choices on the mountain. Ryan heeded the advice as a skier, but it was evident that he also was becoming interested in the protocol, planning, and judgment needed to be a professional mountaineer.

Initially, Ryan's admiration for another adult stirred some jealous feelings. I was hardly an extreme athlete or outdoorsman, so it made sense for Ryan to defer to Ben on skiing matters, but quite honestly, I hadn't experienced success coaching or teaching Ryan *anything*. No one had. He was so sensitive to criticism that even the smallest correction caused him to conclude that he failed, effectively ending the activity or exercise. So why wasn't he resisting Ben's coaching? At first, I assumed Ryan simply looked up to Ben because he was so talented and shared his ambition to ski every intriguing slope in existence, but that wasn't particularly unique for a ski guide at a major resort. Unlike other instructors, however, Ben cared deeply about Ryan's progress as a person, so his comments were delivered at an appropriate time and in a thoughtful manner. He never denied Ryan the opportunity to ski something based on his age or skill level, and if Ryan wasn't ready to tackle an extreme slope, Ben focused instead on what additional runs Ryan needed to master before moving to the next level. In contrast to the doctors, teachers, or other adults in his life—including me—Ben wasn't making corrections to restrict or limit him. He was helping Ryan improve so he could ski more advanced terrain, travel to more exciting destinations, and experience even more freedom. In those instances, the fact that Ryan wasn't melting down when Ben suggested alternative plans indicated to me that he trusted Ben's motives and, for the first time, allowed himself to be opened to improving in the one area of his life that mattered most. As a result, Ryan stopped viewing technical corrections as signs of weakness, viewing them instead as opportunities for advancement.

We traveled extensively in the winter of 2015, celebrating the new year at Snowbird and February vacation in Vail. We kept in contact with Ben and visited Big Sky in late January and early April. There, Ben skied with us for half days or full days, depending on his schedule. Ryan's steady partner enabled him to attack extreme runs, while I received technical advice on improving my form. Bit by bit, I improved, while Ryan was skiing the most difficult inbounds terrain in America.

Ben's tactical approach in managing Ryan's drive and ambition was tested by Ryan's obsessive desire to ski Little Couloir. Quite honestly, I wasn't sure he was ready for a run of that magnitude, and I am not sure how Ben would have addressed it. However, Little Couloir was closed during both our trips to Big Sky in 2015, so the issue was tabled for another year.

Although Little Couloir remained Ryan's stated goal, he and Ben found challenging terrain all over Big Sky. I stayed with them whenever I could, and it was interesting to see their relationship progress. Ben had an amazing instinct for timing his feedback on the technical aspects of Ryan's skiing for moments when Ryan was opened to hearing it. It made me wonder about the doctors and educators encountered over the years with perfectly placed diplomas hanging on office walls: Ivy League universities, master's degrees, PhDs, displayed behind prominent desks where they couldn't be missed. Yet, aside from Dr. Delgado, I could not think of a single professional who was as insightful into what made Ryan tick as Ben.

In contrast, Ben's cooperative and tactful approach was inapposite of Ryan's treatment by teachers and staff at school. Even at the eighth-grade level at Parsons, the administration exerted power by clamping down over the dumbest things. For example, Ryan liked collecting rare oddities, especially items with the "most extreme" title, which made sense given his "Extreme Ryan" social media persona. He became interested in peppers and hot sauces, locating and purchasing insanely hot items on the internet. One additive called capsicum was sold in a crystallized form to sprinkle on spicy dishes and was packaged in a vial, resembling something people used in the 1980s to hide cocaine. Ryan brought the vial to school to show his friends, got in trouble, and for the rest of his time at Parsons, was subjected to a *daily search* for contraband when he got off the bus.

In the early summer of 2015, I received a surprising text from Ben wondering if we had ever considered traveling to Chile for a ski trip. The answer was a resounding "no" because I didn't even know people skied in Chile. After a bit of research, I learned that Chile and Argentina are home to several ski resorts that operate in our summer months—winter in the Southern Hemisphere. Ben planned to guide for a company based out of Truckee, California, called the North American Ski Training Center (NASTC), and said NASTC's Chilean trip to someplace called Portillo might be an interesting adventure for us. Mary Beth and I discussed it, ultimately agreeing it was a wonderful opportunity for Ryan to improve his skiing in a unique part of the world. So, in August, Ryan and I boarded a plane bound for Santiago.

I was shocked one day when Dad asked me if I wanted to go on a ski trip to Chile. Of course, I wanted to go! I immediately researched Chilean ski resorts and learned that Portillo was the best resort in the Andes with huge vertical drops. There was even a run called the Super-C Couloir that many expert skiers traveled to Chile just to attempt.

As I feared, Commodore Arturo Merino Benitez International Airport was a study in organized chaos, filled with people demanding to help with our luggage while offering rides to local attractions. Luckily, being part of the NASTC group, I followed the lead of other clients who had visited Portillo before. Things moved very slowly through customs, and the look on Ryan's face during the many long lines said "international incident waiting to happen." As a toddler, he struggled to wait his turn for anything and usually cut any line. In elementary school, IEP reports referenced difficulty raising his hand before blurting out answers, and in middle school, IEP reports included his inability to take turns in conversations with peers. Yet somehow, the impulsive and impatient kid from Sudbury had traveled internationally to South America, enduring thirteen hours on planes and a torturously slow customs and immigration process.

After clearing customs, we gathered outside the airport and boarded two vans bound for Portillo. I was happy to see Ben and for the opportunity to catch up with him during the long ride to the hotel. The other person in our van was a stunning Russian woman named Elaina. I recognized her from our flight, and she looked more nervous than I did as we loaded the vehicle. We soon found out why. Elaina explained that she got carsick easily and asked to sit in the front seat with the window rolled slightly down, but that didn't help. She vomited into a Ziploc bag each time the road narrowed when approaching a cliff. To add insult to injury, Ryan's gag reflex is set to a hair trigger. As a toddler, he vomited at the sight of certain foods like cream cheese and sometimes vomited at the mere *thought* of cream cheese. While he attended SVTA, they forced him into something called "Food Group" as part of the school day. In Food Group, Ryan was purposely exposed to lunch items that disgusted him by watching other children slowly ingest them. He would inevitably wind up restrained, so it didn't do much to squelch his food sensitivity. Each time Elaina vomited, I waited for him to puke in my lap or on Ben.

The flight down was endless, but luckily, I slept most of the way. On the van ride up, we drove on some of the craziest roads I had ever seen. Sometimes, we were right on the edge of cliffs with cars traveling in both directions. A lady in our van even got carsick because it was so treacherous, but we kept going, before eventually seeing snow. Then we hit a section of the road with dozens of switchbacks. We kept climbing until we saw the bright yellow hotel. I was happy to get out of the van to see what 150 inches of new snow looked like, but the parking lot was madness with cars everywhere and people yelling in Spanish.

After checking in, I quickly unpacked and examined the schedule for the evening. The entire NASTC camp then gathered for a brief welcome meeting including introductions and instructor assignments. Ben was one of the instructors, as well as Chris Fellows—who owns and operates NASTC. The third instructor was a woman named Kim Mann. I was assigned to Chris's group and Ryan was assigned to Kim. She seemed sweet with big brown eyes and a warm smile, but I preferred Ben, and worried how Kim could possibly manage him in a group dynamic without knowing anything about him.

The next morning, during our first day of camp, I spent more time eyeballing Ryan's group than paying attention to Chris, fearing he would struggle in an environment designed to be critical of our skiing. Although Chris is a renowned instructor and has authored two books on skiing, he is also a father to three and appreciated I had more to worry about during camp than my own skiing.

I was assigned to a different group than Dad, which surprised me. My instructor, Kim, was nice, but was often critical of my form and even made me switch my freestyle skis for racing skis to help me learn the right way to turn. It was hard to be corrected in front of the group, all of whom were adults, but Kim's tips really helped. Even to this day, I still think about her instruction.

⚊⚊

As camp progressed, Ryan's willingness to alter his skiing would have surprised educators from his past and present. Like Ben, Kim had earned his trust. She pushed him to make technical corrections, and even when he was tired and frustrated, Ryan remained composed, improving each day. As for me, Chris had my trust from the start, but it didn't make progressing any easier. My self-taught skiing style needed to be completely broken down and built back up from scratch, so my lessons included more drills with one ski than two.

NASTC's beneficial instruction aside, the biggest highlight of the Portillo trip was heli-skiing on our day off from camp. I booked a spot for Ben—to thank him for all he had done for Ryan—and the three of us couldn't have scripted a better day. We flew just outside the resort in blue skies to a mountain valley filled with gorgeous terrain. All things considered, I skied well, never falling, while generating decent speed through the soft powder. Ryan was even better, dynamically attacking the long runs with precision while he floated effortlessly in the deep snow.

⚊⚊

Our group for heli-skiing included Dad, Ben, and another NASTC camper named Tristan. We flew out of the resort in the shadow of Aconcagua to a huge valley filled with endless possibilities. Our guide was from Chamonix, and he explained each run before we skied. With the potential for an avalanche, it was important that we stayed within the boundaries that he set, but the runs themselves were endless and in deep powder. Honestly, I felt different skiing away from the resort. In all that terrain, there were only two groups skiing, and even with the noise from the helicopter, it still felt peaceful. It was the first time that I thought about skiing as a way to explore new terrain—rather than just riding up and down ski lifts to ski runs that thousands of people had skied before me.

For safety's sake during heli-skiing, skiers must wait a minute or two between turns to prevent groups from being clustered in the event of an avalanche. On our last run, after our guide skied off, followed by Ryan and another skier named Tristan, Ben and I were left standing on the mountain waiting our turns when he twisted his head to look at me.

"Rob, I want to thank you so much for today. This was one of the best days of my life."

At that moment, I was so focused on surviving the next run that his comment caught me by surprise. I garbled a response, but afterward regretted failing to recognize the incredible positive force he was in Ryan's life.

On the helicopter flight back to the hotel, as I studied Aconcagua, I was struck by Ben's comment. His simple "thank you" helped me recognize how grateful he was to ski with us and helped me realize that I needed to be thankful, too. Only a few years prior, we were advised to lock Ryan away in a residential treatment facility, and it was hard to imagine that path leading to a helicopter in the Andes. We still faced a long journey ahead of us, but that day, Ben made me reflect on how far we had come.

CHAPTER SEVENTEEN

Doctor Discordance

"The doctor should be opaque to his patients and, like a mirror, should show them nothing but what is shown to him."

—SIGMUND FREUD

August 23, 2015. After returning from the trip of a lifetime, there was no afterglow to Chile. As we waited for our luggage to appear on the carousel at Logan Airport, Ryan began ruminating over a much-dreaded start to high school at Parsons. I wasn't surprised to see him move on so quickly because he rarely reflected on past experiences or looked ahead to upcoming events to elevate his spirits during difficult times. Honestly, it was one of the tougher aspects of parenting him as each hour of his life was weighed and measured in isolation.

Mary Beth and I met with Dr. Delgado to discuss the start of the school year, and he expressed his usual reservations about the strict behavioral component of Parsons, but also took umbrage with the school's lack of transparency over recent changes in Massachusetts law on restraining students with disabilities. Dr. Delgado cited reports of students dying during restraints,[1] and explained that the specter of litigation brought

---

1. An analysis by ProPublica and NPR of data for the 2011–2012 school year of school discipline practices from the U.S. Department of Education's Civil Rights Data collection showed the following:
• Restraint and seclusion were used at least 267,000 times nationwide. That included 163,000 instances in which students were restrained.
• In 75 percent of cases, methods of restraint and seclusion were used on children with disabilities.

by parents of children killed or injured during restraints had forced the Massachusetts Department of Elementary and Secondary Education to issue new guidelines. He said once the new laws were implemented, teachers could only restrain when Ryan presented a threat to himself or to other students or staff. Since the law did not become effective until January 1, 2016, he warned us that Parsons still had a few months to adjust their policies. Ultimately, though, he hoped Ryan would soon notice differences in how, when, and where he was restrained.

Unfortunately, Dr. Delgado was overly optimistic. After our meeting, when Mary Beth and I got home and read the proposed guidelines, we worried Parsons still had plenty of wiggle room to continue restraining Ryan. Dr. Delgado was correct: the staff was no longer permitted to restrain him for causing a disruption, destroying school property, or making threats (without the ability to act on the threat immediately). However, they could restrain him when he acted in a way that was perceived as an imminent threat.

Mary Beth and I were concerned that the staff's history of barraging Ryan with discipline and limitations for small matters would cause him to react to the perceived threat of restraint—regardless of the new rules they'd put in place. And any display of anger by him as a result would justify a restraint, so long as their prior attempt to calm him was made without using physical force. In other words, what came first: Ryan's PTSD reaction to the threat of a restraint or the imminent threat to staff that came with his PTSD reaction? Chicken or egg?

Under the proposed guidelines, even prone restraints (i.e., facedown on the ground) were still allowed when (1) the student had a history of harming staff; (2) all other methods of restraint were exhausted; (3) there were no medical contraindications for the student (documented by a physician); (4) there was a psychological or behavioral justification for the use of restraint and there were no psychological or behavioral contraindications (documented by a licensed mental health professional); (5) the program in question had documented consent from the state in writing;

• A 2009 report by the U.S. Government Accountability Office, a nonpartisan congressional investigative agency, counted hundreds of cases of abuse, including at least twenty deaths.

and (6) the restraint was witnessed by at least one nonparticipating staff member.

In my mind, I pictured a laminated flowchart on classroom walls at Parsons.

Is Ryan upset? Yes.

Is he an imminent threat to himself or others? Yes.

Did you try to calm him using words? Yes—proceed directly to restraint by holding from behind.

Is that method of restraint working? No.

Does Ryan have a history of attempting to harm staff? Yes. (He didn't, but that was a question of perception.)

Is he tough enough to withstand a prone restraint? Yes.

Is there a witness? Yes—proceed to pinning him facedown on the ground.

The new laws were constructed intentionally to create semantical arguments that were stacked against students like Ryan. The staff at Parsons faced more paperwork after a restraint but could easily justify most incidents ending in restraint, even a prone restraint. And, on those rare occasions when the staff was unable to justify a restraint, they were still allowed to isolate Ryan. Although the new directives "banned" seclusion as a means of punishment, it allowed isolation when it was classified as a "timeout." What made a period of isolation into a timeout? Generally, if a staff person was able to see Ryan (i.e., right outside a locked door watching through glass/peephole/video), the timeout was legal if it was used to calm Ryan rather than punish him. Again, Parsons could drive a tractor through that loophole.

～～

At the start of the year, I began getting restrained by a staff member who stood behind me. I wasn't sure if this was just how they did things at the high school level, but that method was difficult for staff because I was usually able to wiggle free. So that usually led to a regular restraint on the ground or else I was dragged to the timeout room where they would lock me in until I was calm. They could tell how I was behaving in the room because it was monitored by a camera. The problem for me was once in the timeout room, I felt panicked and couldn't calm down even if I wanted to. So, a lot of times, I ended up stuck there, sitting on a cement floor for hours. As a result, I missed a lot of class time, which seemed to defeat the purpose of attending school at all.

When Ryan began reporting to Dr. Delgado that he was spending long periods in the timeout room, his dubious eye dissected Ryan's experience in the same critical manner he used with Ryan's medication. He informed Parsons in writing that the stress Ryan experienced when locked in a cell was *as suffocating* as someone sitting on top of him. As usual, the administration ignored his admonishment, but Ryan sensed that he finally had an ally willing to fight for him. I couldn't have agreed more.

In my freshman year of high school at Parsons, I realized how horrible the program was for me and that I needed to leave as soon as possible. My typical day began with a partial strip search and usually ended in a locked room. My parents always assumed the worst part about Parsons was having two giant men drag me to the seclusion room. However, even with all the scratches and bruises, that wasn't the part that bothered me most. It might sound crazy, but the main reason I wanted out of Parsons was the academic aspect of the program.

When I moved to the high school building, I discovered what a disadvantage I was at by attending Parsons because my sister, who was in seventh grade, was getting the same assignments as me. Some nights, not only did she get the exact same worksheets as me, but she got them for homework, while we were doing them as class assignments with help from the teacher. When I realized my assigned work was two grades below my level, I was appalled. Parsons wasn't preparing me for the world at all. Teachers weren't helping my classmates grow or learn properly. They were treating us like throwaway children because they assumed we couldn't be successful, so they didn't bother to push us.

After I realized that my sister was operating at the same grade level as my supposed high school class, I brought in copies of her homework to show my friends. To my surprise, no one cared. It was like it didn't matter at all. I quickly concluded if I was to get anywhere in this world, I needed to be around people who wanted more out of life. I wish I could have done more to convince kids at Parsons to demand more from the school, but you can't make someone change their life if they don't believe they need to.

—⁓—

At its core, Parsons was no different from SVTA. Although composed entirely of students on individual education plans, it was a one-size-fits-all model that never allowed creativity or flexibility when challenged. When we raised the concerns of Dr. Delgado, we were invited to meet with the principal, Karen, a short woman with narrow eyes, maroon hair, orange skin, and a permanent frown.

At the meeting, Karen deadpanned her summation of Ryan's struggles at Parsons. "Ryan's biggest issue is that he only complies with rules that he likes. As soon as he disagrees with something that happens in class, we run into problems." She spoke slowly as if each word pained her. Not because she felt bad about what she was saying but that the act of speaking itself caused her distress, like she had a migraine or the worst hangover in America.

Mary Beth countered first. "We aren't here to argue about that. The reason we're here is that we are more concerned about what happens when he doesn't comply."

Karen was ready for that one. "Well, under the law, we first try to calm him using words or allowing him to take a short walk in the hall. But that generally results in a confrontation where we are forced to place hands on him because the staff feels threatened. As you probably know from talking to Ryan, we are trying to use the timeout room more to keep from restraining him."

Now it was my turn. "But, Karen, the result is the same. Didn't you read the letter Dr. Delgado sent? That locked timeout room is causing him just as much trauma as a restraint."

"The room isn't locked."

"So, Ryan can leave any time he wants?"

"Well, no. A staff member is stationed outside to monitor him."

"To keep him from leaving?"

"Well, sure, and to make sure that he is not harming himself."

"Sounds a lot like a locked room."

Karen's frown strained mightily into the tiniest hint of a smile. "Well, we are happy to try other strategies. Maybe Dr. Delgado has some suggestions?"

Karen was smarter than I thought. She knew Dr. Delgado lacked strategies for dealing with Ryan when he snapped. There wasn't a person on the planet with strategies for that, including me. What I wanted her to focus on, however, were the events leading up to his anger. Every incident ending in restraint or isolation could have easily been avoided with the slightest bit of flexibility. But, like SVTA, Parsons was so hell-bent on defending their model that they missed it. By simply affording Ryan the freedom to make mistakes and process them, he would have felt empowered instead of victimized. Instead, Karen appeased us by offering to modify the school's approach, but nothing ever changed.

Ryan continued to attend Parsons without complaint, but I never once heard him talk about something enjoyable that happened during school. His mindset was to survive each day and somehow make it through high school. But, as the year wore on, Mary Beth and I sensed that he was very unhappy and was forcing himself to endure. We pushed Sally, the special education director for Sudbury, for possible alternatives to Parsons, but none of her suggestions were a fit for Ryan.

⁓

After Christmas break, we looked for new schools because I really wanted out of Parsons. The first place I interviewed was the Lexington Collaborative. My mom warned me, "The kids at this school are very different, but we have to look at this program before we look at others, so don't feel like you did anything wrong." That didn't make me feel very optimistic.

When I sat down in class, a kid with black hair hastily approached me. He began talking faster than a machine gun, saying, "Hi, this school is really great. This is our teacher. She's really nice, and at the end of the year we get to fly to Disney World. It's so great." While I observed the class, it became clear the other students were delayed. I felt bad for the students as they struggled to understand basic concepts, but how I was supposed to learn anything here?

That afternoon, I visited another classroom. This one seemed to be a much better fit since the kids were brighter, even if some of them slept through most of the class. After talking to the teacher, he said that I probably wouldn't be in this second class because all his students were in trouble with their district, and some were expelled. He said I wasn't qualified and would likely wind up with the cognitively delayed group. I wanted to scream at him, "So, you think I'm a better fit with students struggling to read and write? Do I even get a say in my education?" Instead, I bit my tongue and went home feeling hopeless.

While we searched for other options enabling me to leave Parsons, there was one thing that my parents didn't know: I was considering other plans for my future. From my first meeting with Dr. Delgado, he sought my opinion about my school and medication and didn't make assumptions about me. When he first saw the medications I was taking, he asked me if I thought I was bipolar. I said, "I know what bipolar is, but I don't really know what it feels like to be bipolar." When he explained it, I said, "That doesn't sound at all like me."

At each appointment, there was no change to my mood or behavior from reducing my medication, so we kept lowering. As the meds decreased and nothing bad happened, I realized I might not be "sick" at all. After that, I concluded that I wasn't mentally ill, and it changed the way I looked at everything. I didn't belong at Parsons or any therapeutic school for that matter. With this in mind, I decided to take control of my own life. If we couldn't find a new school by my fifteenth birthday, I was dropping out of high school. The only person I ever told about my plan was Dr. Delgado, who said if I was serious, we could look into the process of getting a GED. I thought for sure he would tell my parents, but he never did.

If Ben was the first adult that ever believed in me, Dr. Delgado was the first adult that I trusted away from skiing.

CHAPTER EIGHTEEN

F-Bombs

"It is easier to build strong children than to repair broken men."
—FREDERICK DOUGLASS

March 23, 2016. After several difficult months, we requested a meeting with Sally, the special education director for Sudbury, in her office at Lincoln-Sudbury Regional High School (LS). At the meeting, we argued that Ryan was decompensating, and all the progress made during his stint at Bridger regulating his fight or flight response and trusting adults was in jeopardy at Parsons.

Mary Beth opened the discussion in her usual measured tone. She paused before speaking to pull a yellow legal pad from a giant expanding pocket folder packed with neatly tabbed manila file folders. "Sally, Ryan seems to be running into more trouble lately at school. He's spending a lot of time in seclusion, and we're worried that we are seeing some of the same defensiveness and even combativeness that he displayed at SVTA."

Mary Beth finished and adjusted the yellow legal pad on her lap, cocking her pen to await Sally's response. While she looked toward Sally, she struggled to push the pocket folder away from her feet. By this point, each manila file was so stuffed with doctor's letters and IEP reports that the expansiveness of the accordion folder had reached its limit.

Sally then cleared her throat and sat up straight. School administrators always did that around Mary Beth. Her serious nature intimidated school officials. They usually comported themselves as if they were testifying at a deposition. Not because Mary Beth was bitchy, but because her body language said *I am taking this seriously, so you better as well.*

Despite her formal tone, Sally countered with her usual bullshit. "Ryan is a complicated case due to the lack of programming for someone with his profile. We need to be very careful in how we manage his care. The last thing that I want is for him to have a setback. I just want—"

I cut her off midsentence, interjecting, "At this point, why can't he just come back to school here at LS?"

Sally appeared stunned by my question, and the utter disbelief in her eyes while formulating her answer told me she had never once contemplated Ryan's return to public school. Quickly deflecting, she muttered something about needing to make another appointment with her boss, Ada, who handled the special education program at the high school. "Ada makes the call about students returning to the district, so I can schedule a meeting with her in a few weeks," she summarized.

After years of frustration, I finally snapped, "Who the fuck is this Ada person and why are we just hearing about her now? This fucking process feels like something out of *Alice in Wonderland*. Every time we get over one hurdle, you invent another!"

Sally reacted by stiffening in her chair, and as she clutched both armrests, tears welled in her brown eyes. Visibly shaken, she clenched her teeth. "In all my years here, no one has ever cursed at me."

I took a deep breath to calm down. "Sally, my son is forced to go to school forty-five minutes from my house where the staff does physical and psychological damage to him. So, forgive me for losing my friggin' temper, but I'm sick and tired of waiting for you to help him."

In a matter of minutes, we found ourselves in Ada's office, who was clearly warned that I was losing my shit. Without even the slightest debate, she suggested we "look at the Stonebrook Academy," a "non-traditional" collaborative program among the towns of Sudbury, Concord, and Acton, "for students needing a less intense high school program." She emphasized that Stonebrook was not a "therapeutic program" and lacked most of the services and interventions of Ryan's previous school programs. She raised one eyebrow while awaiting our response and clearly expected that the moment we heard "not a therapeutic program," we would be dissuaded. Little did she realize that eliminating therapeutic was Stonebrook's main selling point.

After the meeting with Ada, Mary Beth and I fought the entire ride home. She typically avoided conflict with school administrators and liked Sally on a personal level, so she worried making an enemy of her made it harder to navigate the special education system. As I drove, she balled both hands into fists and pressed them against her knees.

"Being an asshole isn't going to help. Unless you are ready to home-school him, we have zero leverage here."

Rather than fighting back, I appeared contrite. "Listen, I'm sorry if I lost my shit in there, but she just pissed me off with that same crap about not having any programming. That fucking school revamped the special education program last year to allow more kids on the spectrum. Notice that she has never once mentioned that as an option?"

Mary Beth tilted her head toward me with the same shocked expression as Sally. She pointed back in the direction of LS. "You really think Ryan can go to school there? In that giant building with two thousand kids?"

"Yeah, I do."

She shook her head. "He can't make it through most days at Parsons, and they have a staff member dedicated to him. Someone that literally follows him from class to class to make sure he doesn't get into trouble."

We had been down this road many times. "Maybe that staff member does more harm than good. Maybe Ryan would do better in a place that couldn't tackle him or lock him in a room."

Mary Beth was getting frustrated. She realized, however, that we needed to make peace before we walked in the house to Ryan, so she made a stab toward conciliation. "Look, I'm not happy about Parsons either, but I won't set him up to fail. Let's check out this Stonebrook place and see if it might be a fit."

My tone softened in response. "Okay. I will also shoot Sally an email to apologize for being a jerk."

"Good," she said. "Because she hates your guts."

In reality, I had no plans to apologize to Sally and simply wanted to appease Mary Beth to end the battle before we got home. Truthfully,

I hadn't acted irrationally at all. My temper tantrum was planned for a while, and I had been waiting for the right time to explode. A few weeks before, during the long flight home from Chile, I decided that Sally and the rest of the special education system needed to see a touch of crazy from me because our diplomatic approach using Mary Beth's color-coded files and tabbed expert reports wasn't getting us anywhere. We were being played, and I was furious with myself for not seeing it years earlier. The more we acquiesced, the more the system patted us on the head and told us everything would get better. Yet, fueled by Dr. Delgado's observations, I could finally prove that Ryan was getting worse at Parsons. So, when we walked into the meeting with Sally, I decided that it was time to change our approach and demonstrate my willingness to fight. Fortunately, summoning a dose of rage for her to ingest did not require any stretch of my acting abilities because it accurately represented how I felt about Ryan's decade-long treatment by the system.

⌐~~⌐

A few weeks before my birthday deadline to quit Parsons, my parents came home from a meeting with the school district. As they walked into the house, they seemed mad at each other. Apparently, at the meeting, Dad went crazy, and they were almost thrown out of the building. One good thing did come out of this meeting, however, as we were given one more option: Stonebrook Academy. Although I'd never heard of Stonebrook, it sounded better than the other places I visited. Stonebrook wasn't a therapeutic school, so the staff couldn't restrain me, and it wasn't a school for kids with cognitive disabilities or kids that were in trouble with the law. Even if every other thing about Stonebrook ended up terrible, it still sounded better than Parsons by a long shot.

The day before my visit to Stonebrook, I met with Karen, the principal at Parsons. My only experiences with her were bad. She would get called in when I was restrained or later when I was dragged to the seclusion room. She was nasty in those situations but acted super nice when my parents were around. Karen always seemed to have a special hatred for me because I called her on her bullshit. She told me there was no way I could leave Parsons because I was "only capable of behaving during preferred activities." I disagreed, telling her that, for years, I shut my mouth whenever adults told me I'd never be a con-

tributing member of society. I had spent years in schools that treated me like I was dangerous or a criminal. I told her, "If you think living like that is what I prefer, maybe you're the crazy one."

Later that same day, my teachers met with me to discuss my refusal to do a school assignment. I knew that I was seeing Stonebrook the next day and might leave Parsons, so why bother with the assignment? The conversation got heated, and I was told to leave the room. In an effort to avoid the seclusion room, I ran out the front door and headed toward the middle of campus before climbing into a tree. Karen appeared and said the school planned to start videoing my issues for the state. I responded, "You won't need to bother with that because I'll be on my best behavior tomorrow when I visit Stonebrook, and after today, I'm never coming back here."

That was my last day at Parsons.

— • —

After the dustup with Sally, a few days later, we visited Stonebrook, and there wasn't much to see. The entire school consisted of a handful of rooms inside a daycare center in the neighboring town of Acton. Approximately twenty-five students between ninth and twelfth grade attended Stonebrook for a variety of reasons. On our tour, most students looked like those encountered in other therapeutic programs, and we recognized two students from Ryan's previous schools.

The rest of the tour went well. Stonebrook was hardly impressive, but at least it was not defined by the rules and procedures of Ryan's prior therapeutic programs. Whether the ABA model was a symptom or a cure, most of the students at therapeutic programs would wind up in jail or in adult residential facilities. And by utilizing behavior modification systems exploiting physical punishment and isolation, difficult students like Ryan were conditioned to remain compliant within an authoritarian power structure to prepare for institutionalization in some capacity. If nothing else, Stonebrook was a step toward freedom, even if it was a small step.

A few days later, we heard that Ryan was accepted, and he started at Stonebrook after April break. In our introductory meeting, Lisa, the director at Stonebrook, did not sound overly optimistic about Ryan's probability of success.

"So, Ryan is on a forty-five-day evaluation here. Just so we are clear, we are not a therapeutic program and cannot manage his behaviors like his previous schools."

Mary Beth stopped taking notes and looked at me out of the corner of her eye. She raised her left eyebrow and gave me the "please don't" look that I received many times in our marriage. But there was no stopping me. Lisa opened this door. Wide enough for me to drive a truck through.

"Lisa, we're not looking for you to manage Ryan's behavior. We want you to educate him."

She cleared her throat. She started her retort with "Well, of course, but I just mean—" She paused to regroup. "We're not here to restrain kids and put them in timeout rooms."

My god, she was making this easy. "Well, that is so great to hear, Lisa, because Ryan is not here to be restrained or to be put into timeout rooms. This sounds perfect."

Mary Beth snorted and shook her head. She fought back a smile and gave me another look that I had seen a million times. One that read, *I can't believe I married this crazy son of a bitch.*

Lisa's body language at the meeting told me that none of the staff expected Ryan to last more than a few days. It was the ultimate irony. Because the staff was precluded from isolating or restraining him, Stonebrook's administration was likely warned by the special education department that this experiment could not possibly succeed.

"One last thing, Lisa," I said as Mary Beth, and I got up to leave. "You're about to make me look like a genius."

She stood up from her chair to walk us out. "How's that?"

"Because Ryan is going to be a star here."

Lisa smiled back at me nervously, like she was instructed to humor me along with humoring this attempt at schooling Ryan.

CHAPTER NINETEEN

Into the Backcountry

"It is not what you look at that matters, it's what you see."
—HENRY DAVID THOREAU

JANUARY 21, 2016. Throughout Ryan's life, I have owned and operated a job placement agency with a clientele of highly pedigreed lawyers and major law firms. For obvious reasons, it is beneficial to pretend that my business is in a downtown office building instead of squirreled away in a home office. Over the years, especially when he was younger, my professional charade was often jeopardized by Ryan barging into my office while I was on the phone to play skiing videos from all over the world.

Just prior to our annual Big Sky trip, he showed me a video on his phone of a skier slashing through deep snow in a place called Lone Lake. He explained how easily the skier traversed off the ridgeline to an area outside of the Big Sky resort boundary. In response, I asked the obvious question: "How did he get back?"

"He hiked back up to the ridgeline from the lake. It takes about thirty minutes," he casually remarked.

"Yeah," I said, "Thirty minutes up the side of a mountain, carrying skis. I'm not sure that one is for me."

As Ryan expanded his mind with research on potential backcountry destinations, his physical appearance was reshaped by a devoted exercise regime. More importantly, by finally eliminating all medication, puberty kicked into gear, and he grew taller, leaner, and more muscular. Pictures of him in 2016 look like the Ryan we see today without an extra twenty pounds of bloat. In looking back, I should have challenged the ease in which medication was prescribed to him, but my opposition quickly faded once Dr. Schneider came on board and diagnosed him with a disability. Later, when Dr. Norman convinced us Ryan was a threat to himself and others, relying on medication was a given. Dr. Delgado, however, was willing to peel back the drugs to see what kind of boy emerged, and in my heart, I already knew the answer.

Our skiing that year included trips to Snowbird, Big Sky, Park City, and Chile in August, intertwined with a solid season of East Coast skiing. On skis, Ryan looked more like a man than a boy, strong on his feet and powerful in his turns. He skied the toughest runs available and explored features in the terrain parks while also seeking to launch from small cliffs. He skied aggressively but always smartly—never taking unnecessary risks. One of the reasons Dr. Norman advocated medicating Ryan so heavily was her belief that his "aggressive" skiing masked a desire to harm or even kill himself. On the contrary, he was searching for a way to live.

It was Ben who led Ryan on his first real hike to a skiing expedition outside the boundaries of a ski resort. The excursion took them two hours, and I met them afterward for lunch along with Ben's girlfriend, Hannah. Hannah had spent the morning working on my skiing within the resort while Ben and Ryan hiked and skied in the backcountry. At lunch, Ryan talked about how beautiful it was behind the resort, and Ben seemed thrilled with Ryan's progress as a skier and adventurer, emphasizing his improved physique and cardiovascular conditioning.

———

The next level of skiing for me was beyond the boundaries of resorts, where only those willing to hike can access. In January of 2016, I traveled to see Ben for another Big Sky adventure, but this time, Ben used his day off to ski with me so we could ski outside of the resort to Lone Lake. I was really excited about my first-ever backcountry experience at Big Sky. We met in the morning to make sure that I had enough water and to conduct a beacon check. We then hiked across the ridgeline and skied down into the Lone Lake area. It was so quiet and peaceful back there. Ben and I were the only skiers among the thousands of acres—we even got to ski on untracked snow. That made it so worth it, even if we had to hike out of Lone Lake to get back to the resort boundary.

In the afternoon, we hiked Trident Chute on the north side of the mountain. That chute is only accessed by hiking from the bottom up. Although it took some effort, the snow was deep and untouched, and we both crushed it. Afterward, Ben said he was impressed with my new level of fitness and that we wouldn't have been able to do this type of hiking the year before.

Backcountry skiing requires research and study because skiers must first assess the weather and propensity of the zone for an avalanche. Ryan relied on the internet to view hundreds of videos, and he learned that even the most sanguine eastern mountains offered various ways to ski off-piste—off the defined trails. On our usual Saturday trips to Loon in New Hampshire, I quickly found myself skiing alone while he was off exploring the woods. He made friends through his YouTube channel and discovered an entire community of backcountry skiers that regularly tackled places like Tuckerman Ravine in New Hampshire.

In February of 2016, our entire family traveled to Park City, Utah. Ryan was excited because Park City and the Canyons recently merged and were now linked by a tram—making it the largest ski resort in the country. The combined resorts offer skiers 350 possible runs including dozens of runs rated as double black, but Extreme Ryan was after a run named East Face. Although East Face was technically within the resort boundary, it required hiking across the ridgeline and opened only when the ski patrol determined it was safe. Like most avalanche-prone slopes—depending on the weather, steepness, and aspects such as directionality toward the sun—East Face only opened a few days per year. In that respect, it was similar to Little Couloir at Big Sky, and Ryan never had any luck timing our trips to Montana when that legendary run was open.

On our first day of skiing, Ryan noticed patrol was working on the ridge to East Face, so we hovered for an hour but gave up when the rope for the hike remained closed. An hour or so later, Ryan saw skiers on the traverse, and we raced down and back up again on several lifts, returning to the entrance. Mercifully, it was open when we got there, and he started his hike. I skied down to take some pictures when he entered the run, but after several minutes, I never saw Ryan, or anyone enter it. So, I gave up and skied to the base area.

Eventually, Ryan appeared and was furious. He explained that he completed the entire hike and when he reached the point to start skiing, a ski patroller closed East Face for the day due to high winds. I tried to reason with him.

"We're in the biggest ski resort in the country with 349 other trails to pick from, so we shouldn't be upset about the *one* trail that is closed, right?" However, this was not the answer that Ryan wanted to hear, and he quickly skied off, avoiding me for the rest of the afternoon.

East Face eventually opened two days later, but I realized something during the prior incident. When the ski patroller closed the trail, Ryan was upset, but he gathered himself to ski for the rest of the day. Even after my botched attempt at consoling him, he gritted his teeth and moved on with his life. If this type of incident occurred at school, the administration at SVTA, Bridger, or Parsons would have focused solely on his anger during the conversation and would have restrained him or dragged him into seclusion instead of allowing him time to process his disappointment.

After April break, I began school at Stonebrook. When I got in the van for the first time, we drove to the other side of town, picking up a girl wearing all black with heavy makeup. She didn't bother to say hi. This was an introduction to what Stonebrook would be like. Everyone there looked as though they were in their own private hell. The school had about twenty students in total, all of whom seemed to be misfits of sorts. I tried to stay open-minded. After all, if I could manage this, I had hope of returning to regular public school. At the same time, I didn't see how this was even a school. It looked like a program that should be within a larger school. It was literally upstairs from a daycare center and all the classrooms were within a foot of each other.

Among the small group of students was someone I'd known from Bridger named Justine. It was normal to see people from previous schools in new ones. A lot of times, kids like Justine never found the right fit, switching between five or six schools before graduating. Another student I recognized from Parsons was a boy named Jack. He claimed, as a student at Parsons, his shoulder was dislocated during a restraint. While I had no way to confirm this, it wasn't a stretch in my eyes.

The first thing I remember about Stonebrook was the adjustment to the academic requirements. I was up until midnight for the first three weeks trying to complete my homework, and the sudden adjustment back to my grade level required help from Dad, the internet, and any other resource available to learn the material. Even then, it took hours. However, once I learned the first unit, classes got easier since I had a knowledge base to build on.

After I adjusted to the academic requirements, school went pretty well. I was more relaxed without worrying about being restrained or thrown into seclusion. Stonebrook was still very strict, and I did have a few angry outbursts over some of the rules that seemed dumb, but they also gave us much more freedom than the therapeutic programs. For example, on Fridays, we were allowed to leave school to walk to Dunkin' Donuts. I do not like coffee and wasn't eating unhealthy food anymore, so I just went for the walk and to be with my classmates because my other schools wouldn't even let me go to the bathroom without a teacher's aide, let alone leave school grounds.

Toward the end of the year, my family began making the push for public school, but we were met with a lot of resistance from Lisa, an administrator at Stonebrook whom I greatly despised. She cited multiple incidents where I cracked under the academic pressure, but that pressure wouldn't have existed if my every move wasn't scrutinized to determine whether I could go back to regular school.

In June, we met with Stonebrook's director, Lisa, and Ada, the special education coordinator for Sudbury to discuss Ryan's placement for the following school year.

Lisa began the meeting by admitting that Ryan had performed better than anyone expected. "Ryan is off to a solid start here. We knew that he would be able to handle the academic piece, but we are all surprised by how few problems he's run into with his peers."

Mary Beth jumped in before I could ask the obvious question about Ryan's return to regular public school at LS. "That's good to hear. We all know how hard Ryan is working and that includes how hard he works on relationships and friendships."

Lisa and Ada nodded and smiled in unison, but I was not going to let them off the hook yet. "So, can he go back to regular high school next year?"

Lisa and Ada looked at each other as if begging the other to speak first. Finally, Ada summoned the courage to dive in and said, "Well, we think he is a lot closer than we thought when we first suggested an evaluation at Stonebrook, but we just think he would benefit from more time here."

"Benefit how?" My tone was sharper. Ada looked at Lisa as if to say, *Okay, your turn.*

Lisa sat up in her chair and folded her hands on the circular table. "We just think he needs more time before we try a big place like LS. We are recommending that he remain at Stonebrook for the start of sophomore year with a scheduled revaluation before Christmas break."

I was bitterly disappointed when we left the meeting and dreaded seeing Ryan when we got home to tell him that he was facing another year at Stonebrook. When I walked in the house, he looked up with so much hope in his eyes. It broke my heart, but I knew that I needed to spin this positively. So, I swallowed hard and searched my brain for something uplifting.

"Listen, buddy, they want you to start the year at Stonebrook with a reevaluation after Thanksgiving."

His head dropped into his hands. "I knew they would say no. I'm never going back to regular school. They won't even give me a chance."

"I know it sucks, buddy. Mom and I disagree with them, too, but we have to just shut up and take this for a little while longer."

"That's what you always say, and nothing ever changes."

"Come on, Ry, that isn't fair. You've come further than any of these administrators in Sudbury ever thought you could. Even if today didn't go the way that we wanted, you should try to do something that I learned from playing baseball."

He lifted his head and looked in my eyes. "What the hell does baseball have to do with this?"

"Because in baseball you fail all the time. You make outs seven out of ten times you bat. But if you dwell on those failures, you'll never get a hit the next time up. So, right before every at bat, I tried to visualize a hit. I wanted to imagine success and imprint that image in my brain before I got in the batter's box."

"Did it work?

I laughed. "Not always. But do this for me anyway. Picture your first IEP meeting after you are back and thriving at LS and how, at that meeting, we will make every single fucking administrator apologize to your face for doubting you."

He smiled through the sadness in his eyes and said, "I hope we get that chance."

In August of 2016, we took our second trip to Portillo with the NASTC camp. Ben was on the trip and Ryan was assigned to his group. I was back with Chris Fellows, but moved into the middle group, with several weaker skiers comprising the third group. Also, hoping to balance Ryan's desire to ski off-piste (out of the resort) in Chile with our NASTC camp program that focused on making perfect turns on groomed runs, I reached out to Chris Davenport, one of the world's most accomplished backcountry skiers. Chris had hiked and skied all over the world and was in Portillo running a camp for young Olympic hopefuls, offering race training during the morning and off-piste exploration after lunch. My plan was to have Ryan stay with the NASTC crew in the morning and join the Davenport campers after lunch.

My split-camp brainstorm never really worked out. Ryan skied with the race kids in the afternoons, but the other boys in camp knew each other so well that it was difficult for Ryan to assimilate. While it was a positive experience for Ryan to ski with boys his own age and with a legend like Chris Davenport, I suspected the challenges of breaking into a previously defined social group was a preview of what Ryan faced should he ever be allowed to attend LS.

In the summer, I began hiking to get my nature fix. I even joined the Lincoln Sudbury High School Outdoor Club, which accepted me as a member because I lived in the district. This made my summer more fun, though it came with challenges. I found it hard to make friends because of my school situation. The first question was always, "What school do you go to?" How was I supposed to tell them I attended a school for kids with disabilities? If they gave me a chance, they wouldn't see me as dumb or crazy, but I couldn't figure out how to get past the first conversation and found it easier to just stay quiet.

CHAPTER TWENTY

Circling the Bases

*"Ryan would benefit from explicit instruction in initiating and sus-
taining conversations with peers."*
—IEP Progress Report, Stonebrook School, November
2016

Sophomore year at Stonebrook produced a milestone of sorts. Ryan
landed his first serious girlfriend, but the relationship progressed in
severity faster than anyone expected.

———

*Stonebrook gained students one by one throughout the year as kids left their
local high schools. Luckily for me, the newer students seemed to be friendlier
than the small group that started the year in September. Among the new students was Adriana, and my first interaction with her was interesting. I got up
from the lunch table to go to the bathroom and accidentally backed my chair
into another girl. For some reason, my lack of spatial awareness translated into
Adriana calling me sexist. It was a big jump, since it could have been someone
of any gender behind me. After clarifying it was accidental, we started talking
like civilized human beings. The next day Justine, my old friend from Bridger,
approached me, and she was practically dragging Adriana by the arm.*

*"Adriana has something to say to you," Justine stated. Adriana looked
away and was blushing. After Justine kept probing her, Adriana confessed
to liking me and asked for my phone number. I said, "No thanks," because I*

wasn't interested in dating anyone at Stonebrook. That might sound harsh, but in a matter of months, I planned to be in regular school at LS, and any anchor would make it harder to leave. Both Justine and Adriana walked away disappointed.

Over time, Adriana wore me down, and I ended up giving her my number. We went on a handful of pleasant dates and did basic high school relationship stuff like lots of texting. In February, however, things took a turn when she threatened to kill herself with pain medication over text. She said she had tried before and wasn't failing this time. I ended up calling her grandmother, who had custody of her at the time, and Adriana was hospitalized for a week or so. When she came back to school, she acted super paranoid.

In a last-ditch effort to spite me, she hatched a plan to fake her own death by having Justine text me to tell me she committed suicide because of me, only to see my reaction when she showed up at school. Justine didn't end up assisting Adriana. Instead, she reported it to a counselor.

In addition to his dalliance with Adriana, Ryan attempted to connect with the other students at Stonebrook, but the population was unique. Each teenager had a deeply personal reason for participating in the special program and seemed sad in one way or another. After one particularly bad day, I reminded Ryan how hard we fought to get him into Stonebrook, and he looked at me and asked, "Would you enjoy working at a company where everyone is miserable and only talks about how much they hate being alive?"

In the spring, I was given the opportunity to attend a mainstream sociology class at nearby Acton-Boxboro Regional High School. It was a subject I had no interest in, but it was my only chance to prove I could handle regular school classes, so my time in the building was very businesslike. I walked in, got to class on time, participated in discussions, and walked out. I knew this was a temporary stop, so I didn't bother with making friends. Most people had no clue who I was, and I didn't have any time for lunch. But even though I had never attended real school before, I managed to get an A- on my biggest essay and a B on my final exam.

For the rest of the school year, IEP meetings were held every few weeks, but Stonebrook's administration continuously found reasons for stalling his return to LS. As usual, I tried to counterbalance school with skiing and, from that perspective, Ryan's sophomore year was positive for several reasons. He spent the early season at Loon skiing with new friends Matt and Jared—twins who followed him on Instagram. In their early exchanges, Matt and Jared teased Ryan about his Extreme Ryan moniker, but after their father suggested skiing with Ryan to judge for themselves, the boys became friends. The twins' dad, Andy, was a terrific guy, and we ended up skiing together on Saturdays while the boys explored the glades and backcountry runs requiring short hikes. It was telling that on the mountain Ryan made friends easily with Matt and Jared, further convincing me a return to LS would provide opportunities to meet a more diverse group of kids leading to productive and sustainable relationships.

Away from skiing, the stressful situation at Stonebrook combined with puberty made our home feel like a ticking time bomb. The staff at Stonebrook scrutinized Ryan's every move, and he fretted the slightest misstep would cost him any chance at LS, so he arrived home from school carrying so much pent-up anxiety that his sister or our caregiver, Caitlin, inevitably felt his wrath. Caitlin joined us the previous year after Chloe departed. She was finishing her master's, working part-time while wrapping up her student-teaching requirements. I worried her time with Ryan and Abigail might motivate her to seek an alternative career path. I include Abigail in that calculus because, as a bonus, she was experiencing her own set of issues.

Throughout middle school, Abigail suffered bouts of anxiety. Originally, we viewed it as attention-seeking, comparing her to a sibling jealous of her brother for having cancer because he received so much attention. Obviously, Ryan's issues were not life-threatening, but Abigail never received nearly the attention that he did. And although it took longer than it should have, we finally accepted that her fears were legitimate and sought professional help for her too. Abigail's therapist theorized that witnessing violent confrontations had taken a toll, and she bore the psychological scars of restraints even if she never endured one herself.

Most days, after I headed downstairs after work, Caitlin reported on the family mood, informing me that Ryan failed to complete his homework because it was "hopeless," and Abigail refused to eat dinner because it "looked gross." Luckily, Caitlin was incredibly sweet and persistent, and the kids respected her. Most nights, she worked with Abigail on homework during dinner, distracting her from the cuisine, while I discussed skiing with Ryan—googling any shortcuts available on the internet to assist him with his homework.

Away from the tension inside our home, the rest of ski season was epic. We traveled to Snowbird at Christmas, Big Sky in January, Whistler in February, and then back to Snowbird in April. As usual, Ryan arrived at each destination armed with a list of must-do runs.

———

At Snowbird, I finally got a chance to ski Great Scott, ranked by many as one of the hardest inbounds lines in North America. The run is a sustained forty degrees for a thousand feet. Great Scott also has a reputation for hidden rocks, so skiers can be cruising along before suddenly plummeting to the bottom.

———

As Ryan was dropping into Great Scott, he yelled to me, "If I die, don't let Abigail have any of my shit!"

———

Honestly, I had little trouble skiing it and was just glad Dad let me attempt it without any long debate. He had come to accept that I could ski any inbound run and had stopped trying to ski anything too difficult just to stay with me. It made our trips much less stressful since we were finally working as a team.

———

Obviously, much had changed since our first Utah trip in late 2010. Ryan was certainly a better skier but also a very different travel companion.

He was more self-sufficient, on the mountain and off, and progressions like trying new foods eliminated the stress of having dinner ruined by an unexpected tomato slice. As a result, our time together felt more proportional, and although we would always be father and son, there were glimpses that more resembled old friends. We spent time laughing about my many skiing mishaps but also discussed the important topics in his life like school, girls, and the future—conversations that not only contemplated his career as a professional ski guide but included our first adult conversations about the past and the parenting mistakes that were my responsibility.

"Remember our first time out here when you were nine years old, and you convinced me that we could ski from the bottom of Alta to Snowbird?

"Dad, that was your idea! And if you'd listened to me, we would have taken the right trail. Back then, you always doubted me."

"It wasn't that I doubted you, buddy. That was just a tough time. Skiing was so new for us, and I had no clue what the hell I was doing."

"Yeah, I noticed."

I laughed. I always liked when Ryan tried to be witty, even sarcastic. He was so literal as a kid. Dr. Schneider told Mary Beth and I to never use sarcasm with him because he was incapable of following it. That piece of professional advice was particularly difficult because it was the primary method of communication between husband and wife. So, I was happy to see Ryan continue to prove her wrong, even at my expense.

"That was also a tough trip because you had just gotten released from the hospital."

"I know. I can't believe we came here right after that."

"Ryan, I want you to know that decisions like the hospital and going to SVTA were mistakes. Mistakes that I had a big hand in."

"It's okay. I know that you and Mom weren't trying to hurt me."

"That's true, buddy. We were always trying to help you, but we made some terrible decisions. I think I'll spend the rest of my life wishing I hadn't."

Ryan raised his eyebrows and smiled. "Like trying to ski from Alta to Snowbird?"

I laughed out loud. "Especially like trying to ski from Alta to Snowbird!"

Those dinner conversations were cathartic for both of us.

CHAPTER TWENTY-ONE

Spike It Like Gronk

"There is nothing noble in being superior to your fellow man; true nobility is being superior to your former self."

—ERNEST HEMINGWAY

May 24, 2017. As I sat nervously waiting for Ryan's IEP meeting to begin, Vince Lombardi's admonition to an overzealous kick returner after scoring a touchdown popped in my head, and I reminded myself to "act like you've been there before." Mary Beth warned me not to settle any scores at the meeting, because a victory at best produced a *conditional acceptance*, contingent on a forty-five-day evaluation period at the start of Ryan's junior year. So, even if Ryan was finally allowed to return to public school, better to gently hand the ball to the referee instead of spiking it in the faces of the special education department.

At the meeting, I knew right away that something was different. Like a man on trial relieved to see jurors making eye contact with him after completing deliberations, Lisa and the rest of her staff were relaxed and smiling, even making small talk about summer plans and the Red Sox.

Lisa started the meeting and didn't waste time getting to the verdict. "Ryan is a solid student and, although he faces challenges navigating the social aspects of high school, we feel that he's ready to return to LS for his junior year."

I smiled and nodded. All eyes in the room turned to me, awaiting my victory speech, but I stayed silent. Ryan was outside the door waiting to be brought into the room to hear the decision, and I didn't want him to wait even a second longer to hear the news.

He walked in and looked directly at me for the verdict. "Good news, buddy."

"Really? I can go to LS?"

Ada jumped in. "Yes, Ryan, we are looking forward to having you come to LS. But remember, you'll be on a forty-five-day evaluation at the start of the school year and will be placed in a program called EXCEL, a special subset of students requiring additional support."

Ryan's shoulders slumped and he bowed his head. "So, really, I'm not going to be in the regular school."

Ada jumped in with her sales pitch. "Not at all, Ryan. EXCEL students are considered part of the LS community but take certain classes together and are allowed to retreat to a special break room when feeling overwhelmed."

Ryan recoiled at the word "special," so I tried to close the deal for Ada. "So, he doesn't have to use the break room if he doesn't need to, and he takes most of his classes with the rest of the school?"

"Yes, exactly."

"That doesn't sound so bad, buddy."

———

Finally, after eleven years, I would be in school with the rest of the kids from Sudbury. But just as I was starting to feel great in the meeting, the special education coordinator explained how I would be part of some special program for kids with emotional and behavioral issues. Hadn't I done enough to prove that I was normal? Why did I have to get stuck in another special program? I knew enough about public school to know that everyone would treat me differently as soon as they heard that I was in the EXCEL program.

———

Although Ryan's return to public school came with strings attached, I was pleased. He traveled a long road and succeeded despite a system that long ago rendered him a lost cause. Less than seven years ago, he was in a mental hospital with psychiatrists lobbying to permanently institutionalize him. Now, he was heading back to public school for the first time since preschool while completely free of medication. He had skied in nine states, three countries, and on two continents. On social media platforms, Extreme Ryan was well known as an exceptional skier and was beginning to be recognized by other skiers when we traveled. One young man in Utah even asked Ryan to take a selfie with him and looked giddy after I exchanged places with him so he could ride the chairlift with Ryan. Despite his tremendous progress, we refrained from celebrating his placement at LS because he first had to survive the evaluation period at the start of the year. Any emotional volatility or incidents that hinted he was overwhelmed would find Ryan back at Stonebrook. And as Ryan's most ardent defender, the blowback would land squarely at my feet should he fall apart. Administrators in town, especially my nemesis Sally, would line up at my door to say "I told you so" if Ryan failed.

Ryan and I disagreed on one aspect of his return to LS. In my opinion, entering LS as a sophomore was easier, joining a class that had only been together for a year and hadn't yet formed every clique. LS is a regional high school so, during freshman year, four hundred kids from Sudbury are joined by a hundred kids from Lincoln. As a result, students describe the school as businesslike initially, taking time for friend groups to manifest. Plus, he worked so hard to win the right to attend LS— why not have three years there instead of two?

Ryan was adamant that he was not "staying back" and planned to enter LS as a junior. He feared being stigmatized if other students discovered he repeated sophomore year, and that statement was more loaded than it seemed. Ryan was terrified classmates might uncover his journey through Cambridge Hospital and his years at therapeutic schools. He confided that his biggest fear about attending LS was what to tell people when they asked why he was joining the school as a junior. We could not alleviate his concerns about secrecy because he was correct. Since he had resided in Sudbury for his entire life, some students at LS (especially those who attended elementary and middle school with Abigail) knew he was returning from a long stint in special education programs. I tried diffusing his anxiety by telling him to respond that he was in a secret ski training program for the CIA or was recently paroled. However, we appreciated that when the school year began, his "story" would present a serious dilemma because Ryan hates lying. Although his diagnosis wobbled over the years, his penchant for honesty has remained consistent. Someday, a girlfriend will ask whether she looks good in a pair of jeans, and I hope she is braced for the answer.

Fortunately, we had an entire summer vacation to prepare for his arrival story at LS. In the meantime, Ryan attended overnight summer camps for the first time in his life. Mary Beth helped him select camps with an outdoor focus, and he spent parts of the summer hiking the Long Trail in Vermont and exploring caves and waterfalls in New Hampshire. These camps were cathartic because he attended without labels. He was not "Ryan, the Student with Disabilities" or "Ryan, on the Autism Spectrum"—he was just Ryan from Sudbury. He was thrust into self-dependency and social situations like meeting new people, navigating strange foods, and keeping track of his gear. He did this without parental support or phone contact, sometimes for as long as two weeks, and we were thrilled to see him handle these situations so well on his own.

⚊⚊

The summer after I left Stonebrook was filled with mixed emotions. I did my first proper backpacking trip in Vermont, where I uncovered my passion for hiking. I had hiked many times before, but this was the most immersive experience I'd ever had on any trail. For me, there was a healing quality to spending time in the deep woods, and the friends I made on that trip were unlike any other. When you walk for eight hours a day with the same people, you really get to know them.

When I got home, I set a new goal for myself. I decided to hike all one hundred of New England's highest peaks. The "Hundred Highest," as it is known locally, is an ambitious goal with lots of long days, bushwhacking, and scrambling. Unfortunately, Dad was busy coaching Abigail's softball team, so my peak-bagging would need to wait until the following summer when I could drive myself all over New England. Instead, I did a few local hikes with Mom when Abigail had games outside of town. When her games were in Sudbury, I would go sometimes, but I always got a weird vibe from the girls on the team. I was never sure if they were uncomfortable around me or if I was uncomfortable around them. Maybe it was both? I was so disconnected from our town and feared that any conversation would lead back to where I had gone to school, so I kept quiet around them. Most of the time, I would talk to the other parents about skiing. A lot of them had seen my videos and asked lots of questions. That helped make the games go quicker. A lot of time, however, I found myself looking away from the field and back toward the high school. LS looked so huge. I tried to imagine the hallways, the classes, and the cafeteria. My only memories of public school were from preschool, so it was hard to imagine what it must be like. I had seen enough movies about high school to picture it, but thinking about LS reminded me of my dream to ski Little Couloir. I knew what attending public school in the fall might look like but couldn't picture what it would feel like until I got the chance to make my first few turns in there.

Later that summer, I returned to Portillo, and in preparation for the Super-C Couloir, Dad purchased my first touring setup—special bindings that allowed for easier hiking and enabled me to skin up mountains. I attended NASTC camp in the morning to work on my form, but in the afternoon, I went exploring high above the lifts, usually joining someone else's party, even managing to ski a rare descent called the Upper Toilet Bowl. Unfortunately, Ben was not guiding this year, and without him, I spent the week trying to find another partner for the Super-C. However, in talking to other skiers like Chris Davenport, I heard that the hike across the crux was a sheet of ice and could be deadly. Although I was disappointed, I understood that the Super-C would have to wait until next year.

Dad tried to make up for the fact that I was unable to attempt the Super-C by booking another heli-day. We hadn't been in the valley behind the resort since our first trip two years ago and luckily, we got another great weather day. This time, we teamed with Ken, another NASTC client, and someone Dad and I became friends with after prior Portillo trips. I am not sure if there are many people that love skiing as much as I do, but Ken makes the list. We also skied with Colter, Chris Fellows's son. Colter was an awesome skier who was studying filmmaking in college, and he was in Portillo to make videos for NASTC.

Dad skied really well during our heli-day, and, watching him, I thought back to the first time we skied in the shadow of Aconcagua. Let's just say, he had improved a ton. With NASTC's help and with his lessons in Big Sky with

Ben and Hannah, he was becoming a stronger skier and was able to keep up with our group. He also managed to take some great pictures including one of me jumping off a small cliff.

When I arrived home from Chile, the high of such an epic summer quickly dissipated as I approached a new, daunting environment. Junior year at LS would be an exciting chapter for me, but at the same time, it was terrifying. It wasn't like skiing above huge cliffs, and I couldn't just take a deep breath, turn off the fear, and let my abilities take over. My success wouldn't be the result of my skills or mindset. I knew that once I walked in the door at LS, the opinions of other people would determine my success or failure.

Chapter Twenty-Two

Dale Carnegie Had No Friends in High School

"Our wretched species is so made that those who walk on the well-trodden path always throw stones at those who are showing a new road."

—Voltaire

September 5, 2017. The Governor's Academy in Byfield, Massachusetts, is the oldest continuously operating boarding school in America, and its rich history includes a seal created by Paul Revere and a charter signed by John Hancock and Samuel Adams. Moreover, it is the school that changed my life, and Abigail's brave decision to follow in my footsteps presented an incredible opportunity to forge her own path outside of Ryan's shadow. Yet, it was her first taste of living away from home, which added to an already nerve-racking fall with Ryan headed to LS for the first time. We texted her constantly.

⬥

For the first time in my entire life, I got to ride a regular yellow school bus with the rest of the high school kids in my neighborhood. It turned out to be an eventful ride because our bus driver crashed into a pickup truck on the way to school, making everyone on my bus an hour late for class.

Even on my first day, I saw how different LS would be from my previous schools. Teachers were not hovering in the hallways to watch every student interaction, but everyone still moved quickly and efficiently—never pausing to talk unless it was a free block or lunch. To me, it seemed like everyone walked in, did what they had to do, and walked out, so I wasn't surprised when the other students were not the least bit curious about a new student like me.

In my first week, I noticed a student with big headphones and hair in his eyes. As he walked past me, he never looked up at me or anyone else. I thought to myself, If I don't put myself out there, I'll end up just like him, broken and forgotten. So, I made an ambitious plan to sit at a different lunch table each day—introducing myself to everyone until I found my group. It didn't matter if it was popular kids, high achievers, gamers, artists, or stoners; I planned on trying with everyone. Unfortunately, I never found a group of ski bums, which would have made connecting easier. For the most part, it seemed that people liked me when they met me, but I struggled to make any real friendships.

⸻❦⸻

Like my text exchanges with Abigail, I probed Ryan each day when he arrived home from school. "Was it okay?" "Did you find all of your classes?" "Did you sit with anyone new at lunch?" The poor kid was interrogated each day after walking off the bus. I feared something might happen during the evaluation period that Sudbury would use as an excuse to send him back to Stonebrook.

⸻❦⸻

By October, I managed to understand the social order of LS. Popular kids sat on the far side of the cafeteria near the A200s building. If a boy was popular, he played football or lacrosse. If a girl was popular, she played sports too, or was beautiful, or was dating a popular boy. The far side of the cafeteria near the B200s was called Narnia, populated by nerdy kids, shy kids, or people doing last-minute homework.

Everyone else at LS sat in the middle of the cafeteria with their friend group, and those cliques rarely interacted. I bounced around each day looking for a friendly table, but no matter which one I selected, there was one consistent theme: I always needed to start conversations. Only once did someone introduce themselves to me during my first month. However, when I was able to start a decent conversation, it was like a switch flipped. Suddenly I existed, at least. In fact, some people even seemed interested in getting to know me, but without my persistence in generating conversations, it seemed like it was illegal for people to talk to me.

———

At the conclusion of the forty-five-day evaluation period, we attended an IEP meeting with Ryan. At the meeting, Ryan's teachers reported he was a regular participant in the classroom, had managed his assignments without issue, and most importantly, had avoided emotional outbursts that the school district surely assumed would be a regular occurrence. I never spiked the football by asking for an apology from each administrator, but deep down, it killed me not to gloat. Ryan was vindicated in front of a room full of people who, for years, openly doubted him. Although I kept my mouth shut, I tried to look smug, conferring in the clearest possible terms how happy we were about his return to *regular* school.

The next few weeks confirmed Ryan belonged at LS, but he struggled socially. He stayed tight-lipped about it before breaking down completely one afternoon when he got home. When I walked into the living room, he was sitting on the couch staring in the direction of the television, which was turned off. His phone was beside him, and it was strange to see him ignoring it.

"You all right, buddy?"

"I'm fine."

"You don't sound fine. You sure nothing is wrong?"

"Dad, I'm fine."

"Did something happen at school today?"

"Nothing ever happens at school. No one even knows I'm alive."

My heart sank. "What do you mean by that? People are ignoring you?"

He bowed his head and placed it into his hands, his elbows resting on his knees. He rubbed his eyes, and when he looked up to say something, tears welled up. He began describing how he selected a different lunch table each day hoping to make conversation. He told me, "Most kids won't even look up long enough for me to finish a sentence."

"What do you do when that happens?"

"Sometimes I try again. I sit there for a few minutes trying to think of something interesting or funny to say. But, sometimes, I just give up and sit there eating my lunch. I must not be interesting enough or have so little to offer that people don't care what I have to say." In what is very typical behavior, Ryan's reaction was to blame himself for his lack of success in making friends.

"I don't think that's the reason, Ry. High school is all about status. Everyone is looking for approval. You're an unknown. The other kids are seeking approval from their friends and their little groups to see if you are cool enough to talk to."

"I guess, but I think they've already decided that I am not cool enough to talk to."

It crushed me to hear Ryan so defeated, but I remained optimistic things would improve over time. How could a kid who survived so much and experienced so many interesting people and places not be fascinating to the rest of the students at LS? If nothing else, he was the new guy, and that alone should have generated curiosity. But maybe that's how high school worked in the 1980s when I attended, but in 2017, the new guy was just a nameless person in the hallway who wasn't on any of the cool kids' radars—let alone their Snapchat or Instagram feeds.

We asked Ada for any guidance she could provide on the social fabric at LS. She commented that Ryan melded easily into the classroom scene, but most of his struggles centered on lunch. She disclosed that all the EXCEL kids ate in a small breakroom exclusive to students in the program because they were intimidated by the larger cafeteria, but Ryan refused to do that. I asked Ryan why and he said, "I want to be a regular student, not someone that hides in the breakroom."

Unfortunately, Ada explained his actions cost him two times over. He struggled to connect with the kids in the cafeteria while managing to alienate most of the EXCEL students because he wouldn't retreat to the breakroom.

By late December, Ryan's dream of attending LS risked backfiring. I knew integrating at a large public high school as a junior would be difficult for any student but wondered if he was stigmatized by the "special education" label. The student body at LS was savvy enough to know that a longtime resident does not show up as a junior without a backstory that included a stint at a therapeutic school.

One afternoon, when I walked into the living room to see how his day went, he was once again sitting quietly sans electronic stimulation. "Another bad day?"

"Same as every day, Dad."

"I know, buddy, but it will get better. Soon, winter will be here, and we will be skiing again. Maybe we can find some kids at LS to ski with?"

"Dad, people won't talk to me at lunch. I don't think they will be looking to drive to New Hampshire with us."

I assumed other students knew he was part of the special education group, and it acted like a scarlet letter. However, I worried that by asking him I might alert him to the issue, so I tried to ask about the program in general.

"How are the other kids in the EXCEL program? Any of them cool?"

"Cool? Dad, they're all really nice kids and I like most of them, but people in EXCEL are there because they are antisocial. They don't want to hang out with anyone. They mostly just want to be left alone."

"Do you think it is harder to make friends with non-EXCEL kids because they know you are part of it?" I asked. Ryan demurred.

"I don't think that many people even know I am in EXCEL. I think they just don't like me because of my personality."

He left me an opening for once. Usually, his logical brilliance shattered my counterpoints, or his stubbornness simply wore me into surrender, but today I had him. "How can they not like you because of your personality if they won't even talk to you? They can't know anything about your personality without first talking to you, can they?"

He looked surprised that I scored an argumentative point, but he was not yet surrendering. "Then maybe they just think I'm ugly, or they don't like my face."

Another opening. "Ry, you look exactly like me. I'm great looking. That makes you great looking. Do you own a fucking mirror?"

He laughed. He looked exhausted but seeing him smile gave me hope.

Despite his inclusion in the EXCEL program, Ryan did not fit the antisocial profile he recognized in other EXCEL students. He longed for social interaction and new friendships, which explained why he wanted to hide the fact that he was in the program. I wondered how he could possibly hide his participation, but he truly believed most students had no idea of his backstory.

If Ryan was correct that mainstream students were unaware of his inclusion in EXCEL, I struggled to come up with a reason why making friends was so difficult for him at LS. He was never intimidated by anyone. He wasn't shy, and I knew that his looks were not a hindrance. Perhaps his fellow students simply misread him. For example, in *Talking to Strangers*, Malcolm Gladwell theorizes that strangers are sometimes misunderstood when their behavior is mismatched from their emotional state.[1] Although Ryan's mind never rests and his internal emotional state churns over the desire to fit in, his outward presentation is poised and self-assured. He never embarrasses, is comfortable speaking in front of groups, and makes such great eye contact in conversations that it is unsettling to other teenagers. Adults generally find him fascinating, but to other students, Ryan likely appeared overconfident. Plus, with a reputation for skiing the most difficult terrain on earth as Extreme Ryan, perhaps they wrongly concluded he was a cocky jerk or a confident loner with bigger plans than the mundane world of high school drama.

⁓

LS was certainly more enjoyable than Stonebrook and better than the therapeutic schools by a million miles, but it was stressful socially. I felt like an outsider during the first few months of junior year and got the sense that people were reluctant to talk to me. Whenever I started a conversation, I noticed that the other kids quickly looked around to see if anyone was watching, like they might lose status by speaking to me. Even my friend Mason, who I had known since we were little

---

1. Gladwell provides the example of Amanda Knox, who was wrongly convicted of murder in Italy. Knox's behavior following the murder led Italian police to suspect her because she acted remorseless over the death of her roommate. Knox, however, was described by those knowing her best as awkward and goofy. For strangers judging her in isolation, one could easily mistake her flaky or inappropriate actions following a gruesome murder for a calculating nature.

kids, seemed to hurry in the other direction whenever he ran into me at school. But overall, LS was still a huge upgrade from what I was used to dealing with at therapeutic schools. Most days were pain free, and I had small victories with friendly exchanges here and there.

The hard part was that I sensed Dad's disappointment whenever I talked to him after school because those victories never seemed big enough. He would ask about girls, and even when I had a story about a nice conversation with a friendly girl, he would want to know if I planned to ask her out. Of course, I didn't. I hardly knew the girl's name; how would I date her? I was just happy that she smiled at me when we talked. Or, if I hung with some cool guys at lunch, he would ask me for names and if I planned to hang out with them after school and on weekends. I know that he wanted so badly for LS to go well for me, but he never seemed to understand high school wasn't like skiing. I couldn't quickly move from the magic carpet to the expert runs. This was more like gymnastics. I needed a good score from the judges to move to the next level.

As his social struggles continued, Mary Beth and I theorized that Ryan simply needed more practice being a teenager. In his prior schools, interactions were highly regulated, so I explained to him that body language is incredibly important in making a first impression. I even downloaded Dale Carnegie's *How to Win Friends and Influence People* because Ryan tends to speak in detail when he has familiarity with a subject yet has a tough time making conversations flow easily when discussing a topic he is unfamiliar with.

At LS, one obvious place for Ryan to pursue friendships was the Ski and Snowboard Club, a student group that traveled on Wednesdays in the winter to Wachusett Mountain. Ryan grew up with some of the boys in the club, but since none had sought him out during school, we hoped his participation would elevate his social status.

I joined the Ski and Snowboard Club, and on our first bus ride to Wachusett Mountain, a boy I knew from my neighborhood named Noah introduced me to his friends as "the best skier at LS." I wasn't expecting his praise and wasn't sure if people would be excited or intimidated to ski with me, but in any case, I spent the entire bus ride answering questions about where I had skied and sharing photos. For a moment, I felt like the local pro and wasn't entirely sure I deserved that status, but it was better than feeling like the local loser, which I did plenty of other days at LS.

Once at the mountain, the adult leader of the club, Mr. Wancowitz, told us the rules, then asked, "All right, who thinks they're the best skier on the mountain?" Two people I didn't know raised their hands, but the rest of the bus pointed at me. He laughed and announced, "Okay, there seems to be a general consensus on Ryan."

Although Ski Club was fun, the guys I skied with didn't result in immediate friendships at school or have much of an impact on how I was viewed outside of school. However, it did help build connections, and those connections helped me feel more comfortable at LS.

I also encouraged Ryan to seek activities outside of school to generate new friendships, and the most logical possibility was a job at Nashoba Valley Ski Area, the hill where he first learned to ski. At the informational meeting for new applicants, experienced instructors provided details on the necessary steps to pursue a career as a professional ski instructor. Ryan listened intently, answering several questions during the proposed hypotheticals, before handing his application to an instructor that I recognized. It was Darcy, the instructor with the British accent who taught Ryan during our initial skiing days at Nashoba in 2009.

"Darcy, I doubt you remember us, but a few years ago, you changed this guy's life with a ski lesson," I informed her. She seemed startled and, after struggling for the right words, smiled at Ryan, and replied, "I'm happy to hear that, and thank you very much for telling me—it means a lot."

As we walked through the parking lot following the meeting, I thought to myself, Darcy will never fully appreciate her impact on Ryan's life. If she was a terrible instructor that day, his skiing career might have lasted a few hours. Instead of thanking her for changing his life, I should have thanked her for saving his life.

Ryan was hired by Nashoba and spent two weeks learning how to properly instruct beginner skiers, before he started work after school in January. He enjoyed teaching children and seemed happier than he was in the fall, but that was generally the case when ski season kicked into gear. Although he was back in public high school, his job at Nashoba was to me the biggest progression of all. At each group lesson, Ryan oversaw a half-dozen kids in an activity where injuries are commonplace. Talk about parallel tracks. At school, Ryan was still surrounded by teachers and administrators in the EXCEL program actively monitoring his emotional state, while at Nashoba, parents entrusted him with the safety and security of their young children.

I never considered how hard it would be to teach kids to ski. I guess it just came so easily for me that I assumed most kids would pick it up quickly, but I was so wrong. Some nights, I had as many as ten kids in a lesson, and we were only able to walk around on skis and do basic stance drills because the magic carpet would have killed them. That wasn't so bad, but what frustrated me were the kids that didn't want to be there. I didn't understand why parents forced them to go. I would do everything to make it fun, but some kids just hated it and complained the entire time. It made it harder to teach the group because they took time away from the kids that really wanted to learn. But I did feel good when the more motivated kids got better. I loved moving them to the magic carpet and seeing their faces when they skied the tiny hill that started it all for me.

In late January, we headed west to Big Sky but encountered flat light and blustery days, limiting Ryan and Ben, and once again preventing any opportunity to bag Little Couloir. Despite the restrictions encountered on the slopes, I observed some obvious strides in Ryan's overall maturation. At lunch and dinner, he integrated himself into conversations when other adults were around, and in that setting, wasn't speaking in monologues or dominating the conversation. Moreover, he hung in when the conversations turned to politics or sports—topics that were of little interest to him.

After observing him interact at Big Sky, it struck me that the perception of Ryan by other skiers was the polar opposite of how he was viewed in school. At LS, Ryan's elite status as an extreme skier meant very little. He was not part of a sports team or an artist or musician, and he wasn't overly studious or even a troublemaker. Ryan wandered the halls of LS untethered from any friend group and, to most of the student body, he was the invisible man. Worse, I was certain for a sizable segment of the population at LS, they knew exactly who he was. Ryan was Abigail's brother, pushed out of public school as a toddler because he required help with his emotional issues. For those students, Ryan wasn't invisible; he was unworthy.

※

Three years before I walked into LS for the first time, Dr. Delgado began taking me off medication, and I experienced emotions again for the first time in years. Initially, it was a strange feeling. I was so used to chemicals regulating every-thing that I felt, both good and bad, that the decrease in medicine hit me like a tidal wave. For example, if rain canceled a weekend ski trip, I immediately teared up before I was able to process that we could just go the following weekend. These emotional swings worried my parents and, whenever I broke down or got mad, Mom considered slowing the rate of decrease. Dr. Delgado, however, held firm, and over time, I started regulating my emotions more naturally.

In that weaning period, Dr. Delgado also helped me learn strategies for processing emotions like taking deep breaths during frustration and coun-teracting sadness by thinking about things that brought me happiness. These coping mechanisms come naturally to everyone else, but they were skills that I needed to learn and needed to practice. Oftentimes I was forced to put those coping skills to work as I encountered new situations at Parsons, Stonebrook, and then at LS. Over time, I got better at it, and now that I was free of med-ication for a long enough period that I was unlikely to ever go back, I found myself revisiting everything that happened from preschool to LS.

The part that everyone missed when I was younger was how self-fulfilling a diagnosis of autism or bipolar disorder was for me. With autism, once I was diagnosed, my parents and everyone around me treated me differently. They panicked when I got near other children at the park or when I wanted to organize an activity during a playdate. As a result, I grew up feeling like I was incapable of interacting with people, and despite wanting social interaction, I limited my opportunities to be around others, which only made me appear more autistic to doctors and teachers. That loneliness brought on great sadness and frustration and made it look like I had a mood disorder, even introducing talk of bipolar disorder. I think that one bothered me the most because, even at my worst, I never once suffered a bout of depression or any unexplained highs or lows. Yet, for so long, the bipolar label made me feel like I was too much to deal with, and every time I introduced myself to someone, I felt like I was trying to sell them a defective product. I assumed that being my friend or dating me meant taking on my issues, too, and that didn't seem fair to the other person.

As I learned to handle life without the crutch of medication, I broke through my own self-doubt. Yes, of course I was a difficult kid, but my brain wasn't broken. I realized that doctors and teachers took a difficult kid, and rather than helping, they tried to break me. Then, they told me it was my fault for being put together incorrectly in the first place. And I fell for it.

Finally at LS, however, I wasn't "Ryan with Issues," I was just Ryan. For the rest of the winter, I kept putting myself out there, making connections, resolving insecurities, and living a happier life. It wasn't always easy, and junior year was full of tough days. Unlike my classmates who had already learned to deal with rejection, exclusion, or embarrassment in middle school, I was feeling the full force of those difficult emotions now that I was medication-free in high school. Worse, I was dealing with all that while trying to make friends and impress other kids at LS.

CHAPTER TWENTY-THREE

Little and Big

"You cannot teach a man anything, you can only help him find it within himself."

—GALILEO

February 17, 2018. School vacation offered Ryan a new destination and firsthand opportunity to learn about avalanches. We traveled to Lake Tahoe, skiing at Squaw Valley and Kirkwood, but the supplement to our "vacation" was a three-day certification course on avalanches presented by the American Institute for Avalanche Research and Education, known as AIARE Avi-1. By now, Ryan was expressing interest in a career as a professional ski guide, so knowledge of avalanche terrain was a vital component of his formal education.

Our Avi-1 course enrolled fifteen backcountry enthusiasts—and me. Ryan was by far the youngest, and I was one of the oldest. Most of the attendees, men in their late twenties with cool facial hair, seemed bored by our classroom lecture on the causes of avalanches, but I found it interesting that an avalanche is the product of a steep slope, a weak layer in the snow, and a trigger. Often, the trigger is a person skiing in the backcountry, so my initial takeaway for preventing avalanches was remaining within the friendly confines of ski resorts. However, even if that advice worked for me and most skiers and snowboarders, it was never going to apply to Ryan. Over his lifetime, he was planning to venture in search of untracked snow, and that meant thousands of opportunities to die in an avalanche. I could not stop him from skiing outside of ski resorts, nor did I want to stop him. He was pursuing something in the backcountry that made him happy. I could only hope that courses like this and proper training ensured that he remained safe and, most importantly, alive.

Ryan was enthralled by the material and dove into each case study for clues in determining where backcountry skiing decisions went wrong. He had researched previous avalanche disasters and easily spotted mistakes while offering tactical measures for avoiding tragedy when charged with leading group hypotheticals. Before we broke for lunch, our instructors were already asking for "someone other than Ryan" when they sought input or volunteers for case studies.

The second day of the course was our initial trip into the field, and we walked for a half mile in ski boots while carrying our skis to a small mountain near Lake Tahoe. Most of our group wore high-tech boots made for the backcountry. They looked much sleeker and lighter with a release mechanism in the back to allow the boot to shift forward when it was placed in "walk mode." Ryan was wearing tech boots too, but not by choice. On the flight out, his boot bag came off the luggage conveyor like it had been run over by a tank. Everything inside was destroyed including his boots, helmet, and goggles. We located a ski shop that evening and scrambled to buy him new gear. My bag was fine, so I was still wearing my resort boots. I liked them because they were comfortable, but I was judging that based on skiing, not clomping up a paved road while chasing the rest of my class.

When we finally reached the trailhead, and once our skins were affixed to our skis, we forged ahead in a single-file line. My poor skinning technique was magnified by the increased altitude. As I gasped for each breath, one of the instructors kept prodding me to "slide not step." Maybe it was the fault of my boots, but I just couldn't do it. Ryan and the rest of the group seemed to be skating fluidly across the terrain while I clomped behind like a pony learning to walk. By the time we paused to analyze the snowpack, I was completely exhausted and was breathing like I had just located a pocket of air in a submerged car. So, I made the only logical choice. I surrendered. Backcountry skiing wasn't for me, and I saw little reason to dig a giant hole to determine whether the snow might kill me. Instead, I hung back on the trail while the others dug, bouncing around on my skis to stay warm.

Once our group finished analyzing the snow pit, we skied back to the parking lot and the instructors told us to prepare for a "few hours of skinning tomorrow." I muttered, "No fucking way" under my breath but waited until we got back to the hotel to inform Ryan that I planned to bow out of the final day. To justify it, I told him it wasn't fair of me to slow everyone down and if he was willing to finish the course by himself, I would remain at the hotel. He grumbled in response, but quickly returned to his course homework, analyzing the weather and the intended route for tomorrow's adventure.

The next day, I stayed back and guiltily watched Netflix. As I lay in bed, it struck me that I had never quit anything in my entire life. Not only am I mentally tough, but I once played an entire baseball season with a fractured spine because I refused to quit on my teammates. I was fourteen years old, and I spent that summer skipping rope in my non-air-conditioned attic before games so I could loosen my muscles. I then drove to the field with the heat on full blast ensuring that I didn't tighten up.[1] So, why was I willing to surrender so easily when it came to backcountry skiing? Perhaps I was simply getting older, but there was also an element of common sense at play. The time and effort required to slowly skin up a mountain felt pointless when thousands of amazing runs existed that were serviced by ski lifts, snowcats, and helicopters. To me, backcountry skiing resembled Amish farming. It was principled, even quaint, but it felt impractical and unnecessary.

When Ryan returned at the conclusion of the course, he seemed pleased with his performance during the final day. He received accolades from the instructors who spoke glowingly of his potential as a ski guide and was not upset with me for quitting as we drove that evening to Squaw Valley. Although he had skied in some amazing places, Ryan was really looking forward to Squaw because it is arguably the birthplace of extreme skiing in the United States—made famous by Shane McConkey.

---

1. I did miss the following season but that was only after I woke up from surgery in a body cast and was unable to move my torso for six months.

Prior to his tragic death, McConkey brought extreme skiing to Squaw, and his more famous runs are located within a series of cliffs called "Palisades." I was looking forward to Squaw as well and was curious to see how Ryan would react to being surrounded by some of the best extreme skiers in the country.

Later that year, I took my skiing to the next level. After attaining my AIARE Avi-1, we traveled to the major resorts around Tahoe during school break. On our second day at Squaw Valley, patrol opened the famous Palisades Main Chute, and I stood among some of the best extreme skiers on earth. I was worried about looking like a first timer on Palisades with fifteen badass-looking skiers standing next to me atop the cornice, when suddenly I heard, "Anyone want next drop?"

Feeling confident, I yelled, "I'll take it."

I knew all eyes were on me now, and as I lined my tips before dropping in, I whispered, "Don't fuck this up." Fortunately, I nailed it, landing halfway down the chute at high speed, and even heard cheers from the dudes on the ridge.

While Palisades gave me the confidence to charge a very steep straight line, nothing could have prepared me for a chute called Once Is Enough at Kirkwood Mountain Resort. After the two-hour drive around beautiful Lake Tahoe, we arrived at Kirkwood to a foot of new snow. I instantly fell in love with the rugged free-rider terrain and, after a couple of warm-up runs, we rode up the Wall Chair, where I got my first glance at Once. It looked steep and ridiculously narrow. Normally a doable line, Once was suffering from a dry snow year and was more challenging than usual.

At the top, I looked through the notch of the chute and wondered if it was even possible to ski through without hitting a sidewall. It was a steep drop, barely two ski widths across, and looked like I needed to overlap my skis to fit through. But, gathering my courage, I waved, alerting Dad that I was giving it a shot, so he knew to start filming. I heard him yell, "Are you sure?"

Suddenly, a moment of doubt popped into my head, and I stood there for twenty seconds, debating. Then I went for it, dropping quickly and making the

*critical turn to dodge the rock wall. It went by so fast that I hardly remember
making that move, but I came to a smooth stop and let out a proud "Fuck yeah!"*

*Once is barely a ten-second run, but it taught me something important.
I was a much better skier than I gave myself credit for. It became clear to
me after that Tahoe trip, skiing big lines requires more mental courage than
physical skill.*

⚊⚊

We wrapped up the trip, and Ryan returned to school for a few weeks. In
late March, we traveled to Big Sky, and Ben planned something extreme
for both of us. He thought there was a chance Big Sky's massive snowfall
could lead to the opening of Little Couloir. The Little is an incredibly
steep and narrow run lined with rock. It travels over 1,200 vertical feet
and one misstep at the entrance means plummeting to the bottom. For
my money, it is the most difficult in-bounds run found in any American
ski resort, and Ryan had talked obsessively about the Little since our first
trip to Big Sky in 2014.

⚊⚊

*Upon arrival at Big Sky, Dad offered to sort out some unpacking and logistical
stuff while I skied the remainder of the afternoon. Big Sky was experiencing
record snowfall, and he didn't want me to miss a minute. Before we flew in,
Ben and I talked about the potential for skiing Little Couloir, something he
believed was likely this year. Obviously, partnering with Ben was my only
chance to ski the Little, but this wasn't a run that was typical for guides and
clients. Due to the high risk of injury, no guided party had ever descended
it before, so he contacted the summit supervisor to see if he felt comfortable
allowing us to ski it as a team.*

*While many assume Big Couloir is the hardest line on Lone Peak, Little
Couloir is easily the steepest inbounds run in North America and is far more
technical. The upper amphitheater has a maximum pitch of sixty degrees, while
the remainder of the 1,200-foot run is a sustained pitch of fifty to fifty-five
degrees. With that steepness, it requires wet spring snow to bond to the upper
amphitheater, and on a good year, it only opens once or twice. Even then, only
three or four groups ski it before the skiable snow is sloughed off, closing the run*

185

until it fills with new snow. Big Sky locals are lucky to ski it in their lifetimes, and some exceptional skiers have tumbled uncontrollably to the bottom after a botched turn.

The first time I heard about the Little, I was twelve years old and had just skied the less gnarly Big Couloir. Patrol opened the Little the same day, and it was all people talked about on the tram, so I knew it was special.

Later that season, I saw an Instagram post about it, and I commented, "Looks sick. I can't wait to ski it one day." The author of the post didn't reply with the usual "Yeah man; so sick" or "Get after it, bro." Instead, he gave me a harsh "Be careful what you wish for." So, I did some additional research and found out just how wild it was when I saw videos of top pros rag-dolling down after a fall.

Since 2014, I've looked to the Little as my ultimate test piece, traveling to Big Sky each spring with high hopes of skiing it, only to leave disappointed. This year, despite Ben's optimism before our arrival, my hopes were starting to fade based on the weather. As I rode the chairlift, clouds obscured the peak, blocking my view of my dream line. I then dropped a zone on Andesite Mountain known as Rock Pocket, which featured fantastic pillow lines, and when I finished, I took out my phone on the lift to send Dad a picture. There, I noticed a text from Ben, informing us that persistent cloudy weather would likely prevent us from skiing the Little the next day. I was dejected but knew the weather in Big Sky could change in an instant and still hoped for a miracle.

On our first full day in Big Sky, Ben met us in the morning at our usual spot outside of ski school. As he approached, his casual pace was replaced with a frenetic blur. Talking faster than usual, he looked at Ryan and said in a raspy, almost out of breath manner, "Patrol is opening the Little, but we need to lock in a spot."

Ryan responded with a grunt, and both he and Ben raced ahead to the chairlift, while I hurried to keep pace. When we reached the base of the tram, Ben looked nervous. He had survived the Little in prior years, so he wasn't nervous about skiing it. He was worried about disappointing Ryan if they failed to secure a spot.

Ben usually greeted us with a hug and a smile, but that day he skated toward us with the speed of an Olympic Nordic skier. He was talking fast and demanded that we hurry toward the lift because we might have a shot to ski the Little. Now I understood why he was rushing because to ski the Little, a lot needs to happen. You need an early start on Swift Current lift. Then, you must be one of the first three chairs on the Powder Seeker lift to be one of the first two trams to the peak. And, even then, you're in a tight race with other Big Sky experts to the sign-out sheet to secure a time slot.

On the Powder Seeker chair, as we listened intently to Ben's radio for any sign that the Little was open, I experienced an intense mix of emotions. I was more excited than I'd been in years, but at the same time, I was terrified. The Little would be a test of how far I had come as a skier, but with extremely high consequences. Somewhere buried in my excitement was the frightening image of me tumbling down the nearly vertical headwall.

We managed to make the first tram to the top and, as we rode up, we saw two ski patrollers drop the Apple Core entrance to the Little, shredding the steep terrain as deep slough slid at their feet. A minute later, we heard someone say, "Little is open, just Apple Core, no Direct" over the radio, meaning only one of the two entrances to the Little was doable. Finally, after years of frustration, it was really happening. We just needed to secure a spot, and as we disembarked the tram, a patroller yelled, "Sign-outs are in the penalty box," referring to the shack on the far side of the summit. With that, every skier on the summit began a full sprint to the door. Ben and I managed to secure the third slot of the day, so as long the run was deemed safe after the two groups ahead of us, we were doing this.

After the first two groups survived, patrol reassessed the conditions, and we were finally given the all-clear. I quickly strapped on my helmet and tried not to look at Dad because my heart was pounding, and I didn't want him to make me any more nervous. He was waiting in the shack for Ben and me to get the green light to time his picture-taking efforts, and he planned to ski a run called First Gully that offered a clear view of the Little. He wished us luck as we walked out the door, but I just grunted "thanks" and kept moving. This wasn't the time for any inspirational speeches.

We waited nervously in the ski patrol shack until Ben received the green light. He smiled at Ryan and asked, "Are you ready?" Then, he looked at me and nodded his head confidently while buckling his chin strap. Just a mere sixteen years old, with a mouth full of braces and the slightest hint of peach fuzz over his top lip, Ryan followed Ben out the door without a glance in my direction. I wished them both luck, and off they went.

After we clicked into our skis, we traversed the back side of the mountain and hiked the ridge. We paused momentarily to look down the Apple Core entrance, and I turned to Ben and said, "It actually doesn't look as bad as I thought." In that instant, the Little was no longer just a concept in my brain, and I visualized my turns.

Ben offered me the choice to ski it first, and I nervously stepped into the couloir. I effortlessly touched the wall of the slope without fully extending my arm, indicating how incredibly steep it was. When I got to the point where it was wide enough to ski, I paused, knowing it was time for commitment, and prepared myself to make the first hop-turn. After one last deep breath, I left my feet to flip the direction of my skis and when I landed, it took a second for my edges to catch. My heart dropped. Had my skis failed me, I would have tumbled all 1,200 feet, so I dug my edges in deeper. Although that first hop-turn was terrifying, at least now I had a feel for the line and knew how to proceed. I then made seven more conservative turns, utilizing a smaller hop in the transition to decrease the chances of losing an edge.

Finally, I reached the "Ballroom" area, where I was able to lay down some real turns before traversing to avoid a large cliff lurking below. By this point, I felt truly secure, and my big sweeping turns in the slough felt great. I then stopped to watch Ben. He made a few sketchy hop-turns at the entrance and then started shredding like he usually does. Ben is one of the best skiers I've witnessed and, while a lot of skiers get credit for hitting big airs or bold lines, I give Ben extra points for what he does. Any brave skier can hit bold lines without being technically proficient, but Ben can ski anywhere in the world without ever changing his technique, and he skied the Little the same way he did any other run.

After pausing in the middle to exchange words of excitement, we still had a line to finish. Ben let me initiate the final turns, and I ripped the powder aggressively, trying not to get cocky. I wasn't spoiling the run of a lifetime by falling on the "easy" section, and I made it to the bottom, stopping at the flat zone known as the "Cue Ball" to wait for Ben to finish. Dad, who had been photographing from First Gully, skied down to congratulate us, and I took off my helmet to speak directly into my GoPro.

"I waited half my life to ski that line," I said, "and I finally got it!"

Then I turned off the camera. To be honest, I was hit with a weird range of emotions. I waited a long time to ski that line and had skied it well, but now the journey was done. I was proud to accomplish it but felt sad that it was over. I passed the test, but maybe things were happening for me too quickly? I was only sixteen, still wearing a "junior lift ticket" on my coat and had just skied something that only a handful of skiers in the world could do. As I stood there, Ben and Dad exchanged hugs and looked at pictures on Dad's phone, but I felt a little empty inside and wondered if it was time for another goal. Or was this really as high as I could go?

———

When I met them at the bottom, Ben looked satisfied and proud. To the outside world, he likely resembled a ski guide puffing out his chest about the accomplishments of his star client, but I knew he felt so much more. When we first hired him back in 2014, Ryan was already a good skier and incredibly enthusiastic about skiing harder terrain. As a student, however, he was recalcitrant, distrustful, and extremely sensitive to criticism. As his father, I stopped trying to coach him on anything related to skiing because his sensitivity made it counterproductive. Somehow, Ben negated these emotional scars and limitations, and they slowly built a bond. He gained Ryan's confidence and opened his mind. Ryan grew to appreciate that Ben's only goal was to make him better and improving meant admitting he was not perfect, placing himself in a vulnerable position that he had rebelled against his entire life. Being vulnerable was only possible with trust—a trust that I had assumed was forever damaged by doctors, teachers, restraints, hospital stays, and my poor parenting decisions.

As Ryan looked back toward the Little, replaying the run in his mind, he looked pensive. That might seem too small of a word for the situation, but it was *never* a word anyone used in describing him—even as an infant. Ryan always ran hot. As a child, he spent every waking moment moving, talking about moving, or thinking about moving. If the body naturally seeks homeostasis, Ryan's mind lived in a constant state of upheaval. Dr. Schneider had described it years before with a bisected oval on her yellow legal pad, signifying the imbalance in his brain. Yet, after conquering the Little, there was a contemplativeness in his expression that I had not witnessed in all my years of peering into his eyes, trying to decipher his feelings.

My deep thinking was interrupted by Ben lightly punching me in the shoulder and saying in his happiest voice, "We did it, buddy; we got the Little!" I smiled back, but he must have sensed that I was having mixed feelings because he quickly followed up with, "What should we do for our next run?"

It hadn't even registered to me that the Little was the first run of the three days I was planning to ski with Ben, so hearing him talk about our next run helped me refocus on the many other adventures still to come. So, I suggested the line I originally planned for that morning, "High Pocket 1" to "T.U." He agreed, and we split off again from Dad to head back up the tram. While High Pocket 1 and T.U. feature forty-five and fifty-degree slopes, everything looked flat after skiing the Little, so I charged these steep lines with a new sense of confidence.

After lunch, as we huddled, planning what to ski next, Ben smiled, turned to me, and said, "Now it's *your* turn."

I laughed, assuming he meant Little Couloir. "I'm not sure I'm ready for that one."

Ben shook his head and smiled. Then, lifting his goggles for emphasis, he pointed toward Little Couloir and said, "Not that one," before twisting his body slightly and pointing a few degrees to the left. "I mean that one."

He was now pointing directly at Big Couloir. "I won't tell you that you *should* do it, but I promise you *can* do it."

"You serious? You think I can ski that friggin' thing?"

He smiled broadly. "I know for a fact that you can ski that friggin' thing." He sounded funny when he said friggin'. Like he was trying to mock my Boston accent.

I took a deep breath. "Right now?"

"No, how about this: Let's spend the rest of the day training for it. I have a few runs in mind to build your confidence. Then, if you're good with it, we can sign up for the first run of the day tomorrow."

I nodded. "Sounds like a plan." In my head, however, my subconscious was already starting to work on ways to get out of skiing it—*stomach flu, emergency work call, pulling the fire alarm in the hotel?* Everything was on the table. I kept flashing back to the first time we traveled to Big Sky, when Ryan skied the Big on our first day. That afternoon in 2014, I skied a run with Ben and Ryan on the back side of Lone Peak so they could show me what the Big looked like from the top. They forced me on to a narrow traverse where all that stood between life and plummeting to my death was a plastic snow fence. I got so panicked that I refused to approach the edge to look down the entrance to the Big. Now, Ben was proposing that I not only peek down the entrance but launch myself directly into the fifty-degree mouth of the couloir.

While I remained quietly skeptical, Ben spent the afternoon taking me to runs with similar aspects to prove the Big was doable. We practiced on slopes with difficult couloir entrances and slopes with a similar steepness or narrowing features, and he even located a steep trail with a sharp bend to the left. By the end of the day, I had handled all the trial runs, so he looked to me for a verdict.

"Well, are you up for it?"

I exhaled slowly while looking back toward Big Couloir, and said, "Sure, what the fuck."

He smiled. "I've been waiting a long time to hear that."

I looked toward Ryan. He smiled and slowly nodded his head in approval but stood strangely quiet otherwise.

When I skied Big Couloir at twelve years old, Dad expressed no interest at all, which necessitated hiring Ben in the first place. Now, only a few years later, Dad had progressed to a point where it was within his ability level. Perhaps he was inspired watching us ski the Little or was just feeling confident in his own skiing ability, but, somehow, he agreed. Although Dad successfully executed the practice runs, I was nervous. The Big tends to have variable conditions, and during my several runs down it, I rarely skied it as well as I wanted to. The top is icy, and the upper and middle sections have weird pockets of powder that catch you by surprise. On low-visibility days, Ben and I have been tossed around, trying hard to keep our balance. Dad tends to get nervous in inconsistent conditions, and I worried he would overturn and generate a bad fall like he did in Hangman's Hollow at Mammoth.

The next morning, Ben set the plan in motion by having us ski an hour earlier than the resort opened in a special program called "First Tracks." Although a guide can only ski with one partner, Ben got ski patrol to allow the three of us to ski the Big together and we worked our way to the top of Lone Peak. Just as I feared, a cloud covered the mountain, and I worried the low visibility and flat light would make it really tough for Dad.

As we rode the tram, I wondered what it must've been like for him to watch me ski the Little. Most parents see their kids play in a championship game or on stage in plays and musicals. They experience stress hoping their children don't mess up and are powerless to help them. However, I tried to imagine what Dad must have felt watching me engage a life-or-death battle with a mountain, using nothing but metal edges to prevent tumbling down. That was next-level parental fear, and on the tram to Lone Peak, I got a glimpse of what it must've been like for him. Not only that, but I knew intimate details about what he was about to feel and experience. I had faith that he could make it through, especially with Ben to coach him, but still wondered if he had any idea what he was getting into. He seemed really quiet during the sign-out process and as we traversed around the backside of the mountain to the famous entrance. He groaned when he saw how steep it was but said he was willing to give it a shot.

Ben let me ski first, and I dropped into the clouds and picked my way down. Once again, it wasn't my proudest line due to the combination of icy sec-

tions with deep slough. As I waited at the halfway point, known as the Dogleg, a deep silence fell over the mountain, and I felt completely alone. I waited for any sign of Dad and after nothing happened for a while, I got worried.

Sure enough, I soon heard the usual grunts that he makes when something is difficult, and he emerged out of the clouds. He was alive, but not in the clear yet, and I remembered how he gets tunnel vision when he gets scared. I flashed back to a line called Spiny Chutes at Alta in Utah that we skied a few years prior. That day, I convinced him to try it, but as we neared the bottom, he had two sketchy options to avoid a rocky section, but he got so nervous that he skied straight toward the rocks. He ended up climbing down rather than skiing around it, and with Big Couloir's giant "Cheese Grater" rock staring him in the face, I hoped that wouldn't happen here.

Fortunately, he began to loosen up and even made a few solid turns on the upper section, and when he got to the Dogleg, he yelled out, "How do you like me now, muthafucka?"

At that moment, I knew he was in the clear, and he skied the next section even better, linking turns and looking more confident. At the bottom, Ben took a photo of us, and although Dad was breathing heavily, I knew he was feeling good. I was really happy for him.

—◆—

As I neared the bottom, I regretted skiing so defensively, but no matter. I had conquered Big Couloir. Despite the terrifying entrance, the lack of visibility navigating a brutally steep slope, the Cheese Grater, and the inconsistent snow conditions, I had skied top to bottom without incident. Even if I almost shit my pants as I stood waiting to drop in, like most tests in life, as it neared completion, the entire experience felt less formidable than I anticipated.

As I skidded to a finish, I was breathing heavily. Ryan skied over and tapped my pole and said, "Good job." He seemed proud of me, which felt a little strange, but I also sensed relief in his expression. At first, I assumed he was simply grateful that I survived. Yet, as we spoke about the run, I realized this was a different kind of relief. It reminded me of a million milestone moments I had experienced when Ryan or Abigail attempted something scary. In those instances, the accomplishment is eclipsed by the demonstration of courage itself, and Ryan was pleased that I finally challenged myself on a difficult slope.

Ben met us at the bottom and congratulated me with a hug. I raised my goggles to look him in the eyes. "You know what? You should be in the damn ski instructor Hall of Fame for leading me to this point. How do I get you nominated?"

He laughed and reminded me of something I said one night after a few beers in Portillo. "Remember when we were in Chile the first time? You promised to ski the Big by the time you were fifty."

"I did say that, but I think I was pretty hammered."

"Doesn't matter now. You did it, Rob."

Ryan was watching and listening. I turned my head to look at him. "Did you hear that? When I say I'm gonna do a thing, *I do* a thing!"

He shrugged his shoulders. "Took you long enough."

Before we skied off to seek our next run of the morning, I took one last look at the Big and flashed back to the moment nine years prior, when I stepped onto the magic carpet at Nashoba with Ryan wedged between my legs. I paused for an instant, shook my head, and whispered to the mountain, "Never saw this one coming."

CHAPTER TWENTY-FOUR

The JV Olympics

"Ryan appears to avoid taking risks in all areas due to his difficulty accepting less-than-perfect performance."
—INDIVIDUALIZED EDUCATION PROGRAM REPORT FOR RYAN
DELENA, SVTA (NOVEMBER 17, 2006)

April 15, 2018. We followed up with a trip to Alta/Snowbird during April school break—just before Ryan would begin the spring semester of his junior year. His perseverance in the cafeteria finally paid dividends, and he was invited into a group comprised mostly of girls who accepted him as a regular at their table. It sounds insignificant, but it made a big difference in his attitude toward the school. Between his lunch crew and the boys he met during Ski Club, Ryan grew more comfortable at LS and reacted positively when I suggested signing up for spring track as a pole-vaulter. Although he had never seen a pole-vaulter in person, he was unafraid of heights and possessed killer core strength. When he was younger, he spent hours training for parkour, negotiating physical obstacles by climbing and jumping, and learned to backflip from a standing position. Whether that background translated into a champion pole-vaulter or not, I hoped team membership might lead to stickier friendships carrying over outside of school.

That spring, I started JV pole vault at LS. It was my first time doing a traditional sport and competing against other teams. Of all the track events, pole vault seemed like the best option for me. Obviously, flying through the air every day after school sounded cool, so why not give it a try?

While I liked learning to pole vault, I enjoyed the company of the team more. It was interesting to see how people acted outside of school. They seemed happier and more social. Overall, it was fun being on a team, and I felt more connected with my teammates than anyone I previously met in school.

As Ryan exited the team bus for his first track meet, he looked nervous. It struck me as odd, since he risked his life in the mountains without flinching, but I understood why. For him, skiing was judgment-free and lacked a scoreboard to determine a winner and loser. He drove himself to be the best skier on the mountain, and aside from a few snarky comments on his videos, his mountain peers refrained from passing judgment on him. Even when a ski day wasn't perfect, a poor performance didn't cost his team victory. That wasn't the case with track, especially vaulting. The results are binary, and with a crowd of classmates gathered around as witnesses, Ryan either cleared the bar or smashed into it.

As I sat in the bleachers awaiting his first attempt, I was more nervous than watching him enter Little Couloir. When he cleared the bar and landed on the mat, he pumped his fist and yelled, "Yeah!" I tried to remain still, holding my phone steady to video his attempt, but replaying it, heard myself excitedly whisper, "Yes," as he sailed over the bar.

Ryan gained confidence from his successful first attempt and cleared his next two vaults before missing three straight times at eight and a half feet. After the meet, he seemed pleased. He even indulged me long enough to take his picture, and as the bus pulled away, I sat in my car and stared at the image. Not only was Ryan smiling, but he was also wearing a track uniform with LS emblazoned on his chest. As a child, he could not even play a board game without erupting if the game did not go well in the first few moves. Now, he was vaulting in front of his schoolmates with every failure resulting in a long walk back to the team. He was just another kid doing his best at a JV track meet, but assessing how far he had come, it felt like the Olympics to me.

As I drove home from the track meet, I pondered the life I expected and the life I got. Perhaps it was seeing Ryan in an LS uniform, but I found myself wondering—what if he was a regular kid? I imagined biting my nails when he walked to the plate in Little League before excelling and moving on to all-star teams, travel teams, and elite club teams. I visualized coaching him and pushing him to take private hitting lessons and finding trainers to work on his speed and agility. I envisioned his name in the paper and the buzz around town about his performance in tournaments and the efforts to recruit him.

Then I stopped myself. Was that better than spending every weekend skiing? Was it better than exploring the country and the world together? Was it better than the quiet moments we shared on top of Lone Peak at Big Sky or the incredible valley in the Andes behind Portillo? Would my life have been better sitting for hours at some dusty field hoping Ryan got a base hit? And, most importantly, would his life have been better?

Not a chance in hell.

As the spring wore on, Ryan's attendance at LS felt routine. He managed his schoolwork with occasional drama but mostly without issue. He seemed to be gaining notoriety, and I felt good seeing other boys gravitate toward him at track meets. There remained one aspect to school, however, where Ryan was failing to make progress. Although a welcoming lunch table and supportive track teammates improved life at LS, no matter how hard he tried, he could not find a girlfriend. Despite good looks and willingness to engage most anyone in conversation, no social connection resulted in anything more than friendship. I was certain that being the new guy set him back initially but wondered if dating is where the EXCEL label hurt him most. It is one thing to befriend a fellow student like Ryan with a checkered past, but quite another to have a relationship with him. And, with prom looming, time was running out.

Ryan's attempts at romance followed a similar pattern. A girl in or around the periphery of his friend group would appear interested. He then built up enough courage over a period of weeks to ask her out only to find out that a boyfriend was already in the picture. One girl even agreed to a date and Ryan was flying high for twenty-four hours, only to have her back out claiming she was getting back together with her ex-boyfriend. To Ryan, having her renege was worse than if she'd just said no originally. Although I encouraged him to focus on the fact that she said yes in the first place, his angst resurfaced, and he fixated on why she suddenly bailed. Had she learned about his past? Had someone told her to stay away? I tried explaining the complexity of a high school relationship and how her ex-boyfriend likely redoubled his efforts to keep her after hearing she was readying to date someone else. Unfortunately, my reasoned scenario was of little comfort to a boy who feels emotional pain more acutely than anyone I know.

By the middle of May, students were fixated on the prom. While he struggled to find a date, "promposals" echoed in the hallways and covered the cafeteria floor in glitter. Ryan asked two different girls only to learn each previously accepted an invitation from someone else. For Ryan, failing to land a prom date confirmed that other students at LS saw him as deeply flawed, and he told me it was time to accept his fate of "living alone in the woods."

I told my parents that no matter what I had done on skis, I didn't deserve to be called brave. When it came to asking a girl to prom, I procrastinated to avoid confronting my fear of having a girl say no, so I ended up missing my chance with both potential dates. My parents said I was too hard on myself since I hardly knew any girls at LS. I probably was, but it still hurt.

Since his release from Cambridge Hospital, I assumed Ryan would always need me to balance the difficulty he encountered in most aspects of his life by constantly traveling places to ski. Nine years after we started skiing, however, he was in a vastly different place. He was medication-free, and we were having initial conversations about college. He was working toward becoming a professional ski guide and I could easily envision a life for him in Big Sky or Tahoe leading backcountry expeditions. His life would include but did not require my presence or participation. He proved everyone wrong, including me, and his future was right there in front of him. Yet, he was allowing himself to be shattered by seventeen-year-old girls. It was so frustrating to see his incredible progress jeopardized by a fucking prom.

I ended up going to the prom with my friend Ava from Stonebrook. I told her one day how sad I was about not having a date, and she agreed that if I couldn't find anyone, she would go with me. But when she came over the night of the prom, I was as tense as a human can be. Honestly, I didn't want to go at all, since this wasn't even a real prom date. We took some photos in the backyard and then got in the Uber my parents ordered for us.

When we walked in, we ended up completely switching attitudes. I'm very natural in party scenes and quickly became the center of attention dancing (without Ava) on the dance floor. I actually had more fun than I thought I would. I then tried walking around with Ava, introducing her to people so she would be more at ease. With each introduction, she seemed to get more uncomfortable. Ava is one of the most badass people I know, so seeing her scared of anything was unusual. After talking to her, she revealed to me she felt insecure around all the "rich girls in fancy dresses." I tried talking to her, but she was still upset.

Ava managed to relax as the night wore on, but I never felt right about the whole night. Prom is supposed to be special because you are with someone you like more than as a friend, or because you are having a big party with all your friends. That night, I had neither.

CHAPTER TWENTY-FIVE

The Super-C Couloir

"After climbing a great hill, one only finds that there are more hills to climb."

—NELSON MANDELA

August 6, 2018. Summer was a chance to reconnect with Abigail—who was home from her first year of boarding school—and coaching her travel softball team resulted in many hours together. Ryan, on the other hand, was away for much of the summer, attending separate overnight camps that climbed each of the highest peaks in seven northeast states and paddled kayaks across Lake Champlain. He returned with many stories to share, and his fellow campers provided a much-needed boost after a stressful year at LS.

During the summer, I attended Camp Wildwood again, this time to climb the New England "high points" and adding Mount Marcy in New York. The camp was led by two of my favorite trip leaders from last summer. Our male leader was Matt, a fun-loving guy with an infectious passion for the mountains. I related to him a lot, and we had lengthy conversations about our love of the outdoors. Megan was our female leader. She was quieter and more reserved, but a few conversations with her in camp revealed an inner badass. She had completed the Appalachian Trail and the Pacific Crest Trail, hiked most of the U.S. high points, and served in the military. As for the teens on the trip, all eight of us had different personalities, held different views, and had very different tastes in music. Somehow, it didn't seem to matter, as we became a team. Even better, we became friends.

The first peak that we climbed as a team wasn't really a peak. It was more of a casual stroll to the high point of Rhode Island, Jerimoth Hill. The next peak, Mount Frissel in Connecticut, was more legitimate but mostly because we suffered through 100-degree heat. The third, Mount Mansfield in Vermont, was pretty easy since a large percentage of the peak is serviced by ski trails. The fourth, however, Mount Greylock, the Massachusetts high point, was a different story. The trail out of the Hopper Ravine was steep and brought out our hiking styles. I tend to grind it out and crush peaks without breaks. A camper named William tried to keep up with me even if it meant not breathing. Everyone else preferred taking breaks. Our team's struggle over pacing made an otherwise easy peak a brutal slog, and several people wanted to quit the camp after Mount Greylock with our two main objectives still to go.

Since we almost failed to summit the nine-mile climb up Greylock, the impending challenge of the fifteen-mile Mount Marcy did not lead to much optimism. The day before Mount Marcy, heavy thunderstorms were in the forecast. I was scheduled to be "leader of the day" for Marcy, so Matt and Megan pulled me aside for the hard truths. Megan showed me the route, explaining what sections were easy and what were tough. She said we would be getting a late start because of the weather and needed to keep a steady pace, so I had to keep the rest of the team motivated. On her way out of my tent, she left me with a few words of encouragement: "If there's anyone who can do it, it's you."

However, as I found out later, everyone else in camp had their own meeting about staging a revolt. No one wanted to do Marcy, especially with me as the leader because "Ryan goes hardcore."

After the dueling meetings, there was almost a camper strike, but Matt talked everyone off the ledge. I then presented the game plan for the next day and went to bed unsure how my team would react in the morning. Although I managed to fall asleep, during the night, I woke up twice. Once from a massive thunder crack, and once when Megan shook the tent to wake us at four-thirty a.m. The storm had moved out early, and she wanted to take advantage of it. I woke everyone else up to get moving, and we ended up crushing the first two miles in a half hour.

After we passed the Marcy Dam, it began to rain on us. Our shoes got soaked, and so did our packs. The trail became an absolute river, but we kept going until we entered the alpine zone. The summit was socked in by the storm, bringing strong, steady winds, yet I motivated the team to reach the summit before we stopped to eat. After lunch, the clouds cleared, providing an incredible view of the Adirondack Range. I felt so lucky to be there and was thankful nature rewarded us for our hardship. It was a powerful moment.

Later that week, after climbing Mount Washington, we stopped at the summit to share stories that shaped our lives. There were many tears, with all of us shocked by the things each person endured. It was only the second time I told my story to anyone other than a therapist or family member. Despite revealing my experience at Cambridge Hospital and the therapeutic schools, I felt welcomed and accepted for who I was—not just the part of me that was easy to understand, but even the parts that were hard for the others to process. That experience brought us all closer and made us a great team for our final challenge, Mount Katahdin.

For that final climb, we spent hours scrambling up loose rock and exposed ridges to the summit of Katahdin. It was a long and difficult ascent, but not one camper complained. We had grown closer over the week and spent the day supporting each other, finding a pace that worked for everyone. I was proud to play a part in driving the group and, when we got close to the summit, I stepped back, allowing a camper named Mikey to lead the final steps to the cairn because his group was turned back on this peak the year before when the weather changed suddenly. We then joined around the rocky point, awed by the 2,000-foot drop to Chimney Pond.

August meant another trip to Portillo with NASTC. We were pleased to hear Ben made the guide team and to see a few familiar faces on the client roster. Ryan was particularly happy to see Ben's name because it provided a realistic shot at hiking and skiing the Super-C Couloir. And as we sat in Logan Airport awaiting takeoff, his optimism soared when he located a recent video of famed extreme skier Chris Davenport in the Super-C.

Upon arrival, we were happy to reconnect with friends from prior years, and there was a new family in camp with a daughter named Ashley. Ashley seemed easygoing, having just finished her freshman year at Tulane University, and Ryan was instantly taken with her. He said Ashley was "hot," but to me she seemed more mature in every possible way. She attended a notorious party school, while Ryan was still in high school with a mouthful of braces with a boyish face and showed no interest in alcohol or vaping.

Most nights in Portillo, guests congregate in the lounge after dinner, where partiers jam into a small dance floor wedged between barstools and tables. On our second night of the trip, I was pleasantly surprised when Ashley agreed to dance with Ryan, but when she returned to our table alone, my heart sank. I asked her what happened to Ryan, and she replied, "He's dancing on a table with Sierra." When I stood up to see what the hell she was talking about, he was indeed dancing on a table next to a tall, striking blond woman. After questioning others in the bar, I learned that Sierra is an ex-racer turned influencer and fashion model. Needless to say, Ryan received his share of approving handshakes when he returned to our table, even though he let Ashley slip away.

The next day, following his table dance with Sierra, Ryan was the star of Portillo. One woman, a documentary filmmaker for ESPN, even stopped us in the hallway to ask Ryan, "Who are you?"

He replied, matter-of-factly, "Ryan from Sudbury."

"Okay but are you somebody important?" she asked emphatically.

"No," he confirmed, "just Ryan from Sudbury." I suppose he should have dropped, "Extreme Ryan from Sudbury," but even his nickname wouldn't have registered unless she was one of his religious followers on Instagram.

———

For our return to Portillo, I trained in the mornings with NASTC and explored more complex terrain in the afternoons free skiing with a kid named Thomas, who I met the year before. On our first day, we decided to do a short hike to a narrow couloir called La Chimney. We broke trail to the top and dropped into a wild couloir, which was barely a ski length across at the top. The next day, we decided to attempt a more complex line, Candelabra Couloir. This involved a steep trail break across a big rock garden, a tricky traverse, and a 3,000-foot ski with a mandatory ice bulge jump. I offered to do the brunt of the work, exhausting myself in the waist-deep snow, and at the top I made ski cuts and jumped on the slope a few times to ensure there was no danger of an avalanche.

Later that day, Thomas asked about the possibility of skiing the Super-C—the crown jewel of all Chilean couloirs. At nearly 5,000 feet long, and with a maximum pitch of fifty degrees, it's a world-class line. However, the Super-C isn't without its challenges. It requires a three-hour ascent, topping out at just above 13,000 feet. The hike also involves a traverse above a massive cliff, and a fall on the crux of that hike can be deadly. Not only was I putting together my own crew for this line, but it was my third attempt at finding the right skiers and the right conditions to conquer it. The year before, I decided not to ski it because the snow was too deep to boot up, and at that point, I wasn't comfortable skinning it. I made the right call, but I missed some all-time conditions. I told Thomas he was welcome to join if everyone else on my team was okay with it.

In camp, I was assigned once again to Chris Fellows's group, and Ryan skied in Ben's group. I was alone on a chairlift with Chris on Tuesday when he leaned over to say he could not let Ben attempt the Super-C with Ryan because if something were to happen during camp, he was liable. For emphasis, he removed his ski goggles, fixed his blue eyes on me, and stated, "You know, there is a part of that hike where you need to tiptoe across the crux of a cliff and if you fall, you die?"

Just before dinner, I informed Ryan of the disappointing news about Ben. He was upset but held out hope that he could find someone else to attempt the Super-C. At the Hotel Portillo, meals are served at set times and most guests assemble an hour before dinner in a room resembling a giant living room. I was chatting with a fellow skier when Ryan interrupted and excitedly blurted out that he was hiking the Super-C tomorrow with Thomas, a boy he had skied with during the week. I inquired whether Thomas was the best pick for a partner since he had never skied the

Super-C either, but Ryan reminded me that Thomas was part of a legendary family in Portillo. His grandfather is the hotel doctor, and his uncle is one of the heli-skiing guides, so Ryan emphasized that any team assembled by Thomas would also include experienced mountaineers.

⌐∼

Everyone else who was part of NASTC camp and contemplated joining my team for the Super-C bailed shortly after learning Ben was out. I was losing hope that I could find capable partners when I got a text from Thomas telling me he was putting together his own team for the Super-C, and he invited me to join them. In our text exchange, I asked him extensive questions about the ability level and experience of his partners, and despite not knowing them, I felt comfortable based on this information.

The next morning, we all met at the bottom. The team included a man named Sean and his daughter Kestrel. Thomas told me that Sean had spent time as a mountain guide in Denali, and Kestrel was an Olympic hopeful as a skier, so that provided a jolt of confidence. Even if our group was young and, aside from Sean, lacked climbing experience, the skiing aspect to the Super-C was clearly not going to be an issue. We just needed to get across the crux, and I felt sure Sean would help us navigate that piece.

After exchanging the usual introductory conversation, we got down to business. We booted up for ninety minutes before eventually reaching the top of the easy section. We transitioned into crampons, and I led the steps to the traverse. As I looked over the ridge, I saw a steep rock wall with some old steps prior hikers had kicked in the snow. The gully below quickly became 1,500 feet of vertical rock and ice. The traverse wasn't overly technical, but even the slightest misstep was potentially tragic. After a brief discussion, I decided to continue leading across the crux and with some strategic handholds on the jagged rock, I got across without a problem. Everyone else followed behind me and made it to the other side without issue. We then made quick work of the upper couloir and crested the ridge.

We walked out to the impressive rock feature that overlooked Portillo and the remaining Andes Mountains. Aconcagua towered above all, its summit shrouded in lenticular clouds. We gnawed on some frozen chocolate and then began the descent. The first turns were steep and icy, but, once through the choke, we were in terrain that is shaded on both sides by a dramatic rock wall pre-serving the snow. We ripped soft chalky snow all the way to the apron below. I was ecstatic. This was the coolest thing I'd ever skied—it felt never-ending.

After our incredible adventure, we ate a huge meal at Tío Bob's. At the restaurant, I talked with Chris Davenport about the experience. He said the Super-C is one of his top five favorites. While I may never be on his level, having successfully skied something he respects so much made me feel a step closer that day.

By Wednesday evening, the Super-C was in the books and Ryan's repu-tation in Portillo grew exponentially. He had danced with a model, hiked, and skied one of the world's signature runs, and we still had two more days of camp left to enjoy. The only guy left out of the party was Ben. It killed him to hear Ryan chronicling the experience with every known skiing superlative and, although he appreciated Chris's position as the owner of NASTC, I hoped he would one day have the chance to ski the Super-C with Ryan.

On Friday night just before dinner, Chris approached me with a piece of paper. He explained, since the camp was now officially over, he was willing to allow Ben to accompany Ryan up the Super-C before our bus departed for the airport if I signed a waiver releasing NASTC of any liability. I agreed, of course, and Ben looked absolutely thrilled. While he and Ryan excitedly discussed their itinerary for the morning, I reflected on the picture Ben took of Ryan leading him across the ridgeline at Big Sky when he was twelve years old. Five years later, Ryan planned to lead Ben across a tricky section of cliffs on a mountain in the Andes that I couldn't have located on a map back in 2014. Much had happened since that first trip to Big Sky. Ryan moved back to public school, weaned off medication, and had grown up in so many ways. Still, as the evening would demonstrate, he continued to wrestle with his share of emotional demons.

On our last day of NASTC camp, Ben informed me that on Saturday, once camp ended, he was allowed to hike the Super-C with me. I felt bad earlier in the week when he missed his chance, and I was stoked to take my skiing mentor on the best run of his life.

After skiing the Super-C, I'll admit that I walked around Portillo like I was the king of the ski world. Maybe I got a little too full of myself because, on our last night, I decided to try to make a move with Ashley. I thought she was pretty, but honestly, I wasn't sure I liked her all that much. On the other hand, all the guys on the NASTC trip were putting pressure on me to try and hook up with her. Even if it was just lighthearted guy stuff, I still felt like I had to give it a shot to save face.

So, once the bar cleared out at midnight, I invited her to the "disco" downstairs. There, we walked into a total mob scene, and when I tried dancing with her, she got sidetracked by some random dude with long hair trying to get her Snapchat. After dancing alone and trying to have fun for a while, I walked out with my head low. When I got back to my hotel room, Dad told me I gave up too easily. So, I walked back down to the disco only to find her dancing with a tall older guy. In that moment, I realized maybe I liked her more than just a little, and I walked out again, this time feeling twice as bad as before. I went back to my room and sat there feeling like shit. Dad tried to give me a late-night pep talk but in the middle of his usual "the future will be great" speech, I noticed that the clock read two-thirty a.m. "Holy crap, I've got to take Ben up the Super-C tomorrow." So, I went to bed and tried to forget the feelings of insecurity.

After the shortest night of sleep of my life, I met Ben. Overnight, we'd received an inch of snow at the base, and we weren't sure what we would find at higher altitude. As we began the hike up, with each step, the snow deepened, but we decided we could mitigate the avalanche hazard by hiking in a zigzag pattern. When we finally arrived at the crux, I noticed that our steps from Wednesday were buried by fresh snow, making it even trickier. I offered to go first since I had crossed it previously, and I replaced the old steps from Wednesday for Ben to use as a guide. Once I got across, Ben took a breath and slowly tiptoed over the crux while gripping the rock ledge for dear life. In that moment, he seemed so human, and it was weird because I'd never seen him scared before.

When we finally reached the ridge, we noted at least six inches of new snow in the entrance to the couloir. It was amazing how different things looked from Wednesday. All the volcanic rock that lined Super-C was covered in snow, and the run looked like a 5,000-foot tunnel into a glacier. Ben made several snow cuts, skiing across the slope as quickly as possible to trigger as much of the dry slough as he could to ensure there was no avalanche danger. Finally, after confirming the stability of the slope, we dropped in, and once around the corner, it was clear the slough ran for most of the run.

Ben let me ski first, and even in my first few turns before I maximized my speed, every pivot resulted in a face full of powder. Although the snow smacking my goggles caused a complete whiteout in a rhythmic sequence, it made the run even more epic. I had to trust the feel of each turn. The weightlessness experienced in soft powder was enhanced by relying less on my eyes, and for a few moments, I was completely connected to Super-C. I was forced to put my faith in the continuity of the slope, the consistency of the snow, and my ability to navigate it. Suddenly, all the noise in my head from the night before was quieted. I was floating, and the only sound was the slosh of snow smacking my face every few seconds.

On the lift back to the main resort, we both stared off into space for a minute, wondering, did that really just happen? *Ben suddenly broke the silence, shaking me back and forth saying, "Thank you! Thank you!" He then took a long breath, looked over at me, and said, "Fuck yeah!" We both agreed it was the best run either of us had ever skied.*

As I quickly showered and dressed for the long trip home, I experienced a crazy mix of emotions because I had moved from the most embarrassing night of my life to the best day ever in a matter of hours. I'll admit that when my alarm went off that morning, part of me wanted to just lie in bed and sulk, but I couldn't let Ben down. I think the lesson is not to let things get you too down and always keep moving, no matter how bad things may seem. If you give up, you might just miss the best day of your life.

Chapter Twenty-Six

People Ski in Antarctica?

"No one asks how to motivate a baby. A baby naturally explores everything it can get at unless restraining forces have already been at work. And this tendency doesn't die out, it's wiped out."

—Ernest Shackleton

September 4, 2018. *My return to LS in September was interesting. At the start of the term, I connected with everyone from the year before and tried making new friends as well. One afternoon in early October, I managed to get some amusing publicity at a school assembly, when I volunteered to rap Eminem's "Lose Yourself" on stage. I hadn't planned or prepared for this opportunity, but a guest speaker was calling random people on stage to guess songs after hearing the first few lines. One of them was "Lose Yourself." He then asked if anyone knew all the words to the song. So, I raised my hand, and he brought me up and handed me the microphone. I crushed the first half of the song before he cut the music and asked me to stop. I think he was shocked that I actually knew the words and wasn't prepared to have a successful singer while attempting to make his point about teenagers learning to handle failure.*

After my performance, more people in the hallways knew who I was, and I felt like a part of LS for the first time. Perhaps I got a bit overconfident because I decided to ask out Grace, a super popular girl whom I definitely had no chance with. I'd known her from the year before, but we didn't talk regularly until after the summer. During those conversations, I realized that I liked her, so

I asked her out after a football game. To my surprise, she agreed, and I spent the following day planning ideas for our date. Then I noticed my text to her from the night before never got answered and knew that was a bad sign. Sure enough, a day later she told me she couldn't go out with me because she had a boyfriend in college.

In late September, I received an intriguing text from Ben. "Have you and Ryan considered ski touring in Antarctica?"

What? I read the text again. Maybe he was talking into his phone, and it autocorrected? How the fuck do we get to Antarctica? Military plane? Japanese whaling vessel?

"People ski in Antarctica?" I replied respectfully, trying to be diplomatic and refraining from asking if he bumped his head recently.

He answered quickly. "They do! I skied last winter with the owner of the company. Take a look at the website. It is called Ice Axe Expeditions. He just emailed me and said they have a few spots left for this year."

"Okay, I'll look tonight." However, when I put my phone back in my pocket, I laughed out loud, picturing a team of sled dogs pulling skiers across a barren stretch of ice, engulfed by a swirling blizzard.

That night, I mentioned Ben's suggestion to Mary Beth, assuming she would laugh, too. She did, at first, before googling Ice Axe Expeditions to see pictures of the company's Antarctica trip from 2017. After a minute or two, she said, "This looks amazing," and spun her laptop around for me to look. There, I was shocked to see skiers in bright sunshine headed toward a cobalt blue sea with massive icebergs floating in the distance, while hundreds of penguins huddled near the shoreline. None of the photos included sled dogs or blizzard conditions.

Over the next week, images of Antarctica occupied my consciousness. Each day, I scrolled through the Ice Axe website, unable to focus on anything else, before I finally built up enough courage to email the company to inquire whether the trip was still available. Kurt Williams, the director, emailed right back to say that a few spots remained. I then replied with several questions, admitting that I was neither an expert backcountry skier nor an Olympic athlete while also alerting him that my travel companion was my seventeen-year-old son—slightly hoping Kurt would find sufficient reason to exclude us. To my surprise, he responded enthusiastically and promised that we would not be out of place at all.

After receiving Kurt's email, it was decision time. To go, Ryan would need to miss two weeks of school, and the financial cost of the trip required some level of justification. Although November marked my fiftieth birthday, my true motivation was rooted in Ryan's journey. After emerging from the dark days at Cambridge Hospital to a point where college was now a realistic option, I wanted to reward him for never quitting. Perhaps, deep down, I also hoped traveling to the bottom of the earth for a skiing expedition made up for my parenting missteps that caused him to distrust adults, fear for his own safety, and denied him years of enrichment in school.

The next day, after securing our spots on the ship, I let Ben know, and he pushed to get selected as a guide. Unfortunately, the guide roster was full, and reality set in that we were now traveling without the one person who would ensure our safety. Antarctica wasn't just an unfathomable destination; it was true mountaineering. There were no ski lifts, snowcats, or helicopters, which meant hiking up mountains each day before skiing back down. Nervously, I suspected that everyone on the trip would be a supreme athlete and a great skier, and after my disastrous performance skinning during the Avi-1 course, I feared embarrassing myself—and Ryan.

While I spent the early fall processing the trip, Ryan embarked on an exploratory journey of his own. He joined the rest of his senior classmates in navigating the college application process. Previously, he debated skipping college altogether to instead pursue the requisite ski guide certifications through the Professional Ski Instructor's Association (PSIA) and the American Mountain Guides Association (AMGA). However, after his academically successful junior year, we convinced him college was an important step in his overall maturity, and he agreed to visit two New England schools featuring degree programs in Outdoor Education and Adventure Education: Plymouth State University in Plymouth, New Hampshire, and Northern Vermont University in Johnson, Vermont. Both programs combined traditional academic courses with applicable field training and promoted active learning to better prepare students seeking careers in nature.

Dad and I drove up to New Hampshire for a college fair at Plymouth State. In the gym, each degree program had a table, and we waited our turn to talk to the director of the Outdoor Education program. I was a little nervous and Dad seemed nervous, too. He kept reminding me to do things that I already knew, like make good eye contact and have a firm handshake. When it was finally our turn, we talked to the director for a few minutes. He was nice and seemed to like the program, but when I told him my goal was to be a ski guide, he said the program did not have much of a skiing component or private guiding aspect.

After the fair, Dad and I went to lunch. We talked about the program, and it seemed like he was trying to talk me into how it could still work for me. Eventually, he just sighed and said, "Hopefully, NVU is a better fit." I was glad that he felt that way, because, after listening to the director's description of the program, there was no way I was going to Plymouth State.

The next weekend, we drove to Johnson, Vermont. The NVU campus was smaller and prettier than Plymouth State. It seemed easier to navigate, and I liked seeing mountains on all sides. It felt peaceful. After a long introduction to the school in the auditorium, we went to the gym and met the director of the Adventure Education program. I didn't waste time before informing her of my career goals, and she excitedly responded how well it fit with NVU's program. Unlike Plymouth State, she said that students from the program are in great demand by local ski resorts and previous graduates used the program to pursue the requisite AMGA certifications needed to become professional mountain guides.

I was really happy with her description, and Dad seemed happy, too. We spent a few minutes walking around campus and even ran into someone I knew from Sudbury named Isaac, who was pursuing a similar path to me but in rock climbing. Isaac said that he loved the program and felt it was perfect for me. That clinched it. I was headed to NVU, even if I was still worried whether I could manage it. To be honest, I wasn't sure I believed Dad—who was convinced college would be fun and much different from the cliques and social pecking order that was such an important part to LS.

On the ride home, I was elated to hear the excitement in Ryan's voice as he talked about the visit to NVU. We were happily engaged in our conversation when a car next to me lost control in the snow and crashed into us. Luckily, we were unhurt, but ordinarily the prospect of dealing with my insurance company and repairing the car would have enraged me. Yet, I reminded myself that Ryan was *going to college*—not even a car accident could wipe the smile off my face.

Throughout the college process, I focused on the programs and not the pedigree of the school. Ryan scored nearly 1200 on the SAT without ever attempting a single practice question and his GPA was near the A- range. He could have applied to bigger-named schools, but none of that mattered. I stopped caring about the college sticker on my rear windshield long ago. At NVU, Ryan found the right program to achieve his goal of bringing groups of skiers, hikers, and climbers into nature to properly demonstrate risky outdoor activities.

I found that so ironic. As a child, Ryan was told time and time again that he was unable to care for himself, which necessitated placement in situations with adults constraining his every move. Yet, NVU provided an opportunity to advance in a career supervising paying clients, relying on *his* judgment to safely explore the world, while pushing their own physical and emotional limitations.

Chapter Twenty-Seven

Fatal Accident

"If you're a leader, a fellow that other fellows look to, you've got to keep going."
—Ernest Shackleton

October 1, 2018. When a list of required gear arrived in an email from Ice Axe, I wondered whether it was time for a crash course in speaking "Antarctic" because most of the items were a complete mystery. Additionally, Ice Axe mandated the purchase of "evacuation insurance," a supplemental insurance policy for rescue situations that defrayed the cost of returning an injured or lifeless body to America.

Nevertheless, on October 31, we boarded a plane bound for Atlanta, beginning our journey to the bottom of the earth. Prior to departure, a quick glance at my travel companion told me he was wrestling with something that had nothing to do with a desolate continent filled with crevasses. A few hours earlier, Ryan had dressed as a skier for Senior Costume Day, enduring an unusually warm late October day in snow pants and a helmet, while other classmates orchestrated group or themed costumes. Once again, he felt like an outsider at LS. I advised him to leave school behind for the next couple of weeks and focus on our journey.

We flew overnight, and after changing airports in Buenos Aires, we boarded another three-hour flight to Ushuaia, where we would remain for the next thirty-six hours before our ship departed for Antarctica. Aside from one of us dying, my most pressing concern was lost luggage, because each bag contained key pieces of equipment. So, when I spotted our last bag on the conveyor belt, I felt exhilarated. That feeling, however, quickly dissipated when one of the other clients at the baggage carousel leaned in and whispered, "Did you see the memo about the guy who was *killed?*"

Unsure if I heard him correctly, I stammered, "Killed? Killed how?" He nodded and replied simply, "Skiing."

After dropping my bags to the floor, I frantically searched my phone, and he was right. There was a memo from Doug Stoup, the owner of Ice Axe, detailing how a guest scheduled to travel to Antarctica was killed earlier in the day skiing in Ushuaia. The letter did not provide details but stated clearly that the incident occurred while the guest was skiing recreationally before the trip technically started and concluded by calling his death a "fatal accident."

Ryan and I stumbled outside to load the courtesy bus, along with the rest of the bleary-eyed clients from our flight. In the parking lot, Ryan snapped pictures of Ushuaia while I debated how and when to broach the subject of the skiing casualty. Word spread quickly on the ride to the hotel, but conversations were respectfully muted as phones were handed back and forth, displaying the memo. Ryan seemed unaware of the dialogue happening around him, and I waited until we were alone in our room to inform him. Unsure of what to say, I read the memo verbatim, and after digesting the news, he seemed unaffected.

"So that happened today?" Ryan looked more surprised than frightened.

"Yeah. Sounds like there was a small group out skiing for fun, and he just fell." Then I felt obligated to ask a fatherly question. "Does that worry you at all?"

His face was relaxed and devoid of the slightest hint of apprehension. "Not at all. That sounds totally different than what we'll be doing. We have guides to lead us, and these guys are super dialed in."

Ryan studied his phone to catch up on the many hours where we lacked service. He paused a minute or two later to interrupt me as I unpacked clean clothes for dinner. "Dad, are you worried?"

I smiled and nodded. "Buddy, I haven't stopped worrying since the day you were born, but I know you can handle this. Me, on the other hand . . . Well, just promise to bury me someplace nice. Maybe near some penguins to keep me company."

He snorted, shook his head, and went back to his phone.

Later, we assembled in the lobby to meet our assigned guide for the trip, whom I assumed would provide additional information about the accident. While other clients and guides struggled to match name tags, Andrew Eisenstark quickly identified the only father-and-son duo in the mix, greeting Ryan and me with businesslike handshakes. He looked younger than his forty years with longish hair tucked behind his ears and an easygoing demeanor that oozed *It's all good, bro.*

After inquiring about our trip down, Andrew mentioned he was guiding for the ninth time in Antarctica. In response, I tilted my head away from Ryan, leaned toward Andrew, and whispered, "Did any of the other trips have tough days like today?" He shook his head and tapped Ryan's shoulder to bring him into the conversation before explaining the unique circumstances surrounding the skiing casualty. In his words, the guest, a fifty-six-year-old doctor from Colorado "lost his balance while climbing up a glacier, fell, and slid headfirst down the mountain on his back, hitting the only rock on the trail." He confirmed that "it was a million to one shot," and he was killed instantly.

Andrew further explained that on the trip we would be roped together when we climbed, so I need not worry about falling. In rebuttal, I looked at him and asked, "Should I be worried about the forty-seven other ways I can die?"

His head snapped back a tiny bit. Although surprised that a guest on a trip designed for adrenaline junkies expressed fear so openly, he smiled and tucked his hair behind his ears. "Robert, I promise I'll get you home in one piece."

We next moved into the hotel restaurant for our welcome dinner. There, I was struck by the age of the other clients, since most were clearly older than me. Given the cost of the trip, I was certain most accomplished great things professionally but wondered if there was something unanswered in their lives that necessitated this type of experience. My motivation, on the other hand, was less textured. I simply wanted to reward Ryan for all he overcame, never considering for one minute that I was searching for something, too.

━━◆━━

That night during dinner, Doug, the owner of Ice Axe, made a toast in honor of the guest that was killed. After that, we never spoke about him again, and conversations during dinner seemed to touch on just about any other subject, except for the man who died on a glacier we were about to ski.

That night, Dad asked me if I was worried that we might get killed on the trip. I said I didn't think so, but that probably didn't help his anxiety level. I knew deep down, after his inability to handle a short hike on relatively flat terrain during our Avi-1 Course, he probably wasn't optimistic about his ability to perform at a level required by this expedition. Now, he was scared he wouldn't survive it. Or worse, that something might happen to me.

━━◆━━

On our way out of dinner, Ryan noticed a girl approximately his age standing near the dessert table. In our planning discussions, we assumed he would be the only teenager on the trip, so we immediately stopped to introduce ourselves. There we met Lindsay, who was headed to Harvard University in the fall and traveling with her mom, Sibylla, who bore a striking resemblance to Bo Derek. After introductions, Sibylla and I quickly bonded over our fears about the trip, while Ryan and Lindsay discussed their apprehension about heading to college. Lindsay was remarkably casual about attending Harvard and never flinched when Ryan told her about his plan to attend NVU to become a ski guide. She seemed genuinely excited to meet Ryan, and I wasn't sure if I was happy or sad that she was so adorable. I had enough to worry about, including staying alive, and needed Ryan to remain focused to help me do so.

━━◆━━

On our first morning in Ushuaia, we woke up to chaos. People were rifling through their bags for gear checks, and it looked like an REI store exploded in the hotel lobby. We found Andrew, and then arranged our travel to the glacier for a practice day. After a quick breakfast, we left the city and headed for the moun-tains. With only one day of skiing under my belt this season, the southern end of Patagonia was certainly a step up from my October laps at Killington in Vermont.

———

The plan was to practice skinning and other mountaineering skills on the nearby Martial Glacier. Our group included me, Ryan, Andrew, and a woman named Erin. I did not remember meeting Erin at dinner but was told she was a thirty-six-year-old doctor from Colorado with plenty of backcountry experience. Kurt, the Ice Axe director, provided her back-story to assure me that Erin wouldn't slow us down. Little did he know, I worried more about Erin speeding us up. When she walked into the lobby, she was everything I feared. As I shook her hand, I assessed her chiseled physique and thought, *Shit, I was really hoping for someone twenty years older and thirty pounds heavier.*

After introductions, our team loaded into two cabs and headed toward Tierra del Fuego National Park. In Ushuaia, taxi drivers strap ski gear on car roofs using bungee cords, and after somehow arriving at the park with our gear intact, we assembled our skis and backpacks, and added another guest named Jim to our practice group. We huddled briefly in the dirt lot and Andrew laid out the game plan. We then began marching up the mountain while carrying our skis and boots, and after a few minutes, Ryan and Erin had pulled way ahead. Jim and Andrew remained just ahead of me, but I could tell they were lingering so that I wouldn't fall too far behind.

After ten minutes, I asked for a break to strip off some layers, but Andrew said to continue hiking until we reached an area with snow on the ground. Once there, we stopped for our next set of instructions, and Andrew asked us to strap on our climbing har-nesses while also attaching skins to our skis. I was a little baffled by the climbing harness, but I didn't want to embarrass myself, so I never asked why we needed it. We then hid our regular shoes in the woods and started to skin up a long flat trail toward the base of the mountain. Ryan and Erin continued racing and shot ahead, while Andrew stayed just in front of me, moving at a slower pace. Jim was nice enough to trail behind me and occasionally offered tips for skinning more efficiently, explaining that an experienced skinner glides up a hill like a cross-country skier. Similar to my experience skinning during the Avi-1 course the year before, I looked more like someone snowshoeing with skis, clomping more than gliding.

After approaching a steeper section, we stopped for a brief meeting where Andrew instructed us to clip our harnesses to a rope that ran about twenty feet from skier to skier, and we initiated our skin up the steep slope in a zigzag pattern. Like riding a bike uphill, the zigzag approach enabled the group to moderate the incline but required frequent changes in direction. The term for turning while skinning is a "kick turn," bracing with one leg while lifting and crossing over with the other. Andrew, Ryan, and Jim made it look effortless, while Erin's were smooth enough for a skiing ballet. On the other hand, I looked and sounded like a pig on ice skates, squealing each time I slid backward on my plant leg.

We ascended through small, scrubby bushes with the massive cirque looming overhead. Once at the foot of the alpine zone, we roped up and ran through a series of glacier travel techniques. After finishing the practice simulations, we decided to continue up the valley to a rocky saddle. We picked up the pace, skinning quickly up the mellow slope of isothermal snow.

With the instruction portion behind us, we traded our boot crampons for skis and began skinning up the rest of the mountain. As I assessed the terrain and the potential for hours of skinning ahead of me, I yelled ahead to Andrew, "Hey, how far up this thing are we planning to go?"

He kept skinning without even the slightest hitch as he slid up the mountain. Then, ducked the question by responding, "Not too much farther."

That proved to be a lie. We kept going and going, and during one of the steeper kick turns, the group misaligned without enough slack in the rope, and I was pulled down, pinning my left ski behind me. I looked like a calf successfully roped during a rodeo, and after watching me struggle for a bit, Andrew unclipped and skied over to help me. "You okay, Robert?"

Although I like the name Robert, Andrew was the first person in my life to refer to me by my given name. Rather than answering, I looked at him seriously and demanded, "Andrew, I *need* to know how much farther we are going. No bullshit, okay?"

Andrew smiled. He pointed high up to another section of the mountain. "See just over that saddle?"

"The what?"

"That ridge there. We are going to skin up to there and then keep going another little bit."

I didn't like the sound of *little bit.* "I need a visual. Can you just point to the stopping point?"

He smiled. "Sure. See that section of jagged rock? We'll end just underneath that."

That was not the answer I wanted to hear. "Way up there? No fucking way."

Andrew chuckled. He seemed unflappable. "How about this, Robert? Why don't you just wait here? But you have to promise me not to ski down until we get back."

I promised that I wouldn't move (mostly due to exhaustion) until they returned. A few feet farther up the mountain, Ryan glared at me, concerned that my willingness to surrender on our practice day might exclude the group from the most challenging runs in Antarctica.

———

Dad had difficulty keeping up. He did his best to stay with the group, but it was harder than he ever anticipated. About halfway up, Andrew decided it would be best to have him rest in a sheltered area, while we continued up for another ten minutes.

———

I then watched the rest of my team skin up and over a rolling section of the mountain, and they were gone for a long time. With all that time to think about quitting, I felt even worse.

———

We made several more kick turns until we eventually ran out of snow. We then continued up a treacherous talus field to the viewpoint. The saddle overlooked a massive glacial valley that immediately impressed me with its vastness. Patagonia has an incredible amount of terrain, and I stood in awe, while I pictured coming back here many times as I got older.

Next, we carefully down-climbed the rocky field back to our skis. After clicking in, I began with an aggressive turn down the fall-line. I was surprised at how well my edges carved this wet, heavy snow. Feeling confident, stable, and alive, I ripped a solid set of turns down the glacier. We then paused to reconnect with Dad and cruised all the way to the snow/dirt line. It felt amazing to explore backcountry terrain in such a unique part of the world.

Eventually the group returned, and we skied for a couple of minutes back to where we started. At some point, during the many transitions in and out of our skins, the sharp edges of my new skis sliced my hands in several spots, and as we walked down the mountain, blood poured from them. When we reached the parking lot, I tried to help load our equipment, but everything I touched was quickly covered in blood. I joked to Erin about needing her emergency room skills to stitch me up, but she looked at me with more pity than grave concern. Andrew then brought over a napkin from the back of our taxi and told me to put pressure on the main cut, before asking, "You good otherwise?"

I nodded my head, but answered honestly, "I don't know how I can do this for a week in Antarctica."

He smiled and put his hand on my shoulder. "Robert, I promise that it will get easier every day."

I thought, *Yeah, that's what your cellmate tells you when you get to prison.* I knew it was his job to lie to me, so I nodded and responded, "Thanks, Coach."

When we arrived back at the hotel, there was a mad dash to gather our bags for loading onto the ship bound for Antarctica. In the lobby, Kurt told me that he was assigned to our group as the tail guide and looked forward to touring with us, before he casually mentioned that Erin was changing groups. He said she wanted to ski with the other doctors on the trip, but I suspected she asked out of our group because I was so pathetic during our practice day. I felt a little embarrassed, but part of me was relieved. She clearly trained hard for the trip, and it was unfair of me to negatively impact her experience. I told Kurt that my biggest concern was having my performance in Antarctica limit what Ryan ended up skiing. He brought Andrew into the conversation, and they recommended that I join the team in the morning to ski something attainable for me. Then they suggested that in the afternoon I tour Antarctica in a zodiac while the three of them attacked more advanced terrain. That sounded like a manageable plan, and I walked away from the conversation with renewed optimism.

When evening arrived, the sun was still high in the sky. Argentinian law required that we travel to the ship by bus, an edict that ensured work for the six bus drivers and luggage porters in a country with its share of economic hardship. So, rather than simply walking across the street, and after the world's shortest bus ride, all 135 clients boarded and excitedly explored our home for the next ten days. The ship, a Russian commercial vessel retrofitted for cruise life, was renamed *Ocean Adventurer*. There were multiple decks on each level and two hot tubs. The dining area was well appointed with dark wood and white table linens, and there was a sizable lounge area with a staffed bar located in the stern. In the lounge, staff passed champagne and hors d'oeuvres, while we were introduced to the captain and various members of the crew. As we set sail, most of the clients congregated outside for one final glance at civilization, while I looked in the opposite direction, across the Beagle Channel toward an unknown ocean, doing everything possible to feign confidence about what the next week might bring.

Chapter Twenty-Eight

Deception Island

"Superhuman effort isn't worth a damn unless it achieves results."
—Ernest Shackleton

November 3, 2018. The *Ocean Adventurer* sailed out of the Beagle Channel and into the notorious Drake Passage, named for Sir Frances Drake. Drake discovered the passage after his ship, the *Golden Hind*, was blown off course in 1578. That unintended shift to the south, below the Straits of Magellan, revealed an open connection between the Atlantic and Pacific oceans with brutal winds and extremely rough seas— seas that caused our ship to pitch and roll like a child's bathtub toy. We quickly learned that anything untethered in our room eventually wound up on the floor. Clients with stronger constitutions, like Ryan and me, spent time viewing presentations from the guides in the lounge. Meanwhile, the guests who were more vulnerable to seasickness spent time retching in cabin bathrooms or over deck railings.

Doug Stoup, the founder of Ice Axe, is a legendary explorer who has trekked to the North Pole and South Pole more times than anyone in history. He even looked the part with flowing sandy-blond hair, light blue eyes, and linebacker proportions that I was certain traced back to a Viking tribe. Although he was friendly and approachable, his initial presentation in the lounge centered on a solo expedition to the South Pole where he was forced to extract one of his teeth with pliers after it cracked. Clearly, he operated at a different intensity level during expeditions, and as he clicked through images of his trek, I expected a slide on the preparation of penguin stew in a blizzard. Apparently, famed explorer Ernest Shackleton and his crew spent almost two years surviving on penguin (after they consumed the dogs) when their ship, *Endurance*, was crushed by pack ice in Antarctica. Doug described how Shackleton led his men across the Drake Passage in wooden lifeboats to save them and he ended his presentation with a quote about Shackleton: "When disaster strikes and all hope is gone, get down on your knees and pray for Shackleton."[1] Although Doug's admiration for Shackleton told me that we were in capable hands if disaster struck, I decided, looking out at the massive swells in the Drake, that I would skip the lifeboat and planned to go down with the ship.

After Doug's slideshow, we mingled with the other guests and ski guides and met lead guides from mountains in Chile, Argentina, Russia, India, Australia, France, Canada, and the United States. The most recognizable was John Egan, made famous in early Warren Miller ski movies, and a member of the U.S. Ski and Snowboard Hall of Fame. There were also two separate film crews on the ship. One was a heavily financed IMAX movie about Torah Bright, a former gold and silver medalist in the Olympics in the halfpipe event for snowboarders. That film crew was led by Brennan Legasse, an accomplished ski guide, adventurer, educator, and writer who organized the daily shooting schedule to ensure that Torah, the crew, and the hundreds of thousands of dollars' worth of equipment returned safely to the ship each afternoon.

The other content creator was a twenty-four-year-old recent college graduate named Thor Retzlaff, who focused on generating marketing material for Ice Axe. If our group leader, Andrew, was out of ski guide central casting, Thor was out of ski *dude* central casting. He had grown up skiing in Squaw Valley with parents who skied professionally, and he was well over six feet, with long sandy blond hair and blue eyes that he fixed on you when he spoke. Drenched in boyish idealism, Thor posited that the company's content motivated viewers to appreciate the beauty of the planet and thereby influenced human behavior.

---

1. Sir Raymond Priestly, 1956 address to the British Science Association.

Ryan was immediately taken by Thor's ebullience, and his eyes widened as Thor described his work for Ice Axe. In our conversation, Thor asked about our road to skiing in Antarctica, and after hearing an edited synopsis of Ryan's journey, he nodded and smiled before informing Ryan that he would make "sick content for the trip." He asked Ryan if he could feature him in Instagram and Facebook stories for Ice Axe, and Extreme Ryan smiled widely before I interjected, "Thor, he's been waiting a lifetime for someone to ask him that question."

Although the ride across the Drake Passage was full of anticipation, we had two days of sailing ahead of us without any activity, phone service, or idea of what we were getting into. After a rough night of ocean travel, we awoke to open ocean. For most of the day, I looked out of the breezeway windows into the endless blue sea. Waves tossed us constantly, inducing seasickness across the entire ship. At 7 p.m., I walked away from the windows and into the ship's dining room for dinner, and after a heavy meal, Dad and I walked back to our cabin. By 10 p.m., we noticed that the skies cleared, giving way to a perfect sunset. We decided to get some air and made our way to the back deck of the ship, where the few remaining clouds glowed orange above the open water like a maple leaf in autumn.

Everyone who wasn't hanging in the dining room moved to the back of the boat to take in the incredible views. For the most part, everyone was at least thirty years older than me, except for Lindsay. She was eighteen and on a gap year before starting college at Harvard. She was very pretty with a vibrant personality, and I related to her love of adventure. During every moment of sanity, while the ship rocked back and forth, I told myself developing feelings for her was a recipe for disaster. However, this was shaping up to be one of those times when I ignored better judgment, so I invited her out to watch the sunset with me after she finished dinner. When she arrived on the back deck, I talked to her for thirty seconds before a photographer pulled me aside to take "a few" pictures of Dad and me. She then took us through what felt like a hundred different angles and poses while I faked a smile. With every picture, my feet inched toward the back deck, practically pulling me down the stairs. However, when I finally returned, Lindsay was gone.

After two rough days at sea, we were called to the bridge by the first mate for our initial land sighting. From the deck, we saw a rocky beachhead with a handful of older buildings and small wooden boats, abandoned or shipwrecked. I overheard some discussion of a bonus ski day since our trip across the Drake was so quick and was relieved when the guides reverted to the original plan of touring Deception Island on foot. I knew tomorrow meant a long day of skinning and skiing, so viewing penguins and the remains of the whaling industry was fine by me.

The next day, an announcement came over the loudspeaker that tailwinds had moved us so quickly through the Drake that we had time to explore Deception Island, just north of the Antarctic Peninsula. Part of the South Shetland Islands, Deception Island is in the caldera of an active volcano, which last erupted in the 1960s.

Everyone quickly gathered on the top deck and waited quietly. Suddenly, a small pillar of dark brown rock pierced through the falling snow. We all cheered as we entered the small passage into the caldera, and an hour later, we launched our zodiacs and made landfall on the rocky shoreline.

On land, whiteout conditions and foreign geology made Deception Island feel like the set of a sci-fi movie. We crossed several treacherous drainages and hiked up to a spot that Andrew said was named Neptune's Window, where the first sighting of Antarctica was recorded. We wandered up the gravel slope past a few penguins and a large whale skeleton. When we reached the top, we peered over the edge into the angry sea below, taking photos and videos before descending back to the beach. We then examined a few deteriorated buildings, remnants of the whaling industry now for-gotten. I remember thinking, If we're this cold walking around for a few minutes, imagine what it felt like living in those shacks for an entire whaling season.

Just as the shivering started to take the fun out of the journey, the zodiacs returned, and we headed back to our ship. Upon returning, we were treated to a demonstration of the erratic weather in the region. The storm rolled out, and bright sunshine with increased visibility revealed beautiful mountain slopes surrounded by the deep blue waters of the South Shetlands. We then continued south along the coastline toward a more mountainous region, and I couldn't wait to get on skis.

CHAPTER TWENTY-NINE

Don't Forget to Look Around

"Difficulties are just things to overcome, after all."
—ERNEST SHACKLETON

November 5, 2018. The evening sail was much calmer, and for the first time, we slept through the night. At 7 a.m., the first mate came over the loudspeaker to wake us, announcing the daily schedule and weather conditions. After climbing out of bed, I pulled back the curtains, revealing stark white glacial cliffs pressed against impossibly blue ocean water while humongous icebergs drifted slowly by. I did my best not to wake Ryan but couldn't stop myself from whispering, "Holy shit."

After breakfast, I snapped a few pictures from the main deck before waking Ryan. Once he was up and fed, we assembled our gear and confirmed that his pack included the necessary items for a day of climbing and skiing. I struggled with how to dress and, more importantly, how to properly prepare Ryan. Yesterday on Deception Island, we encountered a mini-blizzard one minute and blue skies the next, so I tried different layering combinations before settling on a winner for both of us, and nervously added and subtracted items to our packs.

◆

Our first day of skiing began with a frantic morning. We weren't sure what to do, so we scrambled to get our gear together, eat breakfast, and managed to be in the zodiac on time. In between gear runs to the zodiac launching area of the ship, we paused to examine the landscape. I've traveled to lots of places, but Antarctica was far and away the most beautiful place I had ever seen. The water is bluer than anywhere else in the world. Turquoise icebergs slowly pass by, and the pristine snow that covers mountains in the distance is mesmerizing.

On deck, Andrew pointed to the area where we were headed. It was defined by three open bowls lined with large serac fall zones. A serac is a block of glacial ice, formed by crevasses intersecting on a glacier. Since they are enormous and can topple over without warning, skiing near a serac can be extremely dangerous.

We loaded the zodiac and calmly zipped around massive icebergs to a place Andrew called "The Farm." From the shoreline, he offered a rough description of our intended route to Victoria Peak, and we climbed over a rocky ledge to a snow-covered plateau that served as a staging point to assemble our climbing gear. It was then that I noticed that my skins were not in my pack. Somehow, in my haste to ensure Ryan's pack contained all the necessary gear, I made a major blunder with my own, and I wanted to drown myself in the frigid ocean water. After confessing to Andrew, he seemed frustrated but told me to relax, and he arranged to have my skins sent over in the next zodiac.

When we arrived on shore, we looked up and assessed our first run at the bottom of the world. For me, the excitement and anticipation building toward this moment was immense. We pulled our skins out of our backpacks and got ready to begin the climb. Well, most of us. After emptying his pack onto the ice, Dad realized he'd forgotten his skins on the way out. I don't think I've ever sighed so hard in my life. He begged me not to sigh, so I sighed in the most exaggerated way that I could. We both laughed, lightening the mood.

It took ten minutes for my skins to arrive, but with everyone including Ryan standing around waiting for me, it felt like ten hours. When they finally arrived, Andrew clipped us together for the skin up, and the initial ascent was manageable. It was a long stretch gradually increasing in elevation, but I kept pace until we arrived at the base of Victoria Peak. At that point, the slope increased drastically, and each sliding step was tougher on my legs. We initiated a zigzag pattern and I fared well initially, but as we neared the top half of the mountain, I was expending so much energy on my kick turns that I quickly tired.

We roped up for the glacier and began ascending the mountain before us. It had snowed the day before, covering a thick layer of ice crust with a few inches of fresh snow. On our fourth or fifth kick turns, my foot slipped and pushed the soft snow downhill. I thought to myself, That isn't a good sign, and assumed Andrew noted this as well because it was an obvious indicator that conditions were ripe for an avalanche.

After ninety minutes of skinning, I started probing Andrew for an endpoint. Like a dad playing "I Spy" on a long car ride, he avoided answering by pointing out an interesting facet of the glacier or the penguin colony below. Eventually, after a few more badly managed kick turns on the steepest section, I asked to quit.

"This looks like a nice spot. How about we just ski from here?"

Andrew never broke stride and barely turned his head to shout back at me. "Come on, Robert, you're doing great. All of the really steep stuff is done."

"This still seems pretty steep!"

This time he turned to look at me while continuing his methodical march toward the summit. "Listen, this next stretch flattens out, and it will be an easy push to the summit."

I reluctantly agreed to forge ahead but wasn't ready to give him the last word. "You could at least say something inspirational to motivate me."

Andrew grinned and replied, "Don't forget to look around."

Finally, after another thirty-minute slog, we reached the summit. I fell to my knees, unable to move. Everyone else excitedly transitioned out of their skins, but I remained frozen in place from exhaustion until Andrew forced me to get moving. We then skied for a total of three minutes down the mountain face that we had just climbed in some deep powder, which is unusual for Antarctica because most of the snow is glacial snow—possibly thousands of years old, blowing around day after day.

⸻

We pushed on to the summit and transitioned to ski mode in very windy conditions. Faint cloud cover obstructed our view of the ocean below. It was finally time for our first run in Antarctica. We slowly descended from the ridge before dropping into the bowl. Andrew skied about halfway down and signaled me on. On my first turn, I saw two cracks in the snow and, by the time I completed my turn, a large spider web of cracking snow appeared, sliding directly in front of me. I stopped in my tracks and watched the slope rip away.

Luckily, the sliding snow only went about seventy-five feet before slowing to a stop above Andrew, and it wasn't severe enough to pose a serious threat. He signaled me on, and I descended to him without issue. To be sure, if the snow was any deeper, Andrew would have turned us around. This was more of a mini snow slide that included a fracture in the snow. It was cool to see, but it was only a few inches deep. Obviously, a deeper snowpack that fractures can bury skiers, so if this was just a foot deeper, it would have caused concern because it might have knocked us off our feet and pushed us down the mountain toward the exposed rocks near the shoreline.

After lunch, Dad rested, so Andrew, Kurt, and I crossed the bay to tackle a more difficult aspect to Victoria Peak. On shore, Andrew got us organized and moving, and he set an ambitious pace, passing several groups on the way up. I have never struggled to keep pace with anyone on a mountain, but it was my first-time using ski crampons, and it felt like I was running in flip flops. Luckily, I climbed thirty-four mountains the summer before, so from a conditioning standpoint, I was able to keep up easily even if my technique was lacking.

When the snow started getting firm, we stopped just before the ridge before descending an aesthetic headwall between a serac and some bergschrund (a crevasse that forms when moving glacier ice separates from the stagnant ice above). At that point, we were in a lower consequence bowl and our group shared an incredible ski all the way to the ocean before hopping back into the zodiac.

—◦—

That night we ate dinner while the ship set course for a new location. The dining room had more of a buzz because, at last, people had skiing stories to share and the mood was also livelier without the heavy doses of Dramamine, a prerequisite for the trip across the Drake. Yet, I found myself baffled by the maniacal people proselytizing about our day. I tried playing along but wanted to stand up during dessert and scream, "We hiked for two fucking hours and skied for three minutes!"

After dinner, a guide named Rodrigo moderated a slideshow presentation on heli-skiing in Chile. Rodrigo's heli-operation departs from the top of a skyscraper in Santiago, flying clients to some of the best skiing in the Andes. Guests sleep in beautiful bungalows and, after skiing, are served a five-course meal before waking up to do it all over again. Now, *that* was more my speed. Why couldn't I have taken Ryan there? I closed my eyes and fantasized about Chilean sea bass served elegantly, but I was snapped back to reality when I overheard Kurt promising Ryan that tomorrow would be "the biggest tour of the trip with the tallest summit." I cringed. Today was brutal and, clearly, just a warm-up day. Tomorrow was shaping up to be a killer, and I needed to do better.

The next morning, we awoke to perfectly clear skies, and the sun was high in the sky by the time breakfast concluded. In the distance, I noted several large peaks, with one slightly taller than the rest, and assumed the most prominent peak was our objective for the morning climb. At the ship's launching point, Andrew asked me if I was sure everything was packed correctly, and I bowed my head as if asking for forgiveness. We then loaded the zodiac and crossed still waters to an area called Mount Tennant. I knew we faced an incredibly lengthy skin to the top, but the first hour went well. The initial portion toward the base of the ridge was not too steep, just long and slow—slow mostly because of me, but I continued climbing until we stopped for water and to reapply sunblock. Antarctica has limited ozone protection and, when my sunglasses fogged up, I made a rookie mistake placing them on the top of my head—

which led to my first-ever sunburned eyeballs. I spent the next two days convinced there was sandpaper in my eyes.

After delayering onshore, we began the slog to Mount Tennant. The route was heavily glaciated and required close attention to potential danger zones. The ascent took a few hours to complete, mostly to maintain a pace Dad could withstand.

Aside from the blistering sun, I held my own as we began the second hour of skinning. However, I continued advancing very slowly, and several of the groups passed us as Ryan groaned behind me. It was an interesting method of motivating me, but it worked because I quickened my pace, staying on the heels of the other groups.

As we moved into our third hour, I began fading, requesting several water breaks, and sneaking protein cubes for energy.[1] The sugar boost helped, but toward the end of hour three, I begged Andrew to let me ski from this section. He refused and promised we were getting close to the top. Reluctantly, I agreed to continue, but it wasn't until I saw skiers from other groups begin skiing down with huge smiles on their faces that I knew he was telling the truth.

Finally, after another forty-five minutes of skinning, we reached the true summit. If the weather had been nicer, I might have lobbied to die peacefully there, but it was suddenly cloudy and very windy, and my sweaty clothes turned icy. Andrew helped me assemble the last of my equipment, and after a quick briefing on the recommended route, we started down in our usual order.

---

1. The Antarctica Treaty System prevents eating on land or drinking anything other than water. We were also banned from urinating, although I violated that one, a few times. Before we exited or entered the ship, we stepped in a chemical solution to ensure no foreign bodies were transferred.

Once at the summit, a thick cloud layer surrounded the upper mountain. We began our descent in an eerie fog, but by the halfway point, it cleared completely with the ocean shimmering in front of us. The ski down was long and lasted several minutes. We managed to find decent snow even if it was just wind-blown glacial snow.

The descent was much better than the day before, beginning with a long run down a steep face, followed by a series of rolling sections. My legs were fried from the hike up, so I didn't ski as well as I would have liked, but I still managed to stay on my feet.

When we reached the bottom section, we faced a long pole-planting traverse out to the zodiacs, and Andrew took one look at my exhausted expression and said he had an idea. He clipped Ryan to a rope in front of me and forced him to drag me out of the flat section like a sled dog. Ryan wasn't happy, but I joked that I had dragged him through life for seventeen years and it was time he reciprocated. He complied, but as we neared a steeper pitched section, he intentionally charged ahead without unclipping the rope. I tried to ski in his tracks but approaching the zodiac launching point, we tangled up and crashed, while laughing hysterically. It was a nice way to end the morning.

After lunch, Andrew seemed reluctant to tell me the plan, which meant he had an idea that he didn't want the other guides to steal. We took our zodiacs to an area that he called "Landing C++" on the continental mainland and began ascending a previously untouched face. For what it lacked in vertical, it made up for in snow conditions. We somehow managed to find the only "blower pow" on the entire peninsula before skiing a line that we assumed no person in the history of the world had ever set foot on. While it was difficult to prove that it was a true first descent, I had sought a moment like this since the day that I decided to move away from resort skiing as my primary activity. Ironically, I had talked with one of the guides named Brennan a couple of nights prior about this type of exploratory skiing. He said, "It is still possible to find unskied slopes in the world if you are adamant about finding them."

When he said that, I pictured finding good ones in a few years when I was older. I never thought it would only be a matter of days before I bagged one.

On the ride back to the ship, we saw two humpback whales in the water. They put on an impressive display, lifting their massive tails out of the ocean before diving underneath our zodiac. I got a little concerned when our driver mumbled "holy shit" under her breath before radioing the ship to report the sighting. Many people saw whales that day, but none as close as us.

While we watched the whales in awe, we debated what to name the new line we had just discovered.

After we saw the whales, Thor said, "What a sick day."

Andrew then asked me, "Hey Ryan, what would you be doing right now if you were home?"

I looked at the clock on my phone. "I guess I would be in algebra right now. So, yeah, this is a whole lot better."

Thor smiled and said, "How about we name it 'Better than Algebra'?"

Andrew laughed. "Perfect."

After dinner, I had time to assess my performance in the morning. Despite requesting to quit on a couple of occasions, I had fared better than the day before. The morning trek was a long skin up—close to 2,700 feet—and I made it. For the rest of the evening, I tried focusing on that accomplishment, but looking around at the smiling faces in the lounge, I chided myself for being the only person who wanted to quit before reaching the top. Other clients were older and heavier than me, and some even smoked, yet they managed to make it to the top of the mountain without begging to quit. I promised myself that tomorrow my attitude would be better.

The next morning, however, Ryan approached and excitedly informed me that Thor had arranged to spend the morning with our group. He planned to film Ryan to generate content for the Ice Axe Instagram and Facebook pages. I did not want to limit the footage, so I stopped Andrew heading out of breakfast. "Hey, I am thinking about flipping around my day and skipping the morning instead of the afternoon."

"How come?" he wondered.

"Isn't Thor going with you to film? I was thinking you might tackle something more adventurous if I wasn't dragging you down."

Andrew smiled and tilted his head. "Do you want me to answer honestly?"

I laughed. "I think you just did."

⸺ ⸺

Day 3 began at a penguin rookery near the Gonzales Videla Station, one of the few standing buildings on the Antarctic Peninsula. We realized early on, ascending the newly formed ice crust, that this was a perfect corn-snow day. However, that crust combined with the steepness of the slope made for a difficult skin up. We affixed our ski crampons, a piece of equipment that I'm not too fond of due to its lack of gliding efficiency on ascents. Regardless of the tedious process of ski crampon climbing, it was an exciting day since I was filming with Thor. I met Thor on the boat just a few days before. He was hard to miss with his long hair held back by an "Ice Axe Expeditions" headband. In the ship's lounge, Dad noticed Thor was writing in a journal and engaged Thor on what he was writing. This sparked a long discussion about skiing, social media, and life.

Thor planned to produce a narrative about me in the form of an Instagram story, and we set up different shots as we hiked and skied throughout the day. Our first run was a descent of a glorious bowl with a large glacier at its center. I was surprised by the perfectly edge-able snow, and being from the East, I absolutely ripped this crusty stuff and hoped Thor was impressed.

On our second lap, we ascended a unique ridge feature before skiing a wide chute. Once again, we had perfectly edge-able snow, and our second run finished on a rather serious exposure, above a massive ice cliff at the shoreline. There, we were ready to end the morning, when I heard someone yell, "Ski!" By the time I looked, another guest's ski flew by me at high speed. I tried to shuffle over to stop it, but it sailed over the cliff and splashed in the bay. Thor and another guide climbed down to look for it, while the rest of us skinned up to the exit run. We skied down in softened snow and later got word the missing ski was fished out by a zodiac driver. Luckily, the ocean water in Antarctica is so crystal clear that the ski was visible from the zodiac.

At lunch, Ryan was beaming. Thor filmed his hike up and every turn on the descent, even encouraging Ryan to narrate parts of the day on camera. Ryan couldn't wait to see how it turned out, so I was excited for him and felt better about my decision to stay back in the morning.

"So, did you leave Thor in the dust this morning?"

Ryan paused while eating. He never boasted about skiing, or anything else for that matter. He was quick to chronicle every misstep in excruciating detail, but I never got much from him when something went well.

Sheepishly, he looked up from his plate and with a mouthful of cheeseburger said, "Yeah, I kinda' crushed it. This snow is so much like the East. I can rip this stuff."

I was surprised to hear his level of certainty. "So, what did Thor say?"

He went back to deflecting. "I am not sure. 'Rad,' I think?"

"Rad? Well, you can't beat that in ski-speak. Good work, buddy. You're definitely making a name for yourself."

"I guess so."

"Trust me. These guys are noticing. You'll be leading this trip in a few years."

That afternoon, our ship was trapped in the bay by two giant icebergs, and the captain refused to allow any afternoon skiing because he wanted to take advantage of the first opportunity to escape the bay. As a result, my morning off had turned into a full day of rest. I felt guilty, but quite honestly, I needed it.

We didn't end up getting back out till the next day because of shifting icebergs, but I was satisfied with the runs we got in the morning and really enjoyed skiing with Thor. I felt bad that Dad missed the entire day but knew a day of rest would help him with the remaining days of the trip. He was better on our second day than the first, and I hoped he could carry that momentum into day four.

After dinner, a guide named Todd Offenbacher gave a motivational talk along with a very entertaining slide show titled "Never Complain and Never Give Up." Despite occasionally interjecting humorous slides of his family, Todd chronicled skiing and rock-climbing adventures he has led over the years. In one part of the presentation, he highlighted a man with cerebral palsy climbing El Capitan in Yosemite using a contraption Todd constructed. Several climbers, including Todd, pushed this man to climb the 3,000-foot face, inch by inch, over a period of days. *Never complain and never give up.*

Clearly, I needed to get tougher. Maybe I wasn't in the best shape or the most experienced mountaineer, but during our ski tours in Antarctica, I wanted to stop as soon as I got tired. What kind of example was I setting for Ryan? Whenever he was emotionally exhausted and talked about retreating to a cabin in the woods, I got angry, demanding he keep going. And, since the moment that Dr. Schneider first observed him, he had. Despite every obstacle thrown at him by doctors, educators, and even his own parents, he refused to quit. What right did I have to quit at the first signs of physical exhaustion? I felt like a hypocrite.

CHAPTER THIRTY

Not Your Matterhorn

*"When we are no longer able to change a situation, we are challenged
to change ourselves."*

—VIKTOR FRANKL

November 9, 2018. I awoke feeling inspired. The weather was perfect,
but as we rode to our morning objective on Nansen Island, I wondered
how Andrew planned on initiating our skin up the rocky cliff ledge. From
the water's edge, the rocky shore traveled straight up for a hundred feet,
like a wall comprised of jagged rock and slushy snow. There was no way
to skin up that first barrier, so Andrew proposed that, instead, we climb
the ledge while roped together with our skis in one hand and poles in
the other, explaining, "It provides more balance than having everything
on our backs." When I reacted by looking skeptically toward the ledge,
wondering what happened if I fell backward into the frigid water and
pulled everyone down with me, a skier named Jim from Todd's group
who was sharing the zodiac ride over noticed my reticence and asked,
"Are you nervous?"

I laughed and replied, "Fuck yes!"

He patted me on the back and whispered, "Don't worry. You got this."

After clipping together, we slowly began climbing as a team, and as
we ascended, I tried focusing on each step without ever looking down.
That was easy to do for the first ten feet, but as we climbed higher, I
couldn't help looking back over my shoulder. I wondered what would be

worse: falling backward into the freezing water or coming up short and crashing onto the rocks below? And, since we were clipped together, was I heavy enough to drag everyone down with me?

Closer to the top, I paused before each new step. I tried establishing a climbing rhythm by talking to myself. "Okay, stab your poles into the snow with your left hand. Good? Secure? Okay, now lift your skis and stab them into the snow with your right hand. Seem okay? Sturdy enough to take a step? Okay, good. Now, drive your left foot and dig it into the snow. Atta' boy. Now, same with the right foot. Awesome. Now, rinse and repeat."

When we finally reached the top, everyone stood up, but I continued climbing on my hands and knees with my poles in one hand and skis in the other until there was absolutely zero chance I could fall backward. Todd's group had climbed alongside ours and, when I reached the plateau, I glanced back at him and grumbled, "Okay, I won't give up, but I make no friggin' promises about complaining."

He and Andrew laughed as we completed the transition into our skis and skins and, studying what lay ahead, it registered that Andrew couldn't hide today's plan from me. The skin up led to one place and one place only, a jagged peak that the guides called Not Your Matterhorn.

Andrew and Kurt seemed particularly excited about starting our morning objective, but the zodiac ride took a half hour due to the ice floe that required skilled navigation by our driver to avoid wrecking the motor. When we finally located a decent landing zone on shore, it still left us with a tricky climb up a hundred-foot rock ledge to a steep snow ramp. It took balance and mental toughness to forget about falling backward into the ocean, so the day was difficult right from the start for Dad. However, for the first time all week, I never heard any moaning from him. He even made it to the crest of the ridge without stopping.

As we began to skin up, instead of killing time by counting to one thousand, I slid with my left ski and whispered, "Never complain." Then I slid with my right ski and exhaled, "Never give up." *Never complain, never give up. Never complain, never give up.* I probably repeated it five thousand times before it got tedious, forcing me to rely on the icebergs below for distraction. Since we were now well above sea level, each iceberg in the channel down to my left appeared small in stature. However, even from that distance I recognized the white and teal color contrast above and below the waterline. No matter how massive an iceberg was in terms of tonnage, it was completely silent as it moved through the bay, as if water and ice had agreed on the perfect symbiotic pace.

After gearing up, we crossed a long section of flat glacier, and once we reached the base of the mountain, started a series of steep kick turns to the peak. While just about every view in Antarctica was amazing, this one was the best of the trip. Not Your Matterhorn stood alone along the coastline and the peaks farther inland had insane vertical rise with beautiful ice on them. Some of the peaks looked truly wild and unconquerable, but I thought about someday returning to Antarctica and tackling even more advanced terrain.

As we approached the summit, Andrew warned us that the final section was steep and technical, recommending that we "think through each move to be as surefooted as possible." Since we were roped together, there was no danger of sliding too far, but if I fell on one of the kick turns, I would have slid until I reached Ryan. Perhaps I was heavy enough to cause a chain reaction to take all four of us down the mountain. If nothing else, Andrew wanted me to avoid sliding back to a point where the taut rope would catch me, and I would be forced to skin up that section all over again.

On our final series of turns, his prescient warning proved accurate, and we reached a point where I was unable to lift one leg in the air while executing a kick turn because being on two legs was scary enough. When he heard me gasp at one point, he advised making the turns like the "hands of a clock," slowly opening my inside leg with a series of baby steps, moving from left to right, and then vice versa. On the bright side, as the pyramidal peak narrowed toward the top, the zigzag steps grew shorter and shorter, and finally, after a dozen more breathless clock turns, we reached the summit.

This time, I did not need any reminding from Andrew to look around. The entire scene was majestic with a sky so perfectly clear that it had a deep bluish-purple color I had never witnessed. Down below, the surrounding water was decorated by chunks of ice drifting together in a mosaic pattern disrupted every so often when a massive iceberg parted the field.

Andrew and Kurt had ascended Not Your Matternhorn during previous trips, so they quietly sipped water and applied sunblock while allowing Ryan and I time to process.

After a minute or two, I looked at Ryan. "My god, this is the most beautiful thing I've ever seen."

Ryan turned his head. "Worth the effort, right?"

I snorted and slowly nodded. "Yeah, I gotta admit it. It was worth every step."

Then I turned my head to look directly at him. "Every fucking step."

Maybe I was just exhausted or maybe it was the sheer magnitude of this astonishing place, but in those few moments, I got emotional standing next to Ryan. I found myself contemplating all that transpired to find ourselves in Antarctica. But looking at him, as he stood proudly on top of that mountain—examining the boundless ocean littered with ice floe—I realized that his adventure had only just begun. Regardless of the traumatic experiences he endured in the past or any difficulties that lay ahead, Ryan had the freedom and courage to decide for himself where his life may take him. Perhaps that notion explained the tears in my eyes; it had just registered with me, for the first time, that his long battle over his intellectual and emotional capabilities was finished. Ryan had won.

Dad struggled a bit toward the top, but he was much better today. He even seemed to laugh more and have fun on the way up, and when we did finally reach the summit, he asked Kurt to take some pictures of us. I just wanted to ski this magnificent beast, but I could tell Dad wanted time to enjoy the moment.

At one point, he even looked at me and told me, "Remember this day." I know my life will have plenty of adventure, but did he really think I could forget standing over this incredible ocean scene at the bottom of the world? I knew he wanted me to think about all that I overcame to get to this day and, although I did think about my childhood during the climb up, now that we were standing on top, I didn't want to think about anything aside from how special this place was.

Finally, after a dozen more pictures, we prepared to ski down. Just before my run, I remembered seeing a photo when I first researched the trip of a skier slashing a turn with the ocean in the background. I thought re-creating the shot would be a great way to capture that moment of making my dream come true. I made a big turn for the camera, and then went into autopilot for the rest of the run, cruising through the soft snow. The snow on that line was so perfect for edges that I skied for the first time in full carve and held nothing back.

The top section of Not Your Matterhorn is thirty-five to forty degrees, but Dad actually skied this one really well. Seeing him smile as he neared the meeting spot, I knew he was pleased with his effort and results, so that made me happy. Despite his complaining and mistakes early in the week, he worked hard to keep up each day, and I hoped that he was starting to appreciate backcountry skiing.

Toward the bottom section, we skied down a steep cliff face while tied to a rope secured by Andrew. We did this so we didn't fall into the ocean. It was a little awkward skiing attached to a rope and, at one point, Dad was yanked down when Andrew accidentally led him with too little slack. Part of me wondered if Andrew was getting revenge on Dad for forgetting his skins on day one, but Dad laughed and skied to the zodiac without further issue.

After lunch, Dad took a nature cruise while Andrew, Kurt, and I joined Todd's group to hike a short, steep section. We skied on some nice snow on a rolling section that pitched right into the ocean near an old shipwreck from the whaling days. Overall, this was our best day of the trip, and I was certain Dad agreed.

The next morning, we woke to cloudy skies in a bay in the South Shetland Islands. We traveled north through the night, and our time near the peninsula was over. The plan was to ski for two more days in the

South Shetlands before heading back to Ushuaia, and after breakfast, I bumped into Kurt on deck, and he pointed to a series of peaks pressed against the coastline of Livingston Island. A few minutes later, after loading our gear into the zodiac, we crossed a more active sea through a field of smaller icebergs that jostled our team and forced us to hold tightly to the ropes while Andrew provided details on the morning objective. He described it as "a shorter initial skin up to a very steep face, but with less overall elevation than prior days."

Andrew's description was correct, and the skin up was fairly easy until we reached the steeper face. At that point, my clock-turn kick turns were especially laborious, so Andrew suggested attaching my ski crampons. The teeth of the crampons held me in place to prevent me from slipping backward, but the tradeoff was that each step forward required more lifting and setting, rather than gliding. I proceeded slowly, but I managed, and we eventually reached a plateau to rest. Since we had climbed for only ninety minutes, I was surprised when Andrew slid over and told me that the next section was treacherous and suggested I stop here and ski this main section of the mountain. I didn't want to quit but knew he wouldn't have proposed this option without a good reason. Clearly, the remaining climb was incredibly difficult or dangerous or both, so I took his advice and skied down to the zodiac launch.

Day five went from sunny to cold and windy in an instant. We began our day with a steep skin to the top of an open headwall with a notch in the ridge providing access to a large bowl. Rather than continuing to this bowl, we went around to the opposite side of the rocky ridge through a heavily glaciated area. We wrapped around, heading for a summit capped with blue ice, and were able to get close to the top before we started scraping the snow right off the solid ice underneath. At that point, we realized gaining the ridge would be too difficult because visibility had further decreased, and the wind had picked up. The mountain was telling us it was time to get down, so we dug out a spot for our skis and began descending down a low angle run with lots of exposed ice on both sides. Eventually, we reached the headwall, which had virtually all the snow blown off it. We took it slow, making sure we kept an edge on this steep, icy terrain.

At lunch, rumors were swirling about a surge of hurricane winds heading our way, ensuring that our return trip to Ushuaia would be a brutal one. Skiing and zodiac touring in the afternoon were canceled due to high winds. That afternoon, the captain summoned all clients and crew for a mandatory meeting where he announced that skiing was also canceled for tomorrow. The captain planned to outrun the strongest hurricane winds by sailing back to Argentina immediately, warning us that, by tomorrow, it would be too dangerous to move about the ship without clutching the safety railings.

Instantly, the skiing portion of the trip was over, and I was surprised to feel a twinge of disappointment. Todd's philosophy had elevated my physical performance while conquering the mental and emotional obstacles that previously hampered my experiences in the backcountry. Failure during the Avi-1 course seemed a lifetime ago, and even my willingness to quit during the practice day in Ushuaia felt detached from the person awaiting a hurricane in the middle of the Southern Ocean, feeling dispirited by a lost day of climbing and skiing in Antarctica.

After lunch, we were greeted by a projector screen and an ominous presentation of things to come. We learned the high wind was not just erratic Antarctic weather but the beginnings of a serious storm heading our way. As a result, not only would we be forced to skip our final ski day, but we would be sailing through hurricane-force winds with thirty-foot waves for much of the journey. I was disappointed to lose out on a ski day, but the thought of sailing through a hurricane in the Drake Passage was pretty cool.

That evening, dinner included a special chocolate dessert bar in the foyer while the crew began preparations for a costume party in the lounge. By the start of the party, the ship was already rolling more than we experienced at any point on the trip and any unattended beer bottle or drinking glass quickly crashed to the floor. As we sailed just ahead of the hurricane, I found myself anticipating another potential storm because the costume party was Ryan's opportunity to let Lindsay know that he liked her. Although I assumed it would end in heartbreak, I'll admit that part of me pondered the greatest ending to any date-night movie ever, with Ryan finally landing his soulmate in the middle of the Southern Ocean.

At the party, however, each time I glanced over and saw Ryan doing everything possible to hold Lindsay's attention, I spied Thor and the other young guides lurking in the background like cheetahs in tall grass. At one point, a skier from Vancouver, also named Rob, came up to me and said, "Ryan is really going for it with Lindsay!"

"He sure is, but I think she has a different plan," I said, pointing to Thor. "Isn't he named after the god of fertility?"

<hr />

Another event was happening that night, one that I was absolutely pumped for. The infamous "White Party" to celebrate the White Continent meant that all the ship's clients were required to wear white costumes and outfits. A little-known fact about me is that I love to party. While I never drink or do drugs, I'm probably just as confident as any drunken college student when I am stone sober. I'm not scared of drawing attention to myself, so if there's a dance floor, I'm likely to own it.

The night started slowly, but as the drinks flowed and the music got better, things got rowdier. Just then the girl who I was most excited and nervous to see showed up. Lindsay walked in wearing a white dress, ready to party. We talked for a little bit, danced a little bit, and it seemed like things were going well. Then Thor showed up. Her attention was immediately off me and onto him. Little did I know, Dad and a few others were watching from a distance like I was the subject of a nature documentary. At one point, he even called me over and encouraged me to play hard to get. Apparently, my coach was watching close enough to see that it wasn't going well, and it was time to plan out my defensive plays.

I ignored how uncomfortable I felt and took his advice, walking in the direction of the best dancer in the room, Torah Bright. A former gold medalist in the snowboard half-pipe, Torah was the most energetic person on the trip. We danced together for a little bit until we almost bumped into a table. Torah explained that if something is in your way in a disco, you should just dance on

246

top of it. She demonstrated that by climbing on the table, all while hurricane winds battered the ship. Someone then tried to engage me in conversation, which lasted about a minute before I heard "Catch me!" I turned around and saw Torah jump off the table right onto me. I did not make the catch in time and nearly bowled over a few people.

Any guy would have been absolutely stoked to dance with an Olympic athlete at the bottom of the planet, but my mind kept wandering to what Lindsay was up to. Sure enough, I looked over to see her leaving the room with Thor and a few of the younger guides, and I knew then that I was taking the loss. After all, what was I really expecting?

After Lindsay left, I stayed and talked to Kurt, hoping one of his adventure stories would cheer me up, but he wasn't in much of a talking mood. When it looked like he might just close his eyes and take a nap right there, I got some water. All that dancing made me really dehydrated, so I poured myself a second cup of water and walked out on the deck to get some air. I then climbed to the top deck, quietly rapping the words to a song that was stuck in my head, and on the way up, I stumbled into Lindsay and Thor talking among a group of partiers. I thought for a second about trying to break into the conversation, but I decided to just surrender.

On the walk back to my cabin at the end of the night, I was overwhelmed by emotion, feeling everything from stupid to ugly to worthless. Maybe it was lack of sleep or the grueling two weeks of travel, but I wasn't coming out of this emotional slump any time soon. Apparently, rejection will get you whether you're in your hometown or in the most beautiful place in the world.

***

I stayed at the party until 2:30 a.m. before heading to bed but was jarred awake when the door flung open, and something crashed against the cabin wall. I already knew what Ryan was about to say before he said it: he had lost the battle for Lindsay's heart. Tears welled in his eyes as he said, "I will never be good enough for anyone and should just accept that I'll always be alone."

I started my usual pep talk about the dozens of girlfriends in his future. "Ry, you gotta trust me on this. I have lost out on girls that I liked a million times. Whenever I did, I lost them to a guy like you."

"I doubt that. I can't even get a prom date at a school with a thousand girls."

"Listen, high school sucks. Relationships are all about status and what team you play for or some stupid determination of cool. I'm telling you, starting in college and especially after, it becomes more about the individual. You're smart and good looking, yes, but you're also an incredibly decent person at your core. You're supportive, generous, and never jealous or judgmental. Those qualities make you a good friend to have. Eventually, those qualities start to matter to girls. They start to matter a lot. You gotta' trust me on this one."

He wasn't buying it. "Dad, do you know how many times you have given me this same speech?"

"I know, buddy, but one of these days I'm going to be right. Shit, I must be due. I can't be wrong eight thousand times in a row. It is a statistical impossibility, right?"

He nodded, but I could tell that he was only humoring me. I hadn't closed the deal. So, I quickly shifted gears to why we traveled to Antarctica in the first place. "Look, we came here so you could gain experience to be a great mountain guide someday, and this trip proved that you belong in this world. Even Doug pulled me aside to tell me that he sees you working for Ice Axe someday."

He nodded again, but this time it felt genuine. "Besides, in a few years, you'll be the Thor of every mountain you ski."

He pondered for a second what being desired might feel like, smiled, wiped his tired eyes, and rolled over to sleep.

Ryan survived the long night, and the next couple of days were better. Despite feeling heartsick, he demonstrated improved self-assuredness by spending time with Lindsay and Thor as we headed home. I spent time in the lounge, but as the ship rolled with each swell, my mind wandered to the many "conclusions" about Ryan found in dozens of IEP reports and psychological evaluations conducted over the years. To those who evaluated him, failure by any person, place, or thing to fulfill his expectations risked emotional outbursts necessitating adult supervision to ensure his safety and the safety of those around him. Yet, as I peered through the lounge windows, I saw Ryan and Lindsay roped together on deck as Thor videoed them squaring off against hurricane winds. Although he was suffering inside, Ryan moved on with his life.

As I watched him laugh after he was showered by a massive wave crashing against the bow of the ship, I questioned whether the so-called experts were wrong from the start or if Ryan had simply changed over time. After pondering it for a few minutes, I decided to give the doctors and school administrators the benefit of the doubt because Ryan was a complicated little boy, and his behavior was inconsistent with that of his peers. Doctors and school officials sought to determine why, igniting a chain of events rooted in protocol and procedure. In my heart, I believe every professional in the chain acted without malice, even when mistakes were made. Everyone, including myself and Mary Beth, sought to help Ryan, yet those interventions made his life markedly worse, and without skiing, I might never have realized it.

Perhaps his childhood was analogous to the sailing expedition of Sir Frances Drake. In 1578, Drake intended to sail around South America through the Strait of Magellan, but unforeseen circumstances blew him off course. In the process, he discovered an open passage from one side of the world to the other. Like Drake, Ryan's unforeseen day of skiing was the passageway into a world where he was unknown, unrestricted, and unrestrained.

⬤〜⬤

The next forty-eight hours were long and treacherous. Dramatic swells caused the ship to pitch and roll in the angry sea. A few members aboard were injured, with one man almost losing a finger on the stairs after tumbling down. Plates and glasses broke during lunch, and I was hit with a huge wave on the deck, completely soaking me with freezing water.

Without a ski day, I spent time making funny videos with Lindsay and Thor. We even made a spoof on a safety video that was shown to the entire ship. I really liked hanging with both of them and hoped to adventure with each long after this trip. After all, I couldn't be mad if Lindsay only wanted friendship with me because she found guys like Thor more interesting. Hell, I found him more interesting than me.

In the end, the captain made the right call. The hellish sail home would have been significantly worse had we skied the final day, allowing hurricane-force winds and waves to fully engulf the ship. As we pulled into Ushuaia, we faced two long travel days back to Sudbury, but I was strangely content. Certainly, thoughts of heading home brought on the typical stress associated with work and family, but it felt manageable, and I stared at the rugged coastline in the distance, searching for an explanation to the peacefulness that pervaded my soul. Was it simply the pride of accomplishing something difficult in Antarctica? No, this feeling ran much deeper than successfully testing physical and mental limitations.

As I sat alone on the rear deck during our final day of sailing, I allowed myself to be judged by the one person I had never managed to please: myself. Like any person approaching a milestone birthday, I had suffered my share of days spent pondering my existence—wondering if I was making an impact on the world. Yet, as I looked out across the Beagle Channel, there was one aspect of my life that I knew, with certainty, had mattered. My refusal to give up on Ryan changed *his* world, and that was plenty.

CHAPTER THIRTY-ONE

Redemption

"It does not matter how slowly you go as long as you do not stop."
—CONFUCIUS

November 16, 2018. *I got out of my car in the LS parking lot on a cloudy afternoon after finishing the brutal travel required to return from Antarctica. There was still an hour left of school, and even though we flew all night, and I didn't sleep well, something told me I should go. I'd already missed two weeks and had a lot of work to catch up on, but something else was motivating me as I walked in the front door. For the first time since I had set foot inside LS, I was feeling confident.*

My journey to the bottom of the world helped resolve a lot of things that I'd been struggling with. To this point, LS was certainly better than any of my previous schools and, although I wasn't tackled or locked in a room, I still felt alone. LS hadn't done much for my self-esteem, but I felt good when I burst into my English class and all heads turned my way. My teacher, Mr. Lewis, apologized on my behalf. "Sorry for the interruption. Ryan just got back from Antarctica and is getting readjusted to the schedule."

To miss two weeks of school without getting reported to the state, Dad suggested to the administration that I give presentations on my trip when I returned. So, I put together a PowerPoint presentation with videos and photos, and over the next few weeks, I presented the slide show to all my classes. I hoped the presentation would change people's perception of Antarctica, but I was surprised how, afterward, people's perception of me changed. When I first arrived at LS, Dad said people would find me interesting and mysterious since I was the new guy, but that never panned out. While "New Guy Ryan" didn't turn out to be much of a selling point, "Polar Explorer Ryan" was suddenly in high demand. I was always a good skier, but explaining the history, ecology, and future of Antarctica in light of climate change was relatable to skiers and non-skiers alike. While I never climbed or skied runs like Little Couloir for the sole purpose of receiving attention, I didn't feel bad enjoying the attention I received for skiing in Antarctica. After all, high school is all about how well liked you are, and after feeling like a nobody for so long, it was a welcome change. Guys started giving me props on my ski descents, girls invited me to sit with them at lunch, and everyone wanted to hear about the trip.

In December, Ryan asked me if I wanted to skin up Tuckerman Ravine. It was a dangerous local route, particularly in early season conditions—eleven skiers have been killed on it since the 1960s because of small avalanches or falling into glide cracks. We'd even tried it once the year before, and I ended up spending four hours hiking up a mountain with a fifty-pound pack only to fall during my second turn of actual skiing on Mt. Washington. That aside, our experience in Antarctica made me a stronger mountaineer and, with deep snow already at the base, I wouldn't need to hike up, carrying my boots and skis as we did in the spring. Ryan promised this tour would be "just like Antarctica" because we could skin from the bottom to the top.

We drove up in the morning, and on the ride to New Hampshire, I thought the ski gods were sending a message when I got a flat tire. Then, when I tried making up for lost time, I got pulled over. By the time that we arrived at the parking lot, it was 10 a.m., so we quickly organized ourselves, geared up, and began skinning up the mountain. Despite my Antarctica experience, it was still incredibly tough, covering nearly two and a half miles with 1,900 feet of elevation.

After ninety minutes together, Ryan forged ahead to preview the snow conditions in the ravine to ensure that I could ski safely. Once we separated, I was alone on a quiet trail leading to the top of Mt. Washington, stopping frequently to rest, when it finally hit me.

Although standing still felt good, unless I started moving, I would *never* reach the top. Yet, when I took even the smallest and slowest possible steps forward, I advanced.

As I forced myself to slide my feet forward and up the steep pathway, my mind raced through the last decade. The magic carpet, Loon, Stowe, Vail, Snowbird, Big Sky, Chile, and Antarctica: Ryan and I had traveled so far together and learned so much about each other. But, just like stopping to rest over and over during the skin up, for much of his childhood, I stood in place and allowed others to make critical decisions about his care and well-being. Finally, one day, I started putting one foot in front of the other—slowly, even painfully at times—but I kept climbing. I learned that the experts were wrong about him because I came to appreciate that I knew him better. In the process, I watched my son tackle the toughest skiing terrain on the planet with skill, courage, and determination. He refused to quit until he conquered each run on his list. We started on a magic carpet and wound up on a magical continent where we reached the top of the mountain, but we recognized that the story doesn't end there. Ryan still needed to ski down and then climb back up the next day, and the next. He needed to apply lessons learned on the mountain into his everyday life. More importantly, I needed to apply what I learned watching him ski to his everyday life. I had spent years fighting for his freedom, but now it was time for Ryan to decide where life might take him.

When I finally reached the base of the ravine, we reunited, and he reported that the snow coverage was very thin at the ridgeline and filled with high consequence fall zones. He warned me there were no easy routes on the upper section and any mishap would cause me to "fall a long way." So, heeding the expert opinion of my personal ski guide, I skipped the final ascent up the face of the ravine—because I hadn't come this far to have my story end in New Hampshire. Instead, we skied out of the ravine and down the 2,000-foot Sherburne Trail together, and it took several minutes to reach the bottom. Was it worth three hours of skinning and hiking? Not a chance—but I never complained, and I never gave up.

Although it took me until senior spring to find my people, I certainly wasn't invisible before that, I was just an unknown. Reading through my yearbook signatures, I felt like I was reading about someone else. Pages were packed full of messages about how I made everyone smile or how my many adventures inspired them. Before reading those messages, I never considered for a minute that I made much of an impact. In fact, if you asked me about my social life before I got back from Antarctica, I would've said no one really cared that I existed. By the time graduation neared, however, I realized that it didn't matter how cool I was or wasn't. What mattered more was positively impacting people who knew me.

CHAPTER 32

Reality Graduation

"Do not follow where the path may lead. Go, instead, where there is no path and leave a trail."

—RALPH WALDO EMERSON

June 2, 2019. As graduation approached, Ryan was torn about attending the ceremony. I promised myself that I would respect his decision if he decided not to attend, but after fifteen years of constant struggle to get to this moment, I desperately hoped he would.

Shortly before the last day of classes, Ryan shocked me with a bit of news: he had submitted a speech for consideration to be one of the graduation speakers.

"You did? I didn't think you even wanted to go. Now you want to be the graduation speaker? Don't you need to be the valedictorian or something?"

"No, they pick the three best speeches, so I figured that I'd give it a shot."

We both knew what my next question would be, and I felt my heart skip a beat faster. "What did you write about?"

He looked back down at his phone and paused for an excruciating few seconds to finish a text before looking back at me sheepishly. "My life story."

I swallowed before speaking. Partly to gather my thoughts before reacting. I wanted to convey how proud I was, but I also needed a second to contemplate how his childhood would sound to a graduation audience. "So, you told them everything? Even the hospital?"

He nodded slowly and fixed his eyes on mine. "Everything."

"Wow." I paused just long enough for Ryan to stare at me quizzically, as if awaiting my reaction to his news. In that instant, every single emotion I experienced while parenting him surged in my chest, but the feeling that won out was pride. Pride with a touch of curiosity. "Can I read it?"

"Fine, but I don't want to hear about how I should have said this or that, or that I should change it. I knew if I showed it to you, you'd rewrite it like you did with my college essay."

I burst out laughing. "For god's sake, I only fixed a little bit of bad grammar!"

He smiled and shook his head slowly. "Sure you did, Dad."

Then, he handed me his phone with the speech already loaded up. "Just read this and be cool about it." I sat down on the couch and took a deep breath. I felt tears welling in my eyes before I even read the first sentence.

Good afternoon and thank you for the opportunity to speak on this special day. I would like to start by congratulating my classmates. I have been privileged to share this experience with you for the past two years.

Although graduation speeches are usually a look into the future, I can only offer my story by looking into the past. As I mentioned, I have only attended LS for two years. To talk about all that occurred before attending LS requires more honesty and courage than I ever could have imagined. My journey was long and difficult. However, despite its challenges, the lessons I have learned along the way made everything worth it. So, today, before you step into the world beyond high school, I want to share these lessons with you. To do that, I first need to tell you a story that I've never told anyone before.

Thirteen years ago, my family was advised by doctors and school officials to make a decision that would alter my life forever. You see, I wasn't a traditional learner. I liked to move around and had lots of energy. I also thought when grown-ups said the word "no," it was more of a suggestion than an actual requirement. That made preschool particularly difficult for my teachers, so when I was five years old, I was moved to a smaller school. I am not going to name the school, but it was considered a therapeutic environment, and everyone said this would help me learn better than attending mainstream kindergarten.

Unfortunately, things took a turn for the worse. At my new school, if you misbehaved, you were physically restrained by teachers and staff. The school operated under the assumption that physical intervention would help students calm down. However, for me, it had the opposite effect. I would struggle to escape and wound up wrestling on the floor for much of the school day. I witnessed teachers overuse and misapply the methods for restraint, and there were times when I feared for my safety. These restraints happened almost daily. I went home with bruises and scrapes, but my family was told this was supposed to "fix" me. The school even encouraged my parents and babysitters to restrain me at home. By the time I left that school after almost four years, I developed PTSD and couldn't trust any adults in my life. Shortly after that, at the recommendation of a therapist, I was hospitalized for two weeks, where I was given a medication with a side effect that nearly killed me.

After I got out of the hospital, no regular schools wanted me. To those who knew me at this time in my life, most assumed that I would wind up institutionalized in some manner for good. However, in the midst of all this, there was a glimmer of hope. One day, my dad drove me to Nashoba Valley to try skiing. He didn't have very high hopes, since many attempts to find a hobby had ended poorly. But from the moment I took my first run, it was love at first sight.

Something clicked that day, and I discovered my passion for skiing. No matter how bad things were at my new school, the mountains became my escape, my church, and my proving ground. I improved with each day on skis, and before I was a teenager, I was tackling the most difficult runs that a mountain offered. I quickly progressed from a resort skier to a free rider, eventually moving into the beautiful and challenging world of ski mountaineering, which means climbing to ski without the help of a chairlift. From that first attempt on the magic carpet at Nashoba, skiing has shown me the world. I have been lucky enough to ski great mountains in the Western U.S., Canada, Chile, and even Antarctica. In case you are wondering, Antarctica is amazingly beautiful. And, yes, penguins are adorable. But, they poop a lot.

Through skiing and my love of the outdoors, my life was no longer about pain and hardship. It was a life of adventure and discovery. The endless world outside of school walls allowed me to push the boundaries of human performance in order to discover what's truly possible for me as a person.

After middle school, skiing helped me reach the end of a long healing process. I learned to trust again. I didn't feel the need to run or fight to protect myself. But little did I know, I was just reaching the basecamp for my hardest summit push: getting back to public school. Despite wanting to return to the mainstream school system, I was met with fierce opposition. School administrators didn't view me as a victim, they saw me as a problem. My fight to return to LS wound up taking another three years at two different schools before finally proving that I wasn't the troubled kid that people mistakenly believed me to be.

In September of 2017, I was finally allowed to return to LS. While it did feel a hundred times better to be back in public school, I can't say that it was perfect. It took a while to adjust and make friends. I had to drop a level in math, and I failed pretty epically at finding a date to junior prom. But I'm so grateful for everyone who gave me a chance by putting up with my skiing and hiking stories, introducing me to their friends, and making me feel welcome. To many of you, saying hi to me in the halls was a nice gesture that you probably forgot all about, but to me, it meant so much more, and helped me feel like I belonged.

In the end, there are a few major takeaways from my journey that I want to share with you.

One, treat everyone with kindness, and always give new people a chance. I've been to six different schools since birth, with all different types of people. Oftentimes, the kids who seemed weird, different, or even the ones people warned me about were the nicest. As a result, I have learned to give people a chance, no matter where they come from, and taking that risk has generated some great friendships.

Two, don't ever waste your life doing something you hate. From my time spent at rock bottom, I learned how valuable happiness is. Follow your passion and find a way to make it a major part of your life, or you will never be truly happy.

Three, just because you go through hardship does not mean that it should define your entire life. In 2009, after the hospital, the state wanted me to live in a residential facility to be constantly monitored. Instead, I embarked on a ten-year journey traveling to different mountains, learning what I could from professionals, and trying to be my best self on and off the slopes. When times were tough, my excitement about my next ski day kept me going, and with all the hard work and support from my family, today I'm graduating from a school I was told I'd never attend. I am medication-free, and I am always planning my next adventure.

This fall, I will pursue my adventure education degree at Northern Vermont University, so I can make a career out of my passion for the outdoors. My hope is to one day provide positive experiences to people who love the mountains like I do. During those experiences, I want to give people a chance to realize their true potential. Like me, I know each and every one of us is capable of so much more than people sometimes believe.

To my fellow graduates, I know college and adulthood will present challenges. There will be tough days ahead. But whatever you are going through, don't ever give up. Keep climbing toward your mountaintop. Because let me tell you, the view is a whole lot better from the summit.

As I finished, I tried to fight back tears, but one snuck down my cheek. Ryan pretended not to see, but he seemed pleased that I was moved by the speech. Either that or he was just relieved that I wasn't critiquing it. "Ryan, this is perfect. I really hope you get picked, but even if you don't, I want you to know that it took a lot of guts to write this. No matter what happens, you should save this forever and use it to remind yourself about the road you traveled to be who you are."

He smiled and grabbed his phone. "Thanks, Dad."

For much of the spring, I was in a negative headspace about graduation and didn't want to attend the ceremony. I told my parents that every kid graduates high school, and if I listed the accomplishments that I was most proud of, a high school diploma wouldn't even make the list. After some talks with my family, however, I began to see it from a broader perspective. By graduating from LS, I proved many doctors, teachers, and special education administrators wrong, and I had every right to feel proud. So, when the chance to submit a graduation speech came around, I decided to do something bold and I submitted a very personal speech, detailing my journey. Unfortunately, I received a return email that the speech was rejected.

I walked into the LS graduation mad at myself. This was a day to celebrate Ryan, yet I was feeling disappointed because his speech wasn't selected. As we took our seats, I kept telling myself to let it go, and I tried to elevate my mood by focusing on the back of Ryan's head. His graduation cap was decorated with stickers from various ski resorts from all over the world, and he managed to affix a small GoPro camera in the center.

I sat through the three graduation speech winners, but I had a hard time focusing and kept hearing Ryan's speech echoing in my head. At the conclusion of the last speech, the student speaker quoted *Hannah Montana*, and I felt my frustration beginning to heighten. So, when it finally came time for the presentation of diplomas, I felt antsy and wandered away from the seating area to reflect on the true importance of the day. Abigail left her seat to join me, and when she tracked me down, she must have sensed that something was bothering me.

To cheer me up, she held her phone in her right hand like a microphone and with her left arm pointed toward the sky, shook her shoulders, shuddered, and whispered in her deep singing voice, "Everybody makes mistakes. Everybody has those days. Everybody knows what, what I'm talkin' about—everybody gets that way."

Her throaty imitation of Miley Cyrus brought a smile to my face. "What the hell does that even mean?" I asked her.

Abigail smiled. "Don't overthink it, Dad."

I nodded and laughed. "Probably good advice." I took a deep breath and paused for a minute to listen to some of the names being announced. The initial group was filled with award winners and top academic achievers, and Ryan's name would come later with the alphabetical roster. With time to kill, my mind wandered to the many hours I spent with Abigail on athletic fields behind LS and how the prospect of Ryan receiving a high school diploma was a mere fantasy back then. Now, it was minutes away from happening, and it was time to recognize the magnitude of Ryan's accomplishment rather than fixating on speeches already forgotten by most in attendance.

<hr>

When it was finally time to get our diplomas, as they listed off names, I noticed that some people got huge cheers while others received just the quiet clapping of their family. As I walked up the stairs of the stage, I was afraid that I would only have three people clapping for me when my name was called.

<hr>

As diplomas were handed to students with names beginning with "A," Abigail and I noticed parents moving toward the stage for a picture of their son or daughter. We discussed inching up for a better vantage point, but the mob scene of helicopter-parents jockeying for position was too much to take on. Instead, I motioned to her to follow me, and we positioned ourselves directly behind the ramp students were using to exit after receiving their diplomas. We remained there until hearing the announcement of Ryan Charles DeLena, and while I readied myself to take his picture, I noticed that he received an audible cheer from his classmates, which heartened me.

<hr>

To my surprise, I got one of the loudest cheers, and I grabbed my diploma and smiled. I then heard someone in the audience yell, "Yo Extreme, do a flip!" Despite my parkour background, a front flip off the stage in a full gown was out of the question, but I had to give the kid something. As I walked down the ramp, I took a hard left and vaulted over the railing into the grass below. The crowd erupted, and I returned to my seat knowing I had pulled off a very memorable ending to my high school career.

Ryan then approached us with a big smile and, before I could ask him to pause with his diploma, he *vaulted* over the railing and headed back to his seat. When he landed, an even louder cheer erupted.

As I walked back to the audience, I quickly checked my phone, praying I caught his grand parkour exit on camera. After scrolling through the first few pictures, I located a shot of Ryan launching over the railing. In the picture, his body was completely parallel as he soared off the ramp toward the grass below.

Speech or no speech, Ryan had exited LS on his terms, and it was perfect.

Epilogue

July 1, 2019. *I'd been talking to Thor off and on since Antarctica. Although he is a few years older, he was much closer to me in age than other guides and professional instructors that I met, and he became my first real friend in the industry. He is easily one of the coolest people I know, but I also respect his mountain expertise, and we started talking about skiing a volcano in the Cascade Region in July. Throughout the summer, I called him frequently to get information about the trip. At the time, I'd been talking to a girl named Sara from Stonebrook and, despite the fact that I was heading off to college, we ended up dating for the summer.*

In early July, I took her on our first real date, and as we pulled into the parking lot of the restaurant, a call came over the hands-free system. It was Thor calling to invite me to climb and ski Mount Baker and Mount Hood. That conversation with Thor in front of Sara not only made me look like the coolest guy ever on a date, but it also meant I'd get a chance at a Cascade volcano.

Later that week, Dad helped me with the flight and hotel logistics, and I packed my gear and flew out. Thor met me at the airport, and we caught up on the past year during our long drive. When we arrived in the Mount Baker parking lot, Thor noticed my skis were the heaviest things he'd ever felt, so he offered to take the majority of the group gear. The next morning, we trekked in on dry land in a beautiful old-growth forest. Later, as we got into the alpine zone, we walked a narrow ridge, and I was mesmerized by the sheer beauty, completely forgetting how much weight was on my back. Mount Baker was massive with a glacier capping the upper five thousand feet, while below were lush green valleys. It was like we were standing in the middle of a painting.

As we neared dinnertime, I felt a nagging sense of urgency. There is always so much uncertainty in the mountains, and I wanted to push for the summit right then, instead of waiting a night, but Thor knew the forecast was good and felt we would be stronger after a few hours of sleep. So, we made dinner and went to bed, still in daylight. The next morning, the alarm rang at 3 a.m., and I felt strangely rested. Thor and I secured enough water for the day and made breakfast. We then set out for our summit push, and as the sun rose, an orange glow illuminated the Northern Cascades.

We moved rapidly on the glacier, making fantastic time, and even stopping at the volcanic fumarole to chill out since the sun hadn't even begun to warm the snow. Hikers began noticing we were the only party on the glacier who brought skis, and when they asked where we were skiing from, they seemed surprised when we replied, "The top."

After Antarctica, I honestly wondered if the rest of the world would forever seem less beautiful, but reaching the top of Mount Baker reminded me there was still plenty to be amazed by. The Northern Cascades were truly majestic. The sun still hadn't warmed the snow sufficiently, so we put on extra layers and took a seat. By now, people were staring at the two young men practically taking a nap on the summit—which went against every principle of mountaineering. When we finally clicked into our skis, we began cruising down the glacier, doing exactly what we came to do. Ski mountaineering is like running a marathon and celebrating with a dance. The satisfaction isn't only from reaching the summit; it comes from being rewarded with pristine turns for every brutal step it took to get there. As Thor described it, "Prove your worth, and then celebrate."

We hiked out and had dinner near the motel. The next morning, we drove to Sandy, Oregon, to tackle Mount Hood, and as we arrived, it was not as pretty as Mount Baker. The hike starts in a classic Southern Cascades desert, and by now, some soreness from Mount Baker was kicking in. The approach was strenuous for both of us. When we finally hit the snow line and started up the glacier, I laughed at the fact that we were planning to ski this mountain for fun. The snow hadn't been refreshed in months and was covered in a mixture of ice and dirt with some of the worst "sun cups" I'd ever seen.

Nevertheless, we walked a narrow ridge devoid of snow and tagged Mount Hood, the highest mountain in Oregon. Thor promptly took out his phone and called various family members. Based on his conversations, I could tell it was normal for Thor to show love to his family members in this way. My family, on the other hand, has never really been an "I love you" family. It's not that we don't love each other; my parents are just more about showing love in their actions rather than words. Mom and Dad are such logical people, so I think it is just obvious to them how much they love me and Abigail. Still, something was telling me that I should call Dad.

Though we've never talked about it, I always knew Dad had a vision for me to play baseball like him, attend a top college, and go into law or business like he did. Not only that but he wanted me to do it better than he did and to make twice as much money. I am sure when he originally planned my life, it didn't include six different schools and a mental hospital, traveling to Antarctica, Northern Vermont University, or carrying skis up a volcano in July. But with every twist and turn in my journey, he adjusted his hopes for me and made my happiness his only priority. For him, that meant skiing every weekend even when it was freezing out, traveling around the country to slopes that were way over his head, and skiing runs that almost killed him. He even traveled to Canada, South America, and Antarctica to pursue my dreams. I can't imagine how much money he spent over the years and how many times he said no to his friends because he was skiing with me.

As I started to make the call, I felt bad that I hadn't seen him much that winter, since skiing was our thing. Once I started to ski primarily in the backcountry, our weekends together mostly ended, and the fact that he wasn't with me on my adventures felt wrong. So, the least I could do was share this moment with him, and miraculously, my Facetime video call went through.

"Yo! I'm on the summit with Thor. Check this shit out."

I was able to show him the panoramic views off the summit. Then, I turned my phone to face him. "Dad, I want to thank you for always supporting me on my journey and allowing me to find my own way."

Dad looked a little shocked on the screen. He took a long time to say something, but I wasn't sure if it was just the connection. "Wow, Ry, that's nice to hear, but now you have me worried. This isn't like the call the guy made from Everest to his wife just before he froze to death, is it?"

I laughed. "No way, man. We kicked ass. It is so beautiful up here. I just wanted you to share it with me. I wouldn't be here or anywhere without you."

Dad smiled, but it was a funny smile, like he was trying not to cry. Once again, he took forever to say something. Finally, he just said, "Thanks, buddy. That means a lot."

After I hung up with Dad, it was back to our mission. We still had to ski a crazy sun-cupped dirt-covered glacier in the middle of July, but I was ready to continue the wild journey I'd embraced years ago with open arms. More importantly, I was ready to venture well beyond the expectations once held for me by so many experts. When you live without restraint, there is no limit to where life can take you.

I wished I had said more to Ryan during our video chat. I wished I had thanked him for all he taught me about parenting and about myself. Instead, I sat silently staring at Ryan's contact photo on my phone. Finally, after a minute or so, I smiled and slowly shook my head before admitting, "And I wouldn't have made it here without you, buddy."

Although it isn't a very long list of people, those who didn't doubt me allowed me to thrive. Dad and I reached that conclusion during a long car ride one day. Ben believed in my skiing ability, allowing me to take risks and challenge myself in ways that I couldn't at home or at school. Dr. Delgado took me off my meds and helped me realize that there wasn't anything wrong with my brain. Even the Sudbury special education department (after a lot of opposition) gave me a chance to try public school again. However, the biggest heroes in this story are my parents. Had they given up on me back in 2010, I would have been institutionalized, but something my parents saw in me told them the doctors were wrong. Dad saw it first on our ski trips and eventually, after he convinced Mom, they fought like hell to make sure I had a fair shot at life.

The saddest part to my story is what happened to the kids I met along the way who weren't so lucky. Kids who would be doing just fine right now but are living in group homes or residential programs—all because some doctor or school administrator concluded they were hopeless, and their parents listened.

Don't get me wrong. There are people who need support beyond what is available in public school. However, the fact that I was able to slip through the cracks so easily tells me the system is broken. In my experience, the special education system is less about giving kids help and more about making things easier for teachers. Look at me.

One day, in a psychology class at LS, we took tests to determine our learning styles. I found out from that testing that I'm a kinesthetic learner, someone who needs to do things to learn them. That test made me think about my childhood. I wasn't someone that teachers could just stand in front of and lecture. Unfortunately, this is also the hardest learning style to teach in schools. So, when I was in preschool, all teachers saw was a kid who wasn't paying attention and couldn't sit still. It makes me wonder how many non-traditional learners are banished each day to schools like SVTA, Bridger, and Parsons.

My wish is that mainstream schools would abandon the "one size fits all" approach to learning and try to find what works for students. If someone like me was able to fall through the cracks with two loving parents and a team of specialists at my disposal, imagine what it is like for less fortunate kids. Something needs to change.

The bottom line is that an incredible amount of luck played into being where I am today. Had I stayed home that cold day in January of 2009, I never would've uncovered my passion for skiing. Throughout my difficult childhood, the only thing that kept me going was getting into the mountains come Saturday. One day, I'll help others follow their passions, giving them a chance to learn a new skill or helping them have their best day ever in the outdoors. I want to take after my mentors, like Ben, who did the same for me. Ben taught me that a great instructor isn't just a talker or a doer, he is a listener. He allowed me to pursue my goals safely and didn't say no for arbitrary reasons like "you are too young" or "you are too small."

When I think about the incredible skiers and adventurers that I have been so fortunate to learn from over the years like Ben, Chris Fellows, Chris Davenport, Doug Stoup, Andrew Eisenstark, John Egan, Brennan Legasse, Jim Surette, and Thor, they are all guys like me. I am sure they all heard "no" as kids but disregarded it because they had the courage, drive, and ambition to push limits. My situation was different because it wasn't just that I heard "no"—I felt it. My "noes" were accompanied by a physical restriction, and I was caged, in a sense. But I broke free because I possessed similar courage, drive, and ambition as the guys I so admire.

After everything that's happened, I've gained a ton of perspective on life. Everything bad that happened produced the things that are good about me. When I hit rock bottom at Cambridge Hospital, I learned the importance of doing what makes you happy rather than following the herd and compromising yourself. By growing up in a world where I was denied the right to be my own person, I realized that I wasn't going to be handed anything. If I wanted the best out of life, I had to work for it. Now, here I am, proud to be me.

I know by reliving my story I am risking being forever judged by the improper labels I received as a child, but I received a Facebook message in 2020 that convinced me how badly this book was needed. The message came out of the blue after Claire, a former supervisor at Bridger, friended me.

Claire: *You probably do not remember me at all. However, I want to say how incredibly proud I am of you. I was your supervisor at Bridger. (I hated that place.) I knew from the time you were in the fifth grade that you were something special. I am glad your passion never wavered.*

Me: *Wow. You don't know how much it means that you reached out. Bridger was a dark place in my lifetime. I was still healing from fresh trauma from my last school and trying to figure out where to go next. I think you will be happy to know I did really well with my return to public school as well as my first year studying Adventure Education at NVU.*

Claire: *I am not surprised you did well. Bridger treated you guys like there was something wrong with you, when for the most part you all needed some extra love and a path to guide you. I never deserted the kids there. I was actually asked to leave after I saw one of the guys there hit you. I wouldn't keep my mouth shut about it. I am so glad you have proved them all wrong!*

The craziest part of that exchange is that I do not even remember getting hit by one of the security staff at Bridger. I recall most aspects of my life so vividly, but by the time I got to Bridger, I had been hit so many times during restraints that no single incident stands out. Maybe I was so used to it that it was just another day. That is probably why Dad told me once that the missteps of my childhood give me every right to feel like a victim, but I've tried this approach, and I'm not a fan. Constantly feeling wronged by the world is like carrying an extra burden throughout the day. Yes, I lost thirteen years that I could have spent with the people I'm around today, but in the end, everything worked out and I got to be a part of LS. More importantly, I'm medication-free and advancing in a career I love. Because of skiing and a crazy dad willing to travel the world to help me better my skills, I was given a second chance—one that I have every intention of seizing. Not everything ahead of me will be easy, but I can handle it.

If I was offered the chance to have my childhood over again, growing up like a normal kid, I'd say no thanks. Despite all the pain and hardship, I now appreciate that I'm strong enough to handle anything. I bet there are not too many eighteen-year-olds who feel that way. So, in a weird way, maybe I am lucky. But, if you ask me whether another child should go through what I went through, I will say no way. In fact, the only reason that I wanted to work on this book with Dad was to help parents learn from my story, so they wouldn't make similar mistakes with their children.

If your son or daughter is different from other kids, that is okay. For some reason, we are taught to admire men and women who challenge the status quo, yet, when a child acts differently, parents instinctively try to change them. They even seek out doctors and experts to help break the misbehaving child. Well, take it from me, if you do that, you will not only break your child of bad behavior—you will break them entirely.

I came as close to that breaking point as a person can experience. Had Dad decided to take me to Home Depot on January 2, 2009, instead of skiing at Nashoba, I'd be sitting right now in my room at a group home, bloated by medication, staring out a window, watching the world go by. Instead, the world will spend a lifetime watching me go by as I bring people with me to ski, climb, and explore every inch of this amazing planet.

The end—for now.

About the Authors

Robert C. DeLena was raised in Revere, Massachusetts, and is a graduate of The Governor's Academy, Trinity College, and Northeastern University School of Law. After practicing law unhappily, he founded a small recruiting company called Legal Staffing Solutions, and for over twenty years has advised law firms, lawyers, and law students on legal hiring. Rob lives in Sudbury, Massachusetts with his wife, Mary Beth, and their daughter, Abigail, who currently attends Hamilton College. He spends time skiing with his son Ryan and the great friends he's made during his journey from beginner to reluctant adventurer. Rob has skied all over the United States, internationally in Canada, Chile, and Argentina, and even survived a backcountry expedition in Antarctica in 2018. He is planning to return to Antarctica with Ryan in late 2022.

Ryan C. DeLena is currently a junior at Northern Vermont University studying Outdoor Education. He is widely known in the outdoor community through his social media presence as "Extreme Ryan." He was pictured on the cover of *Backcountry Ski Maps* (2020) and has conquered many of the world's signature ski runs including Super-C Couloir in Chile, Little Couloir in Montana, and Tuckerman Ravine in New Hampshire. Ryan has climbed and skied additional peaks in Oregon, Washington, Utah, California, Nevada, Wyoming, Svalbard, and Antarctica. He is an enthusiastic rock climber, ice climber, and avid hiker, summiting the Grand Teton twice and completing the "Hundred Highest" hiking peaks in New England. Ryan has earned advanced certifications from the American Mountain Guides Association and the Professional Ski Instructors of America. He spends every available moment in the White Mountains and plans on adventuring in Antarctica in 2022.